PISTONHEAD

ARTISTS ENGAGE THE AUTOMOBILE

POWERED BY Ferrari

DECEMBER 3-8, 2013
1111 LINCOLN ROAD
MIAMI BEACH, FL

PHOTOGRAPHS BY KAVA GORNA

Venus Over Manhattan

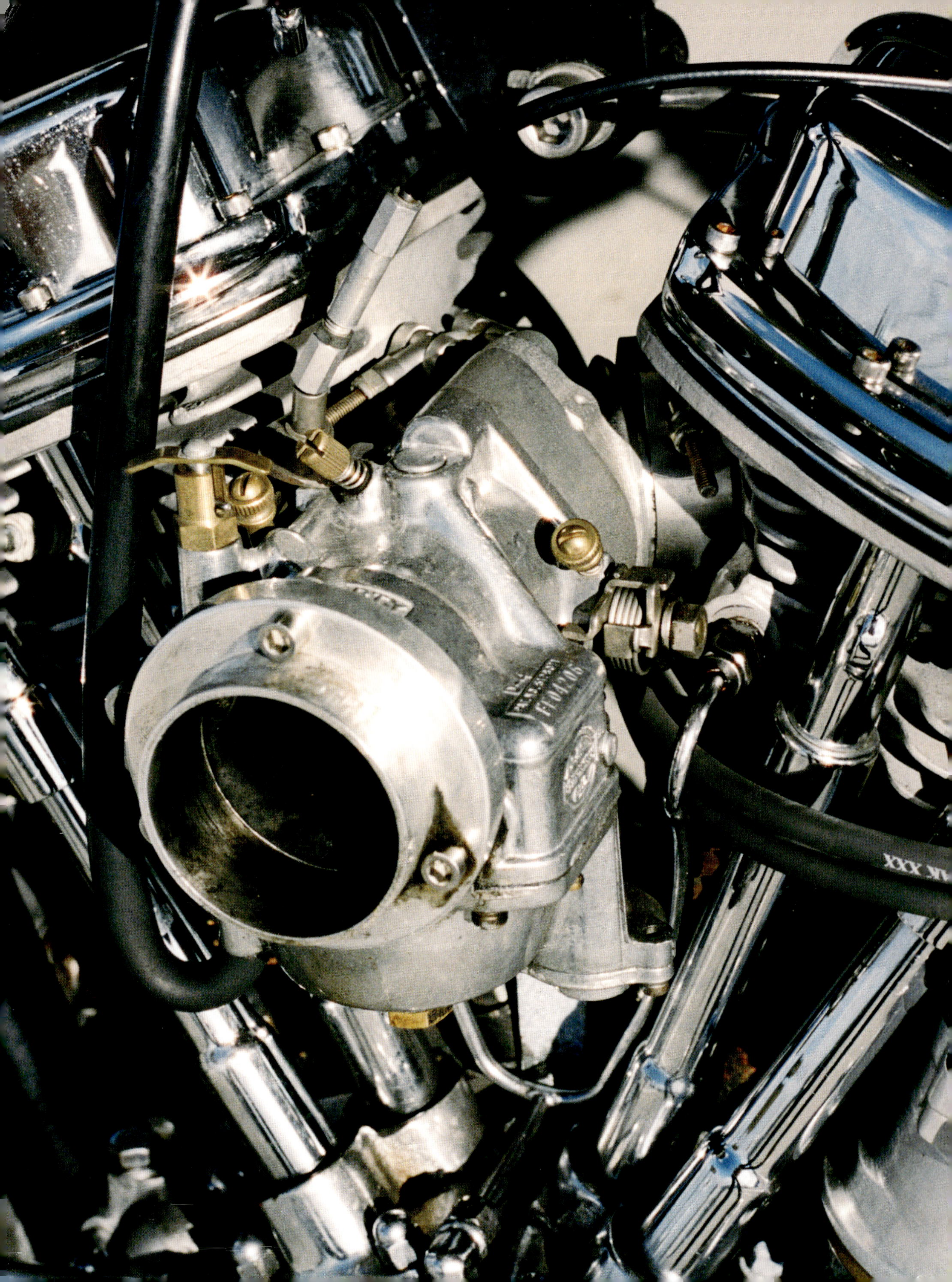

RON ARAD • BRUCE HIGH QUALITY FOUNDATION • DAN COLEN
JOSHUA CALLAGHAN • CÉSAR • KEITH HARING • DAMIEN HIRST
JACOB KASSAY • NATE LOWMAN • SERVANE MARY
OLIVIER MOSSET • VIRGINIA OVERTON • RICHARD PHILLIPS
RICHARD PRINCE • TOM SACHS • SALVATORE SCARPITTA
KENNY SCHARF • LUCIEN SMITH • FRANZ WEST

FOREWORD

The idea for Piston Head somehow sparked out of the intersection of a variety of passions, friends, and dreams. I have loved Herzog and de Meuron's fantastic Miami Beach garage at 1111 Lincoln Road since it first went up. The top floor is, in many ways, the best spot in town. Art Basel Miami Beach has grown into a sprawling art-a-thon that attracts more partygoers than art lovers, a phenomenon I once critiqued in an article in 2011. It was my fantasy to then contradict myself in the style of Marcel Duchamp who famously said, "I force myself to contradict myself in order to avoid conforming to my own taste." What better way than to indulge a fascination with cars, with art, and with architecture all in one show? It was undoubtedly my love for Richard Prince's use of muscle-car culture that inspired me to try to see just how many artist-created cars we could assemble and install in time for the opening of the fair. So we researched what was possible and soon felt confident that we could deliver at least a dozen (in the end, we had 17). I then thought of sponsorship, not only because we would need some financial help to make the numbers work, but also because in Miami, everything must be branded to register. The best brand in the car world is, of course, Ferrari, with whom luckily I enjoy a close relationship. I had bought one years ago from my wonderful friend Lapo Elkann, a shareholder in the company, a great master of style and design, and the grandson of the venerated Gianni Agnelli, the ultimate Italian tycoon and tastemaker. When Lapo once invited me to have a drink with his grandfather, I remember telling "Avocato" that I had always lusted for a Lamborghini Countach, at which point he chuckled, with a twinkle in his eye, and said nonchalantly, "a Lamborghini is a car for a pimp to park in front of a nightclub!" We all laughed and I ended up with a Ferrari. Many years later, and thanks to the generous vision of Marco Mattiaci, the president of Ferrari North America, the gallery was proud to have Ferrari as the sponsor of Piston Head, along with their one-night-only flash of 2014's all-new supercar, the F150, dubbed LaFerrari.

For any art-loving motorhead, Piston Head turned out to be an amazing spectacle, with historic cars like those by Scarpitta, Haring, and West, on to über-famous living artists like Prince and Hirst. We had work by Dan Colen and Nate Lowman but also invited brand-new primary work by promising talent like The Bruce High Quality Foundation and Virginia Overton. All in, the show had something for everyone, and succeeded in putting a smile on most people's faces. Thanks are due to the entire Ferrari team, Marco Mattiacci, Maria Stampone, Krista Florin and Luca Fronti, as well as to the ironwoman of Art PR, Andrea Schwan. The Venus Over Manhattan team of Pablo Alberdi, Anna Furney, Eran Schreiber, Josh Shaddock, and Annie Won, as well as our man in Miami, Shannon Serig, over-delivered on every level. And we all join in thanking the participating lenders for their generous trust, as well as the artists and galleries who supported the show. Lastly, thanks to Kava Gorna who we asked to document the exhibit and whose photographs found in the pages that follow. In the end, it seemed more appropriate to offer this photo essay than to approach the subject from a more conventional perspective. We hope you like it and look forward to inviting you to a second chapter soon.

Adam Lindemann

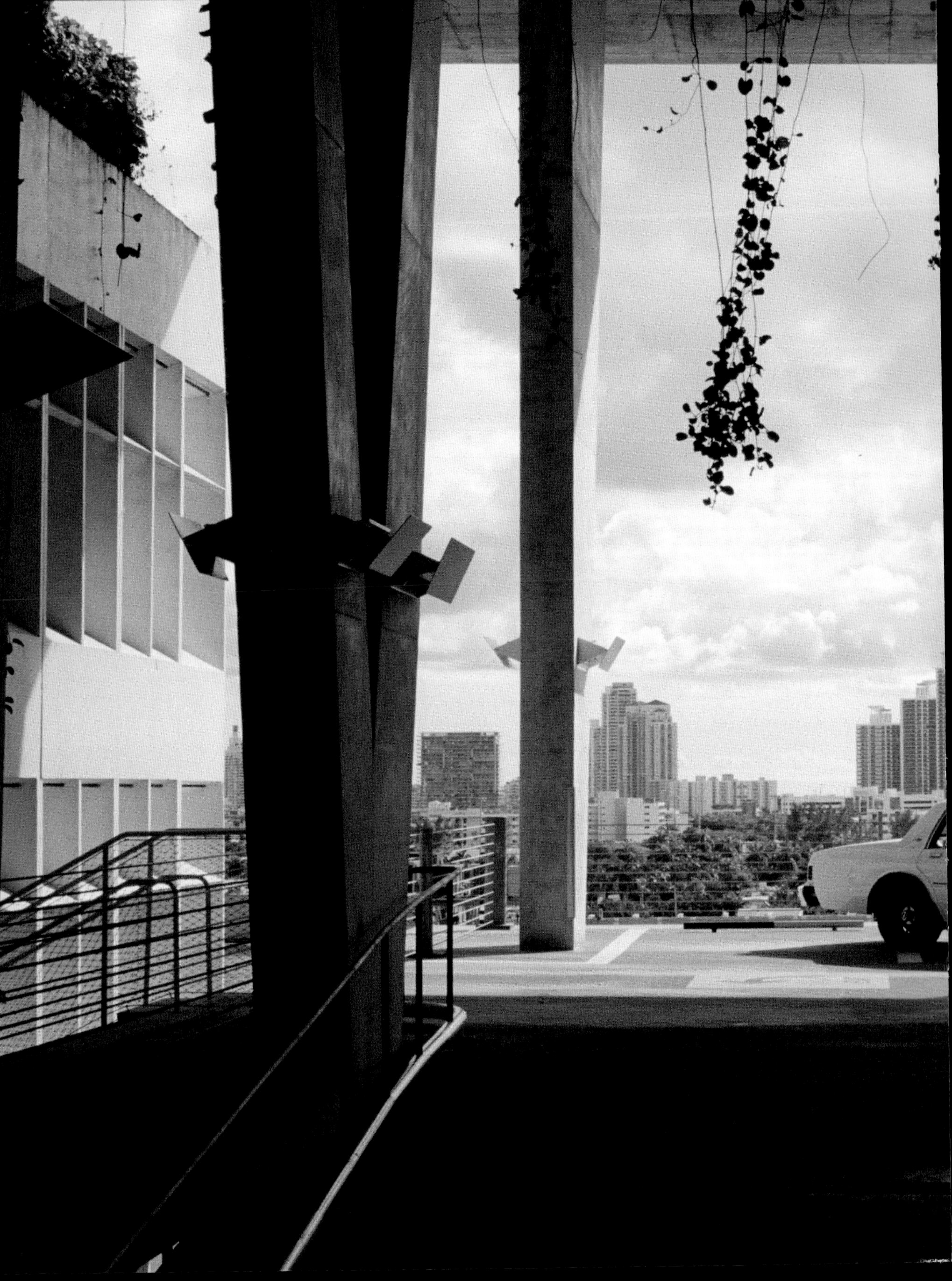

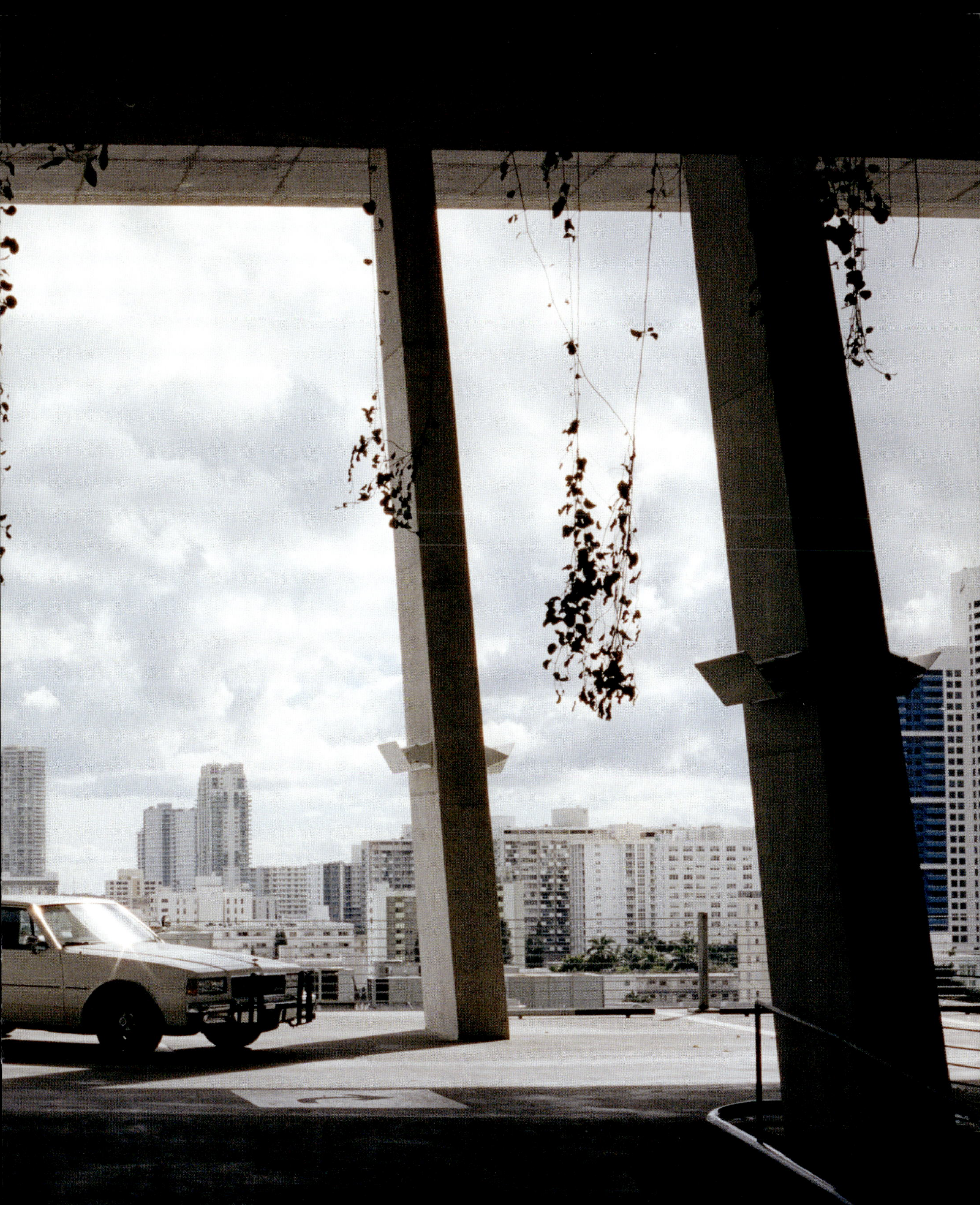

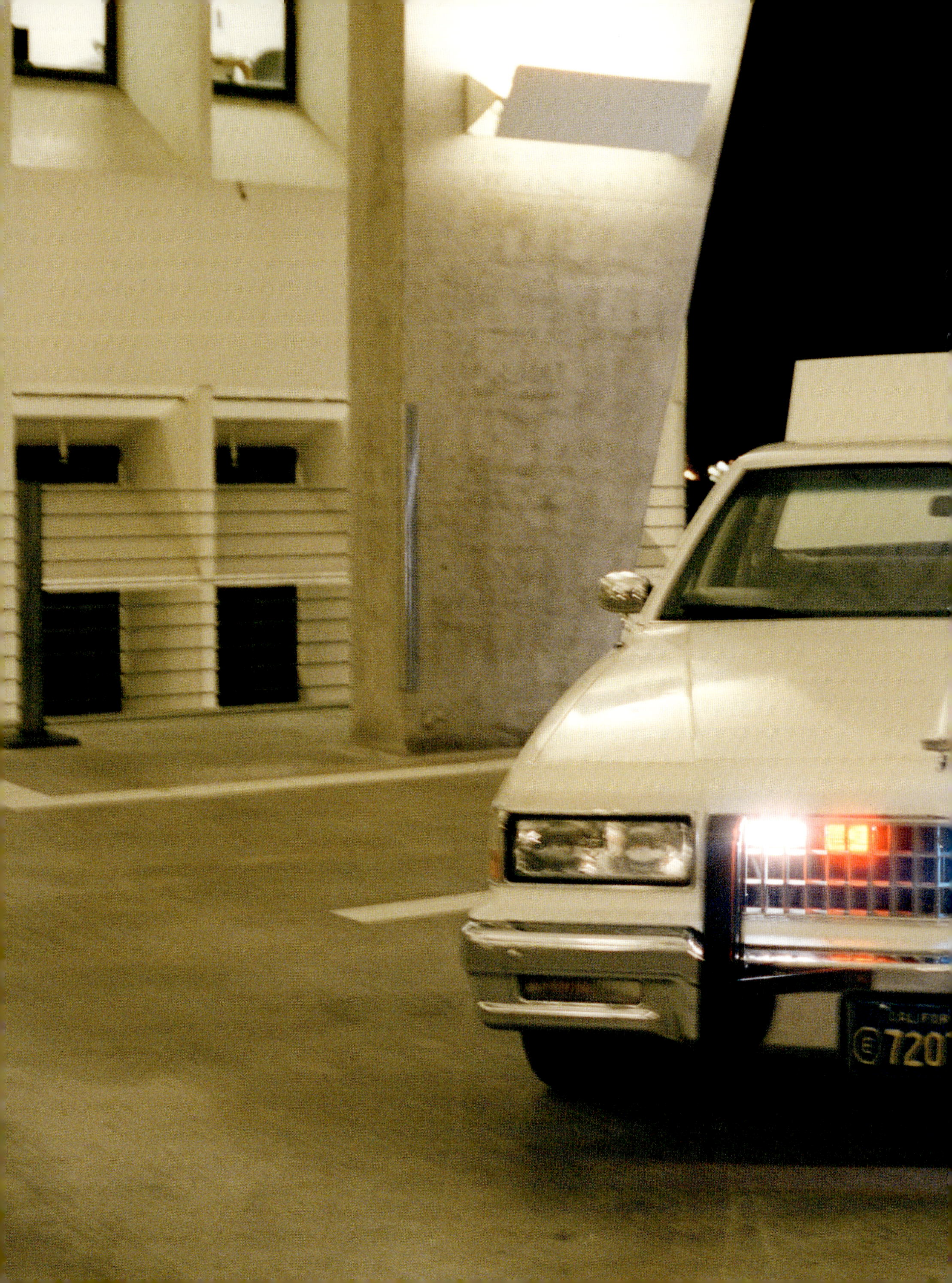

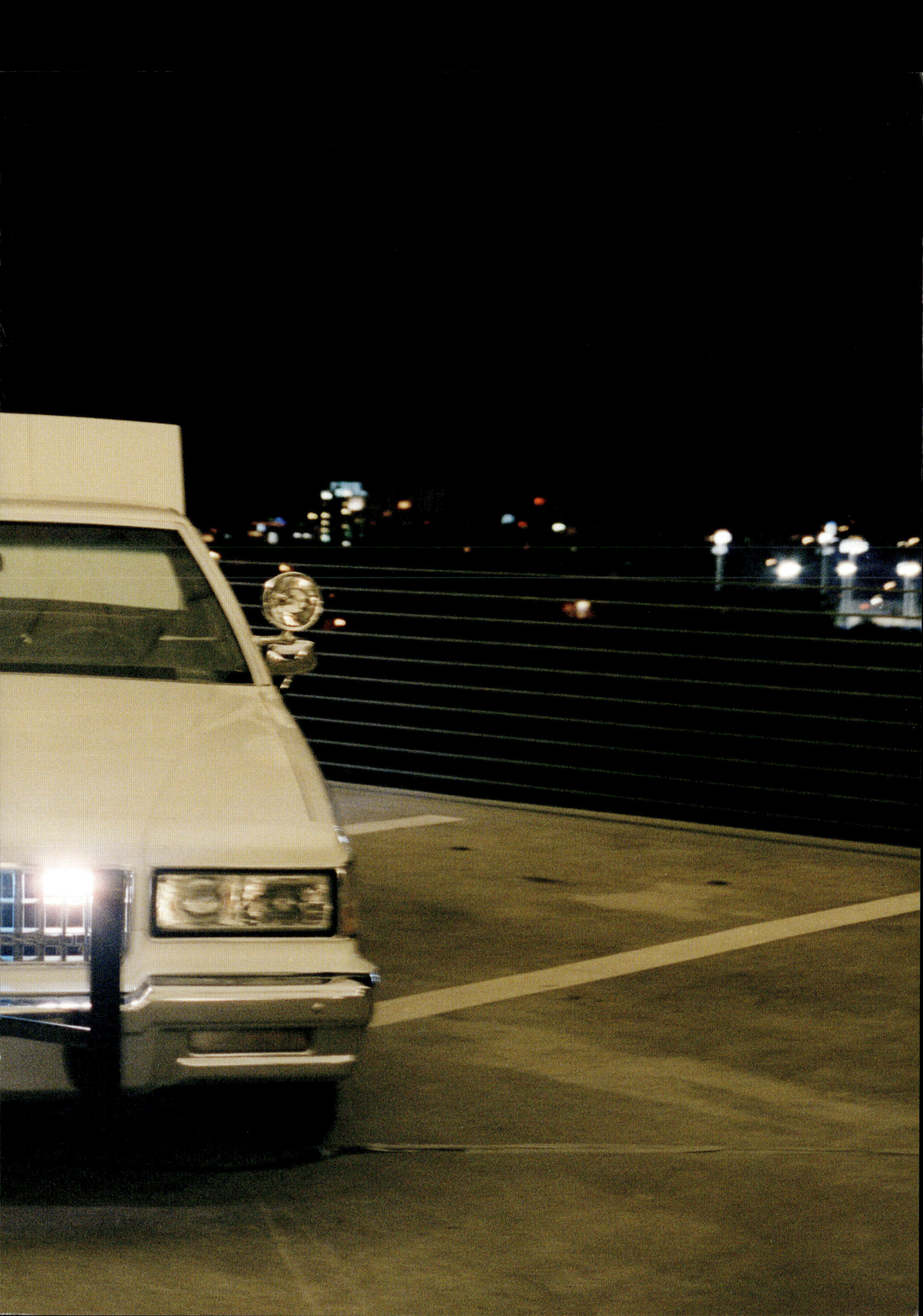

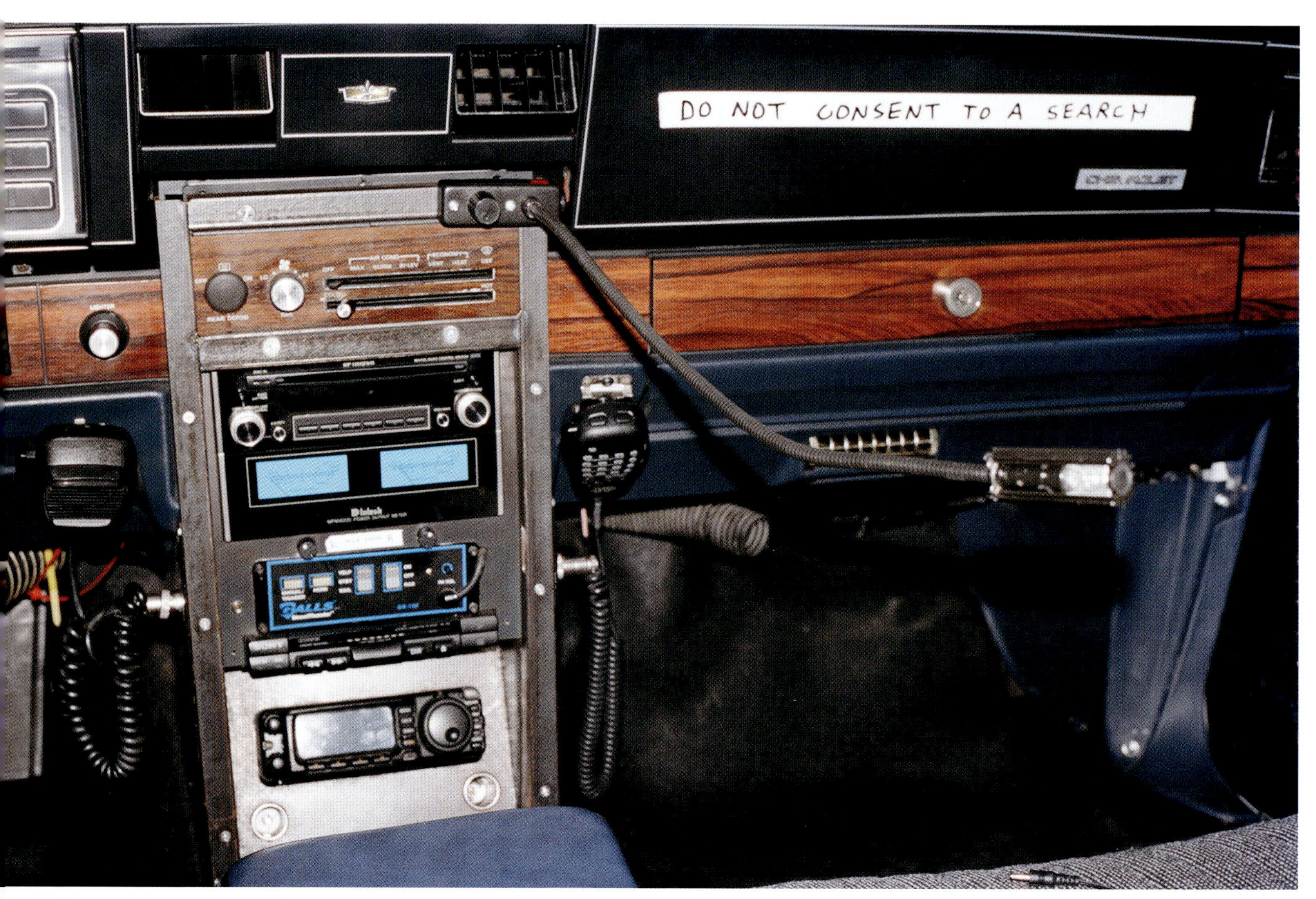
DO NOT CONSENT TO A SEARCH
CHEVROLET

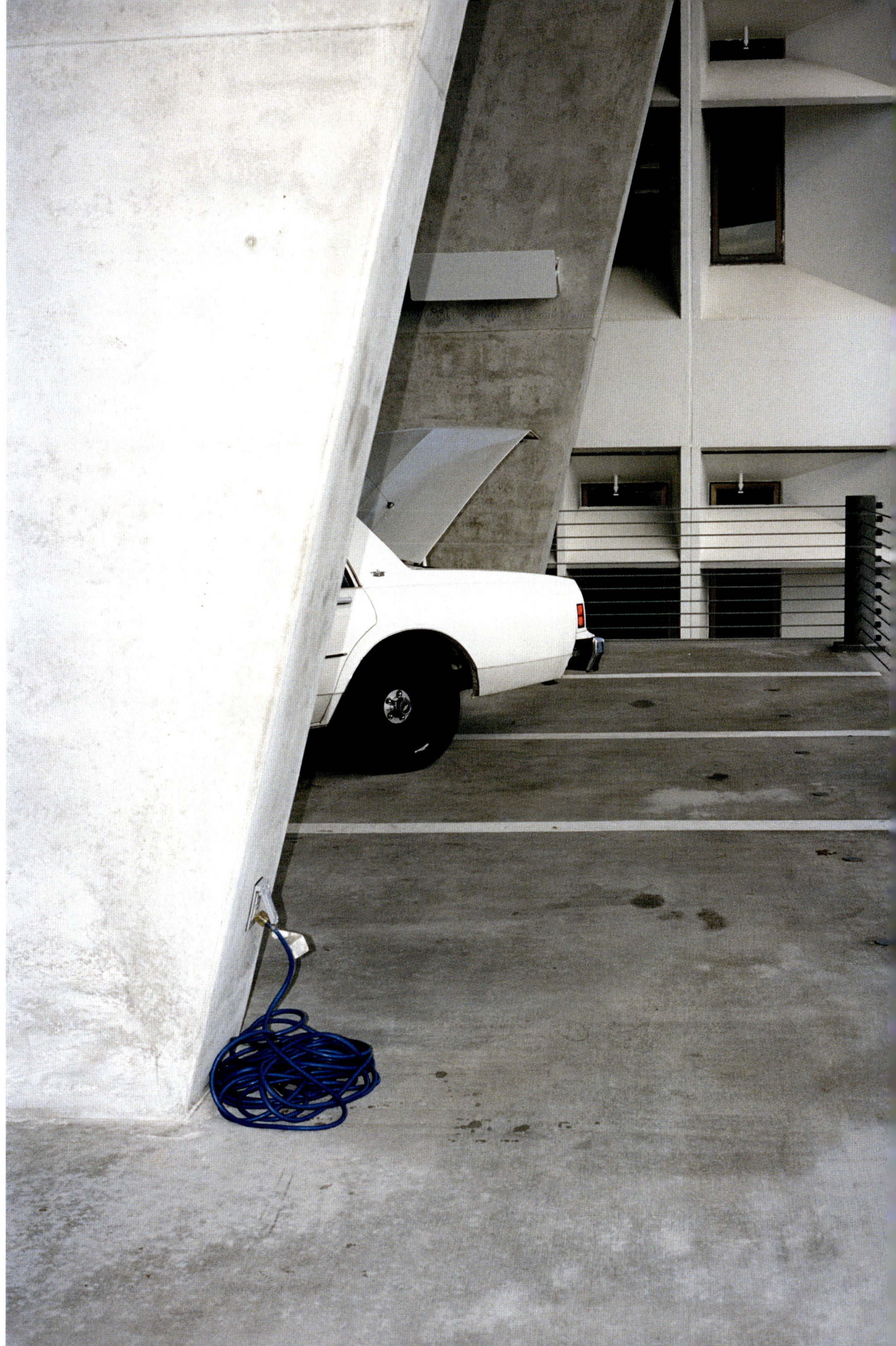

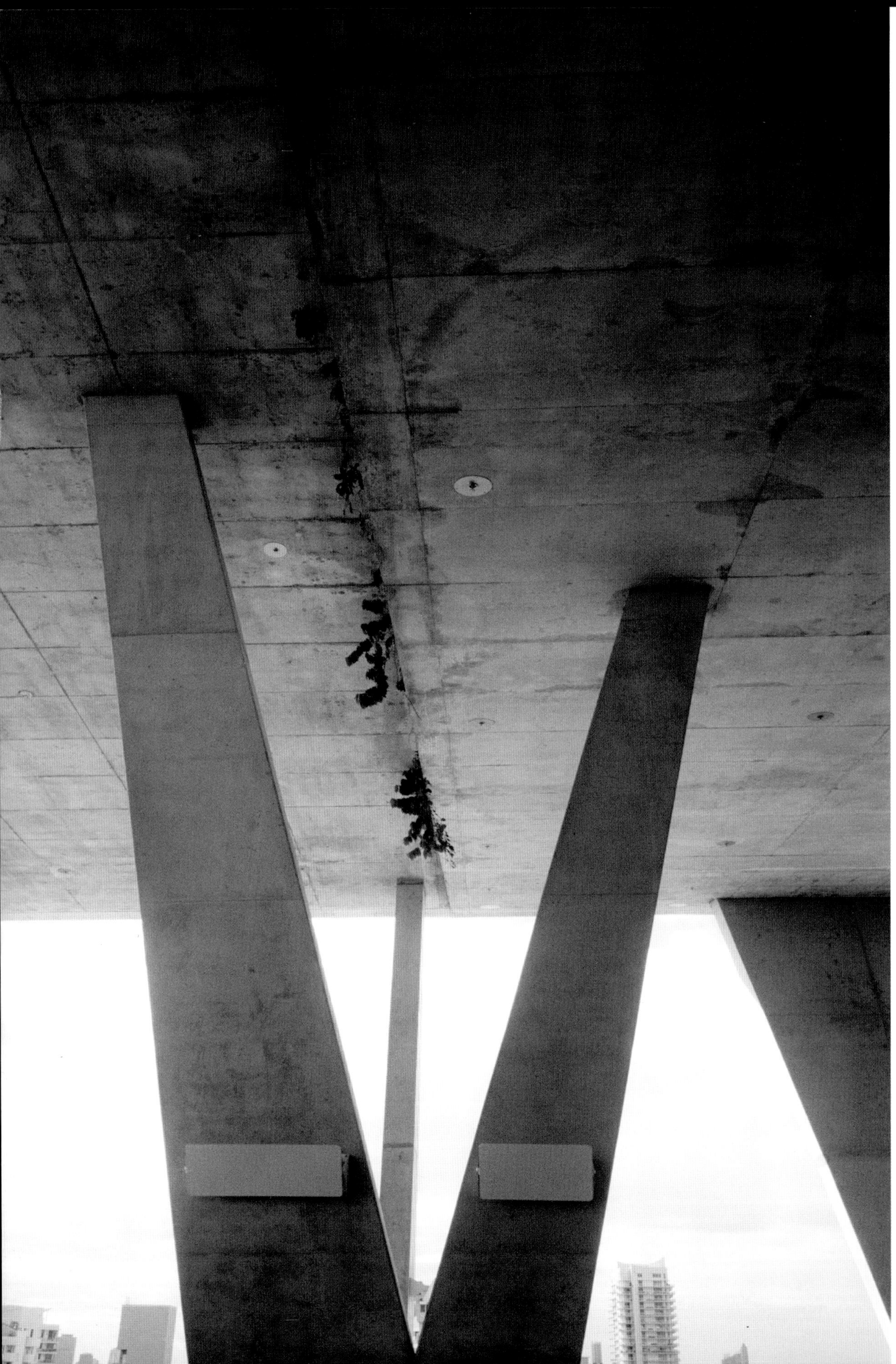

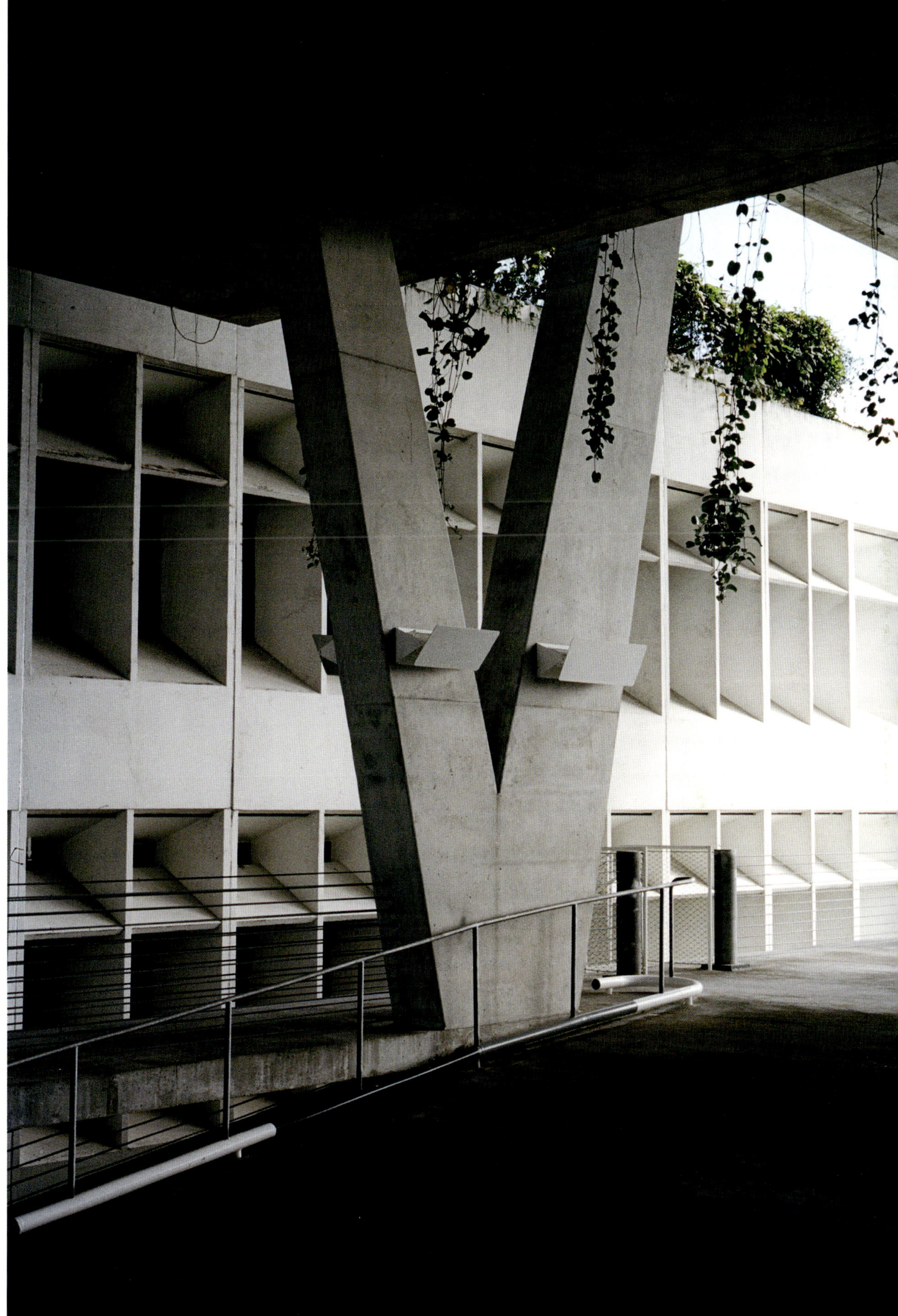

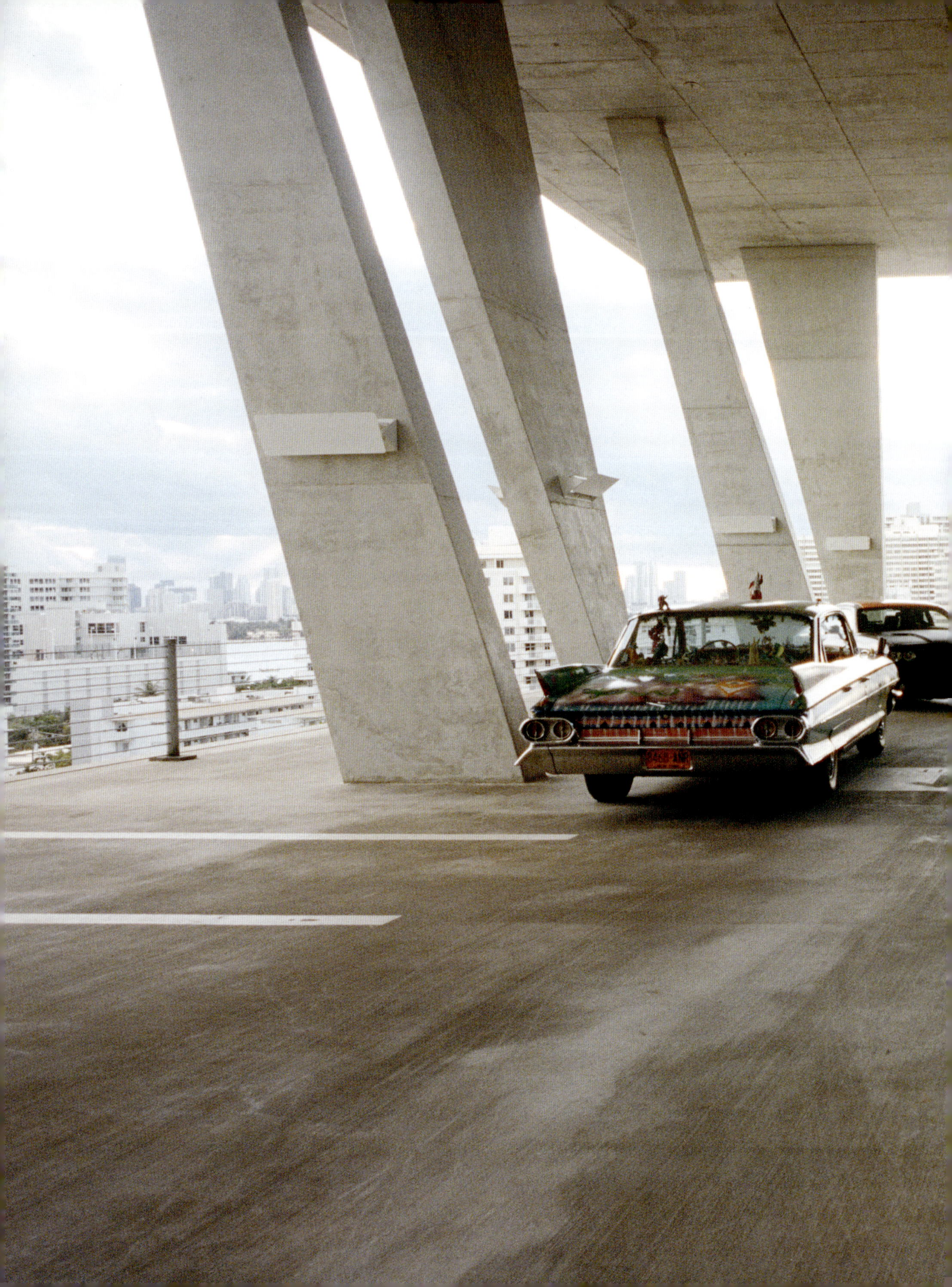

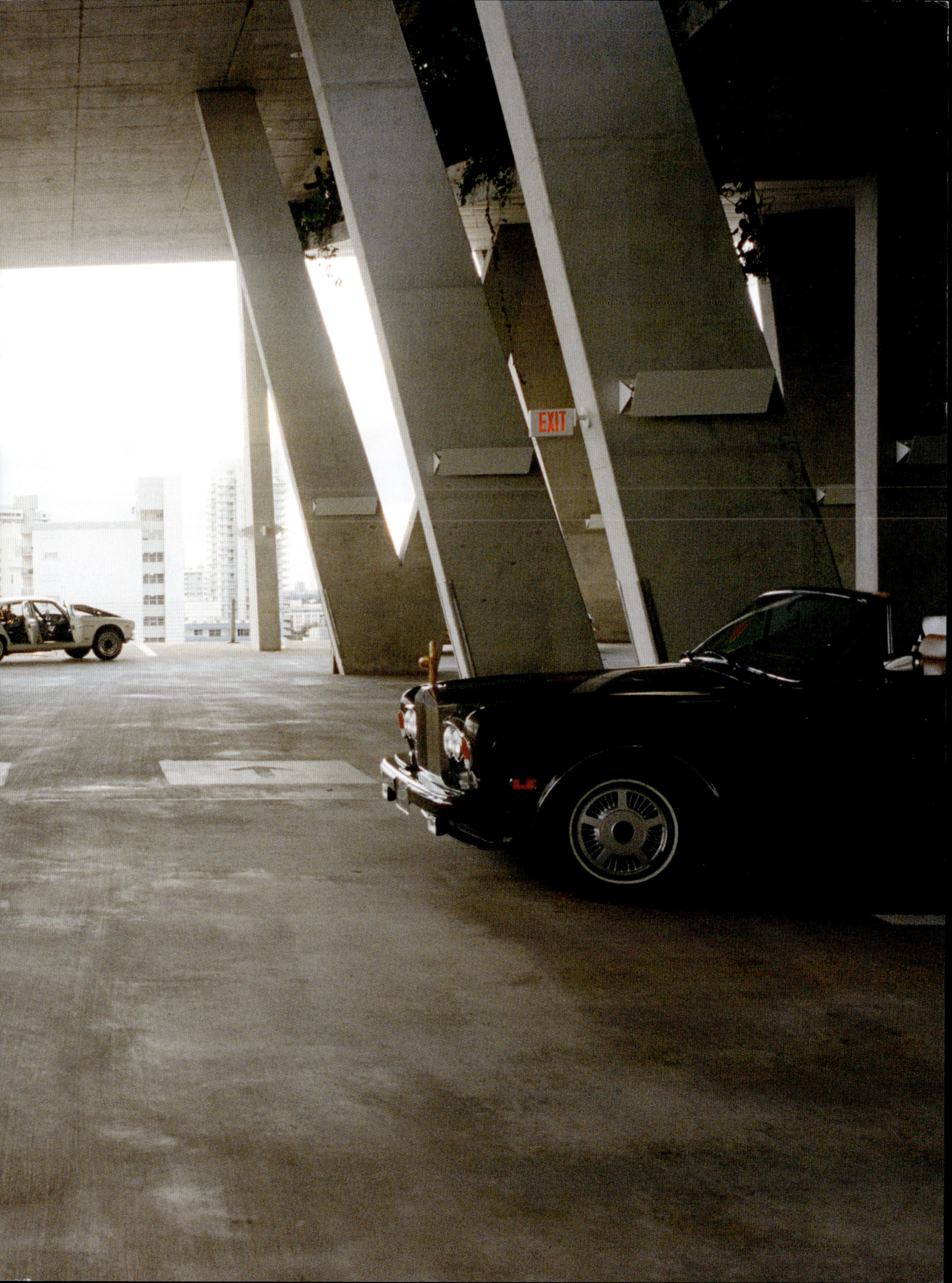
EXIT

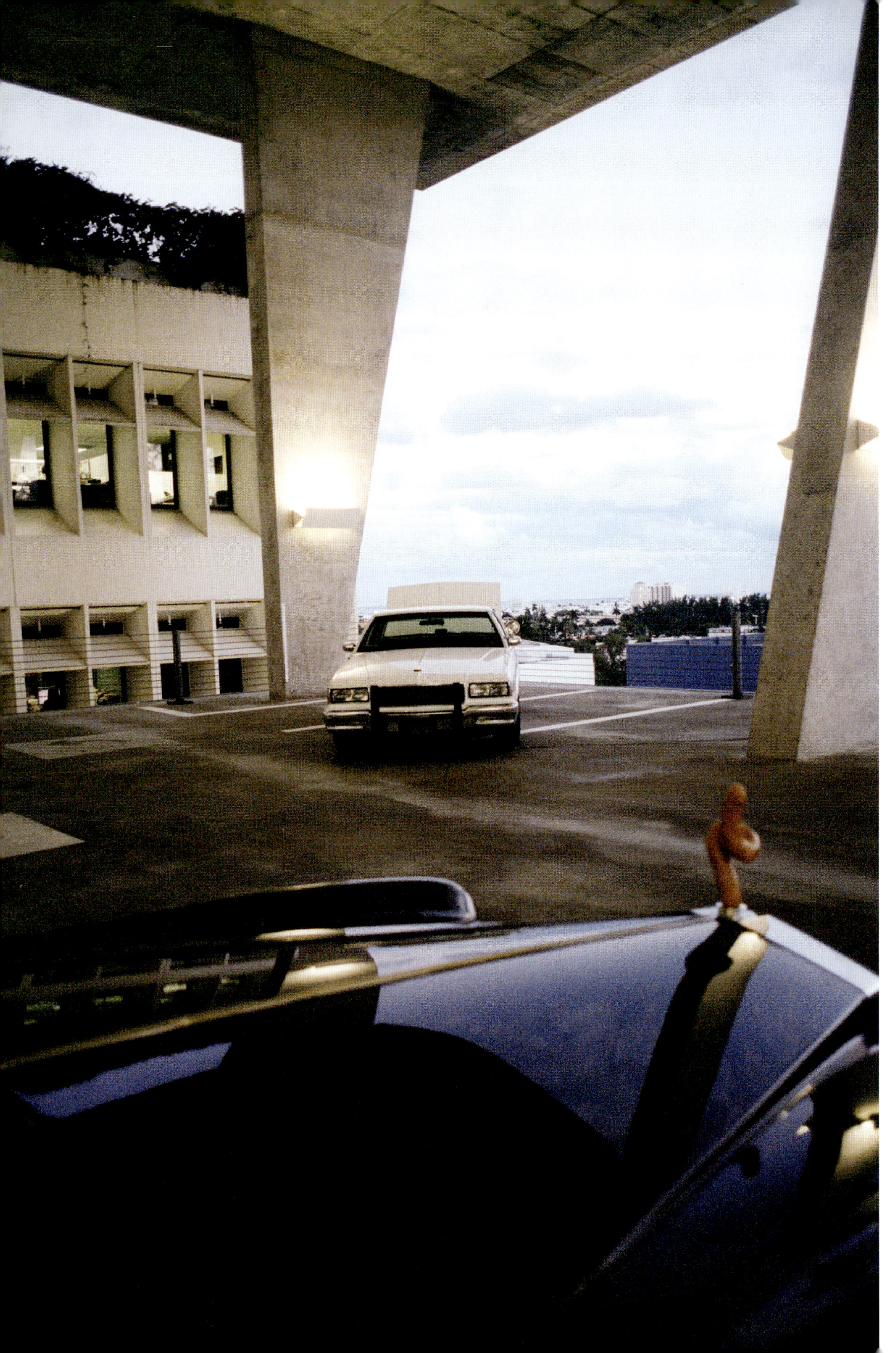

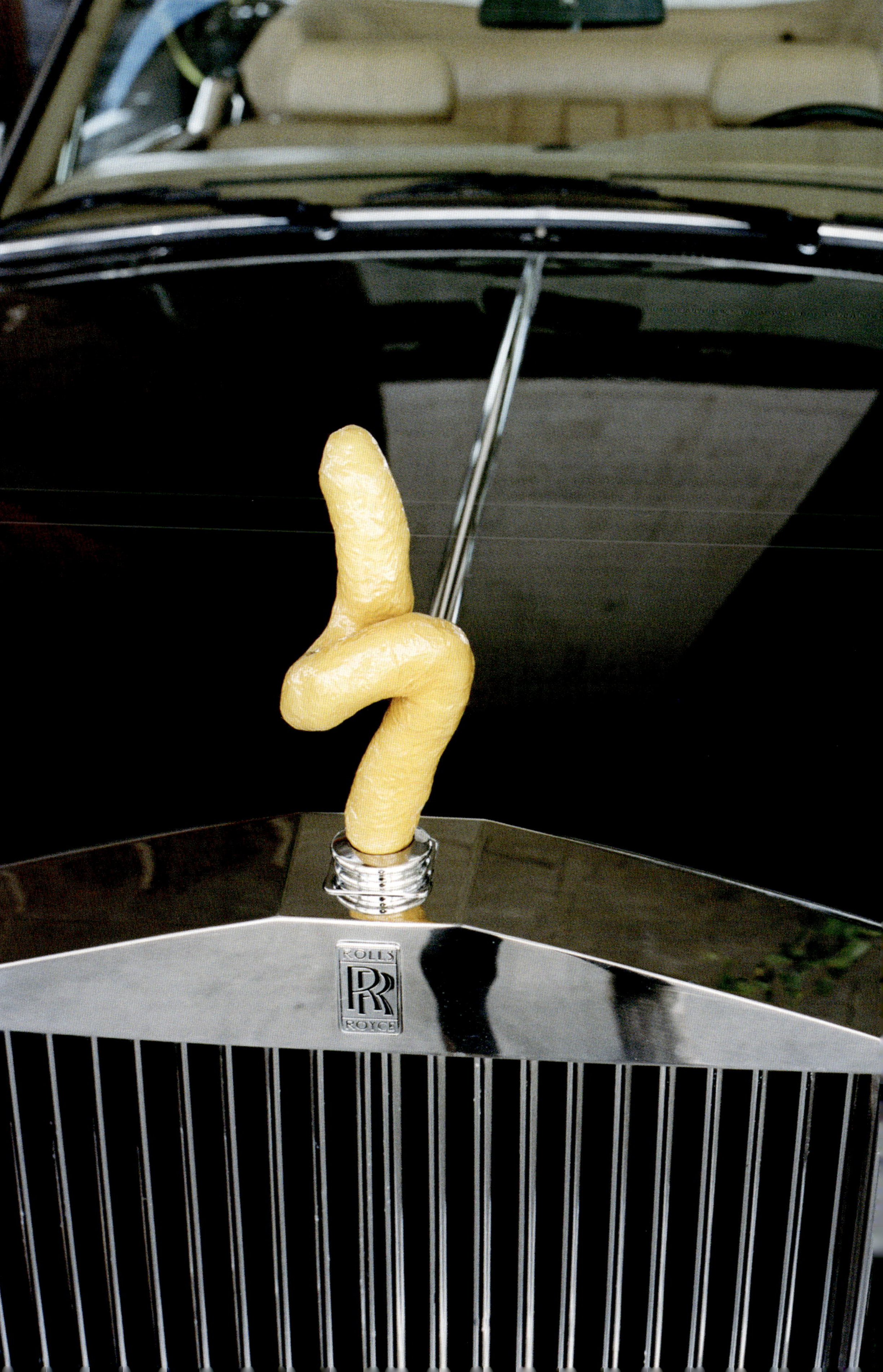
ROLLS
RR
ROYCE

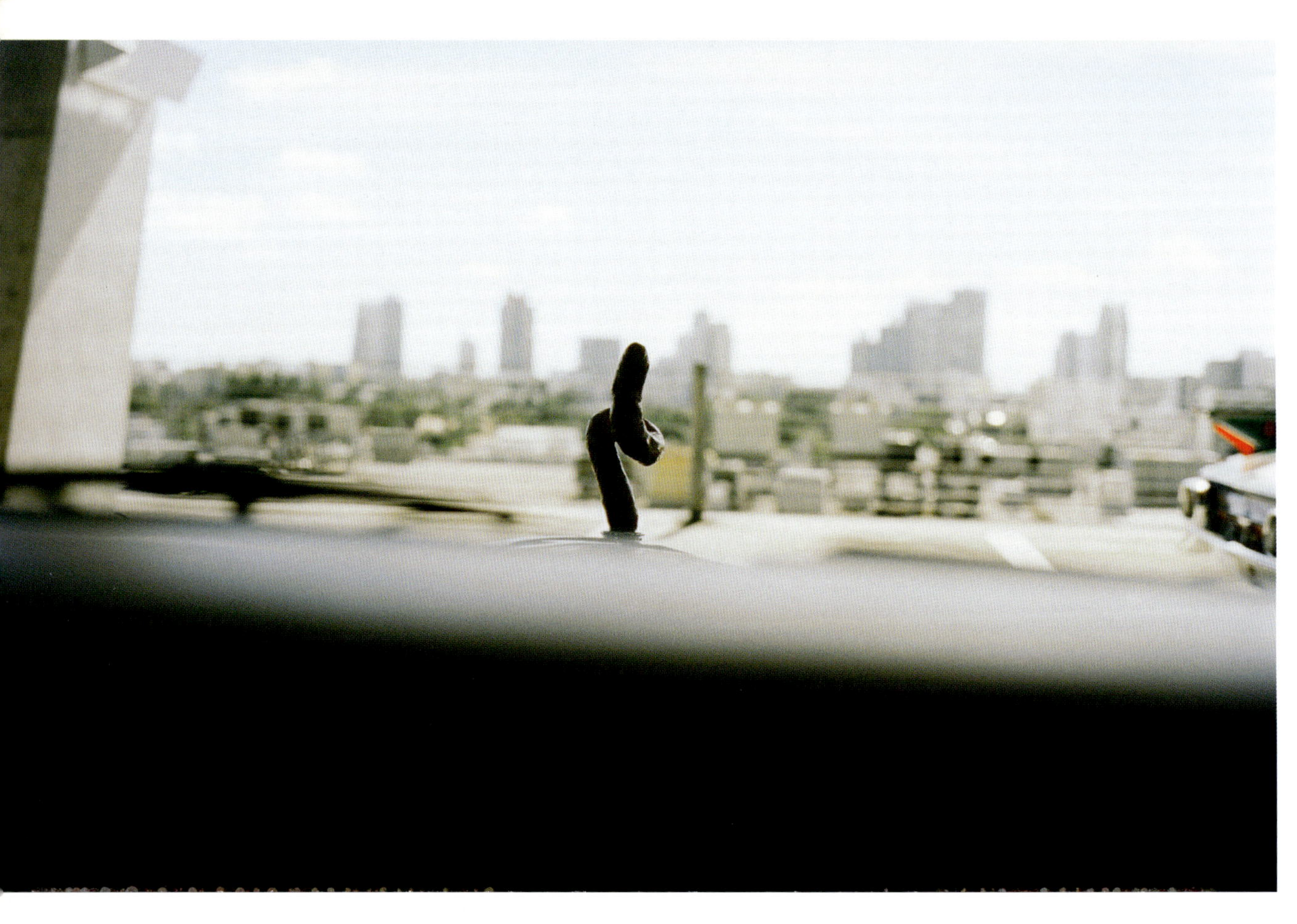

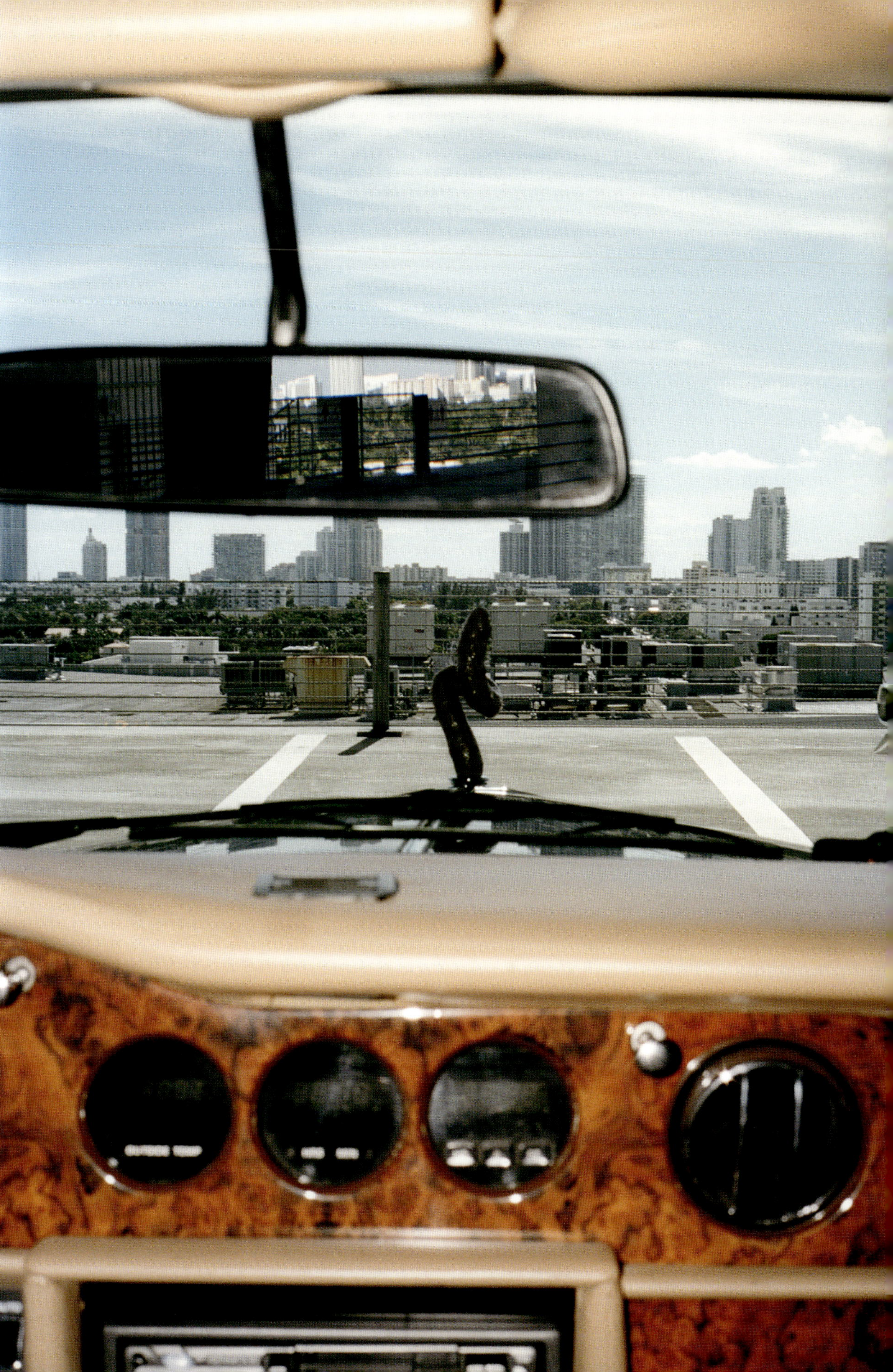

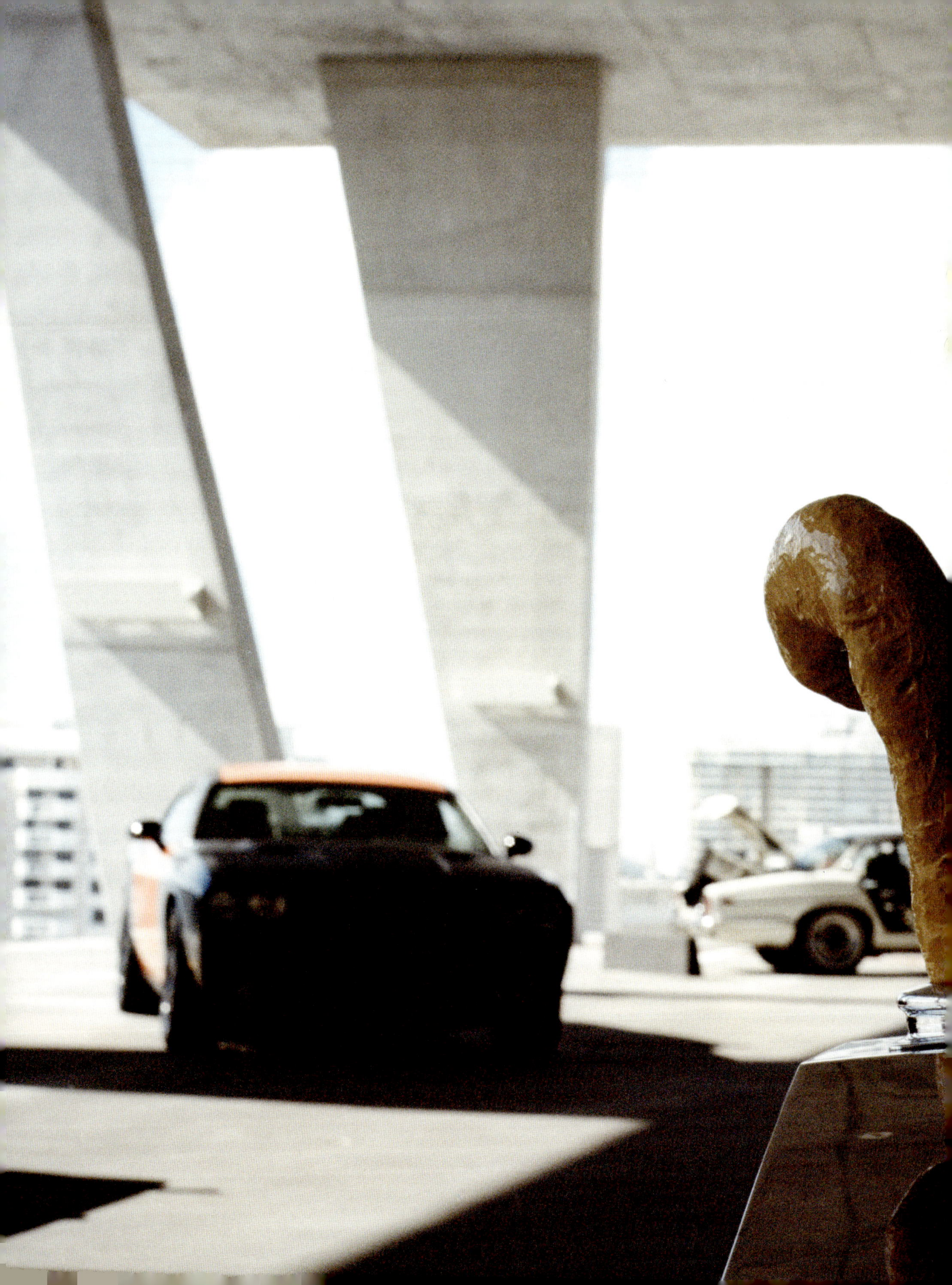

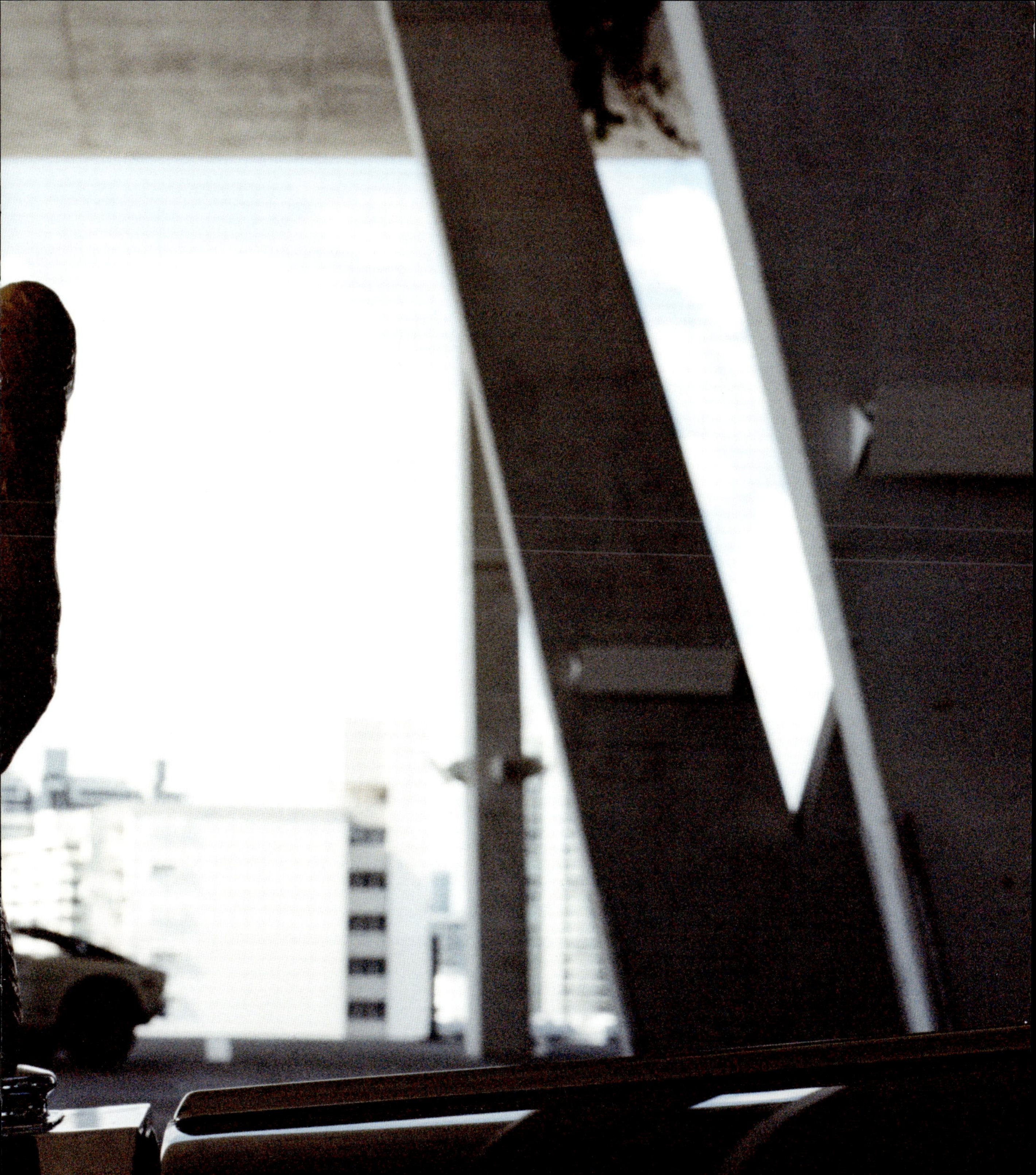

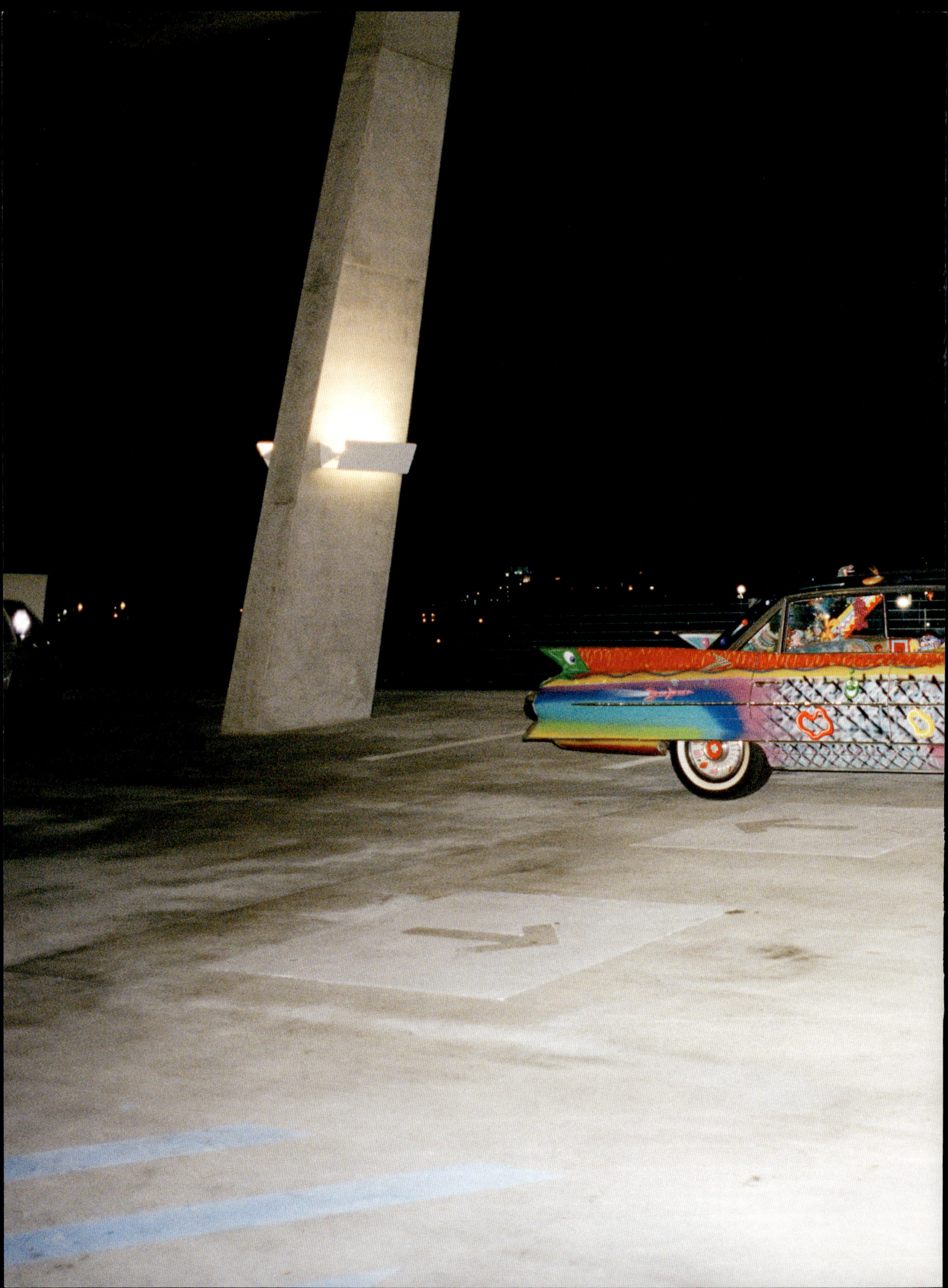

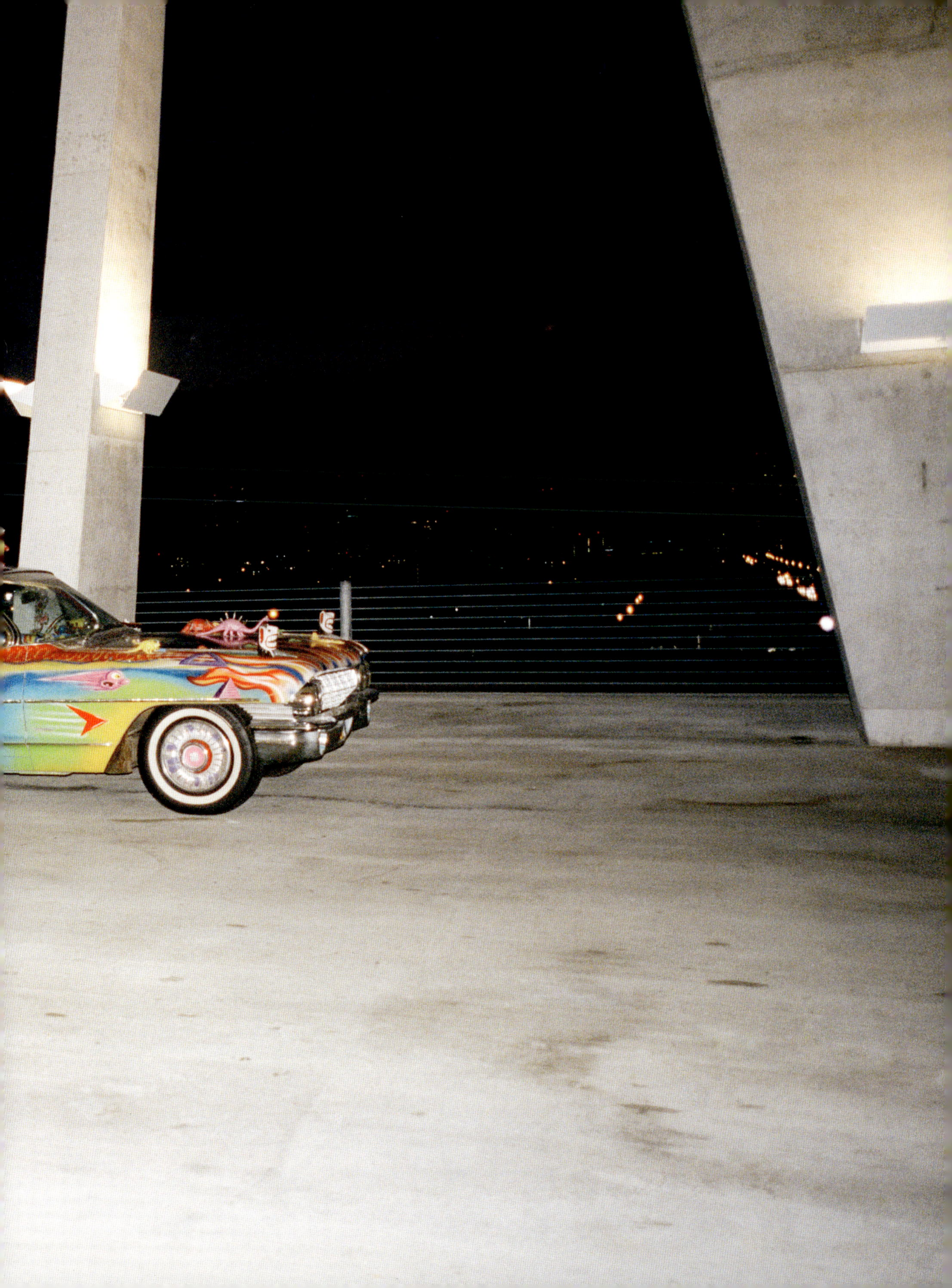

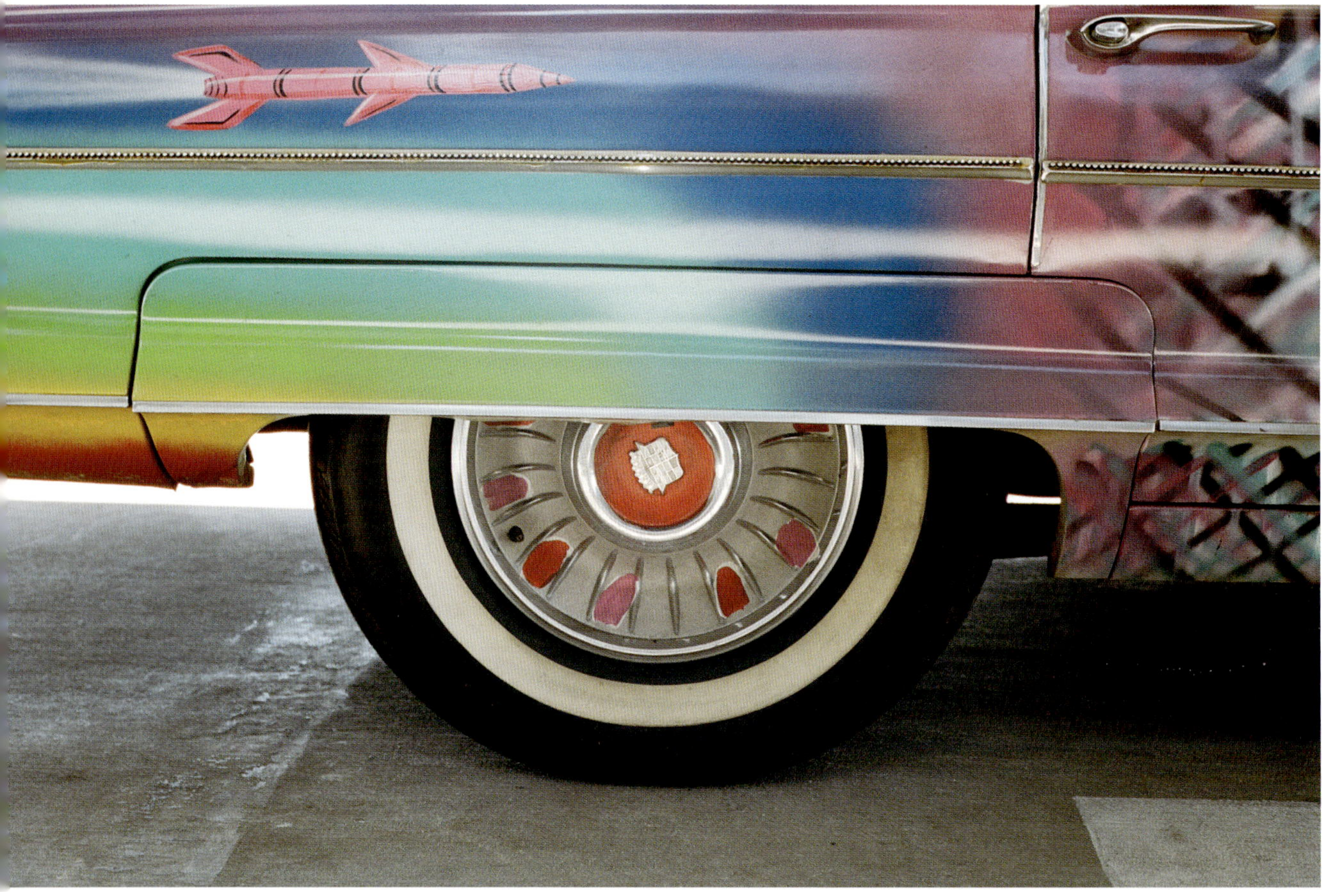

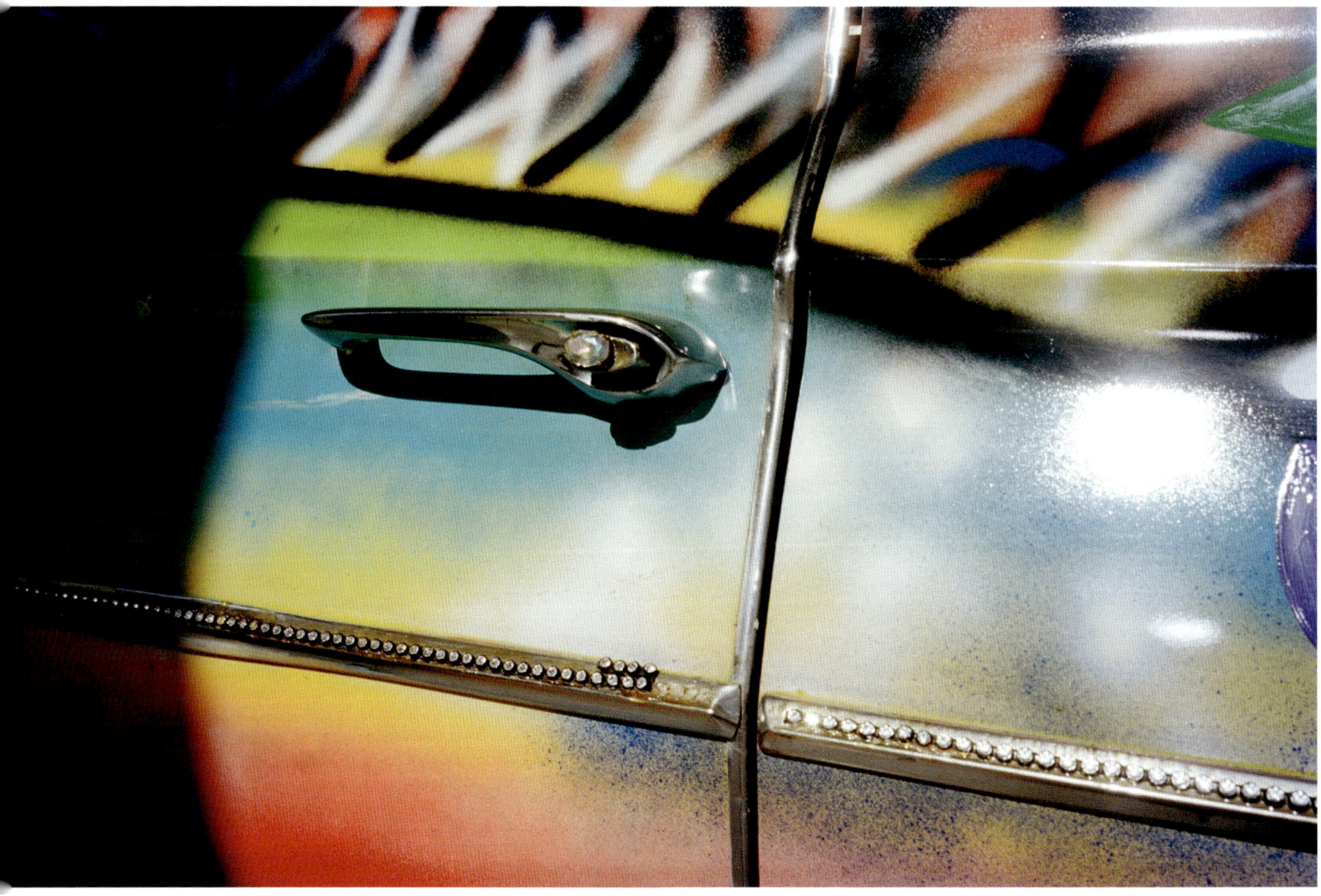

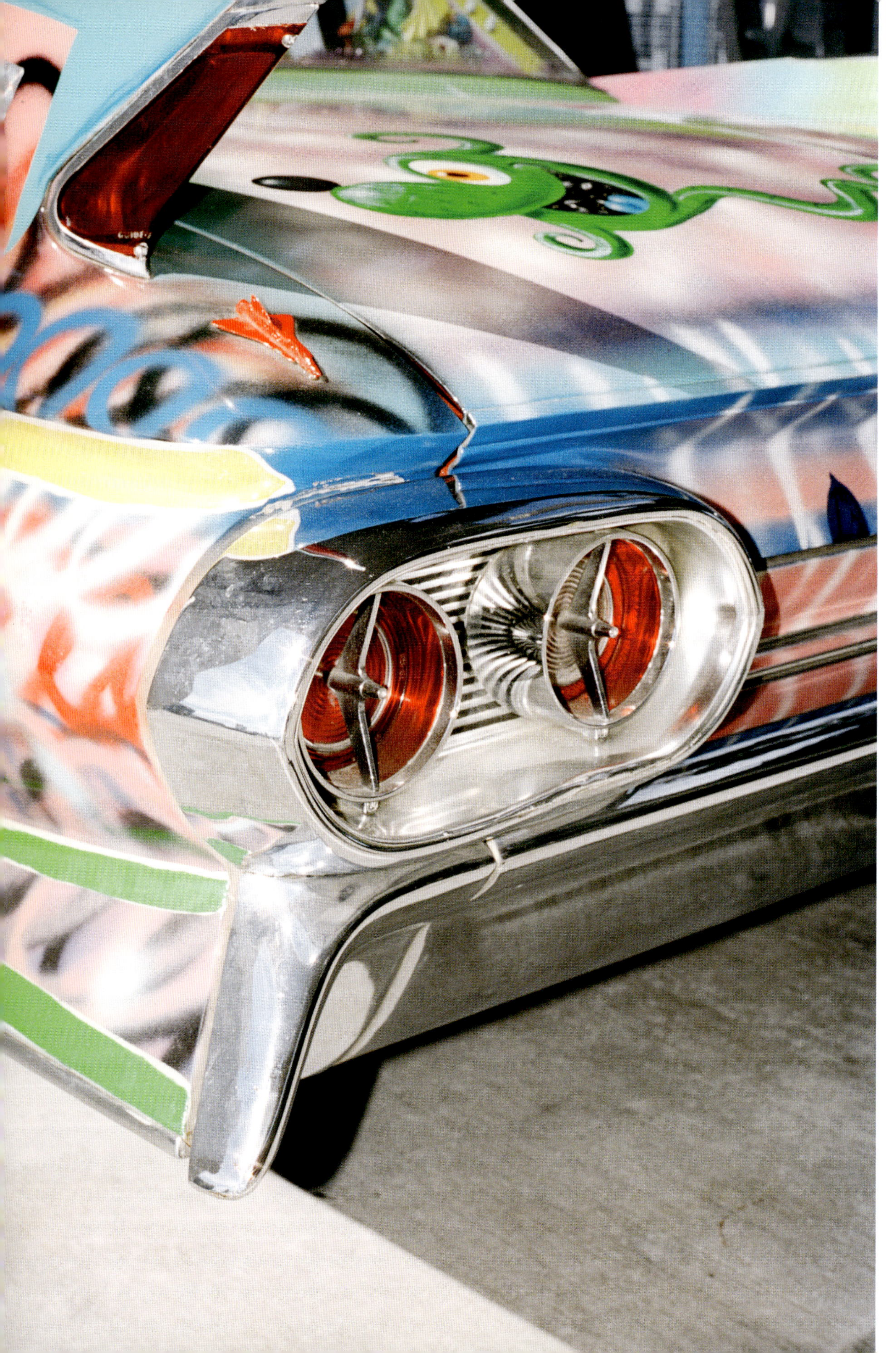

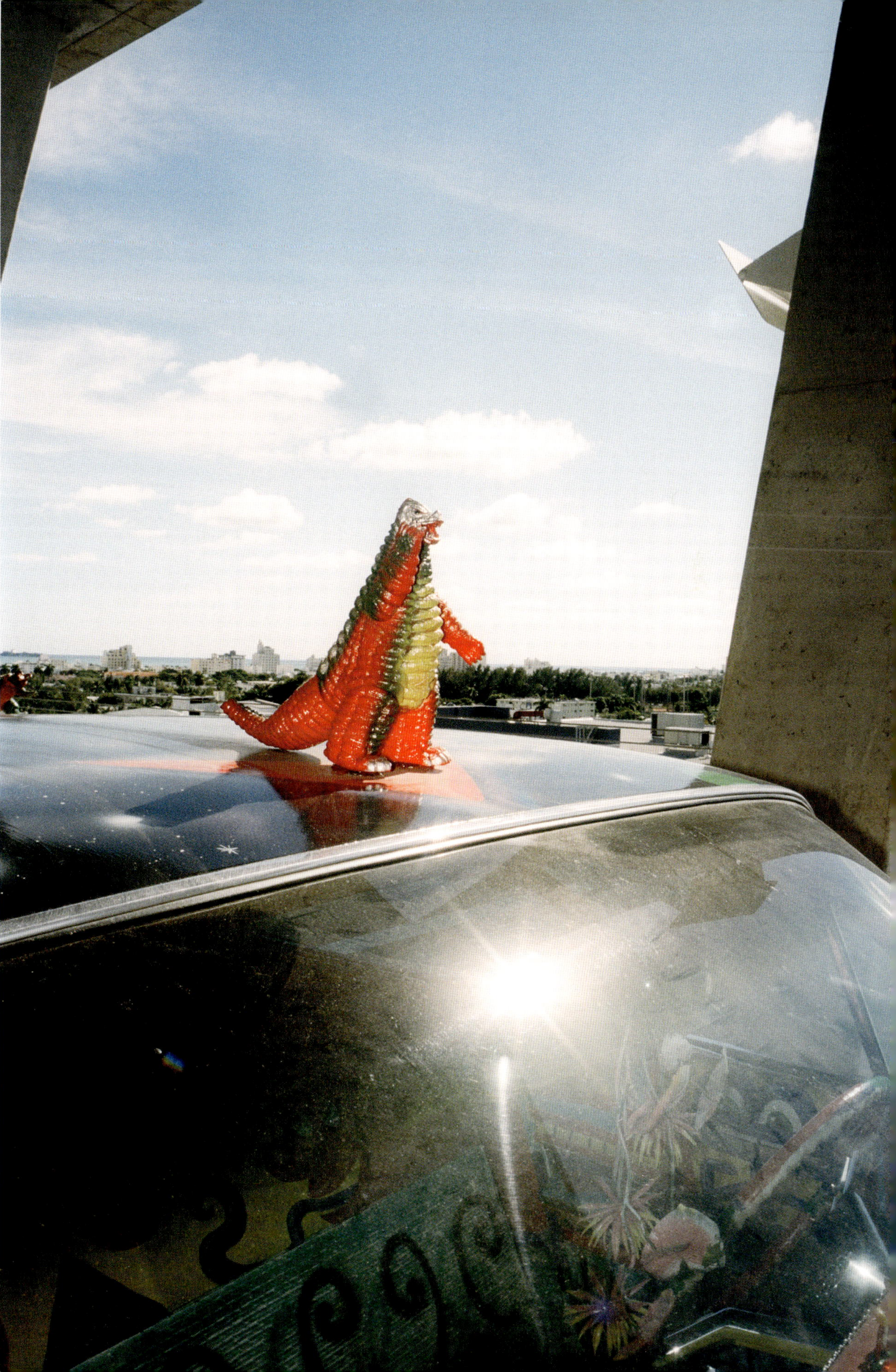

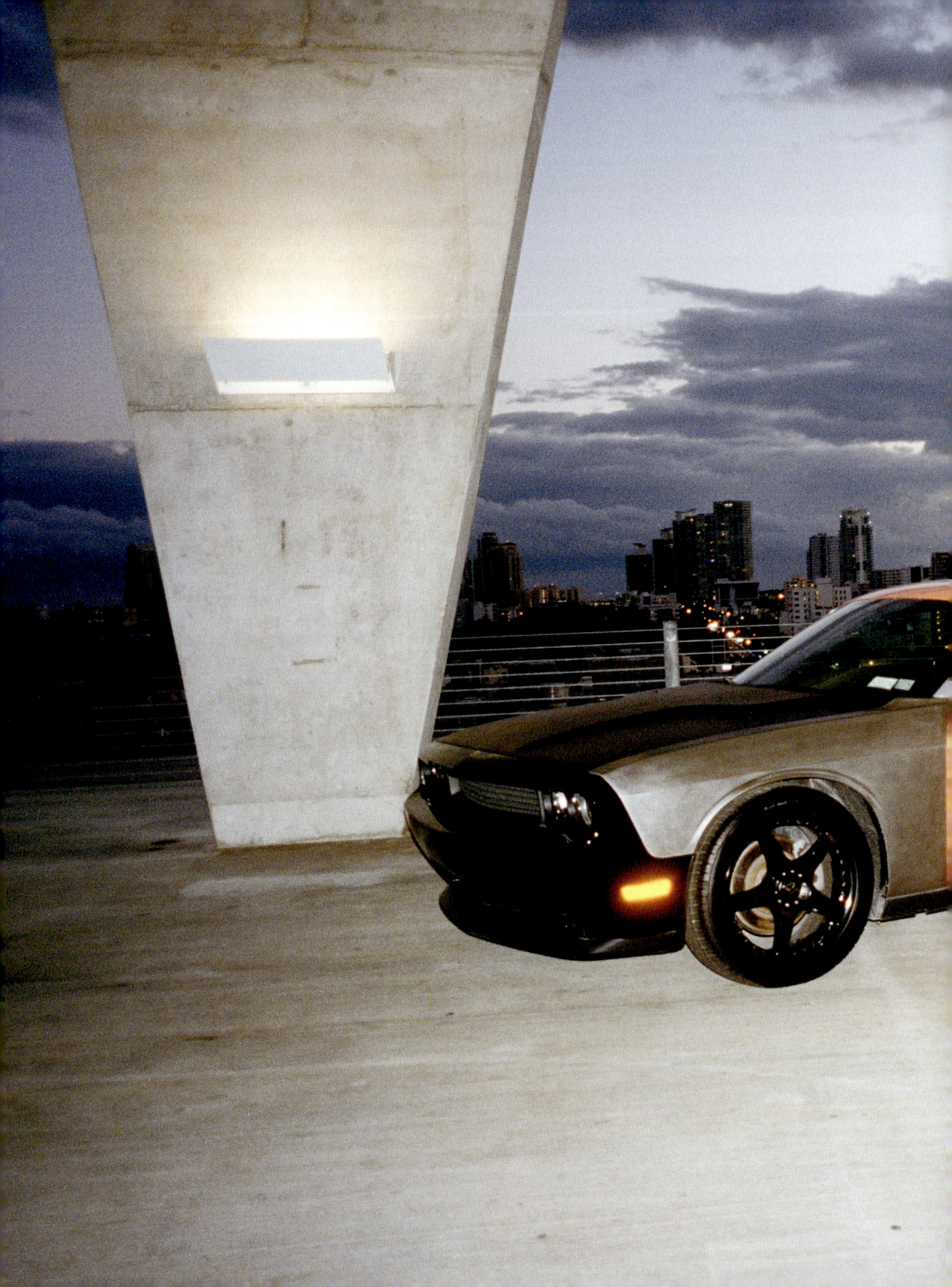

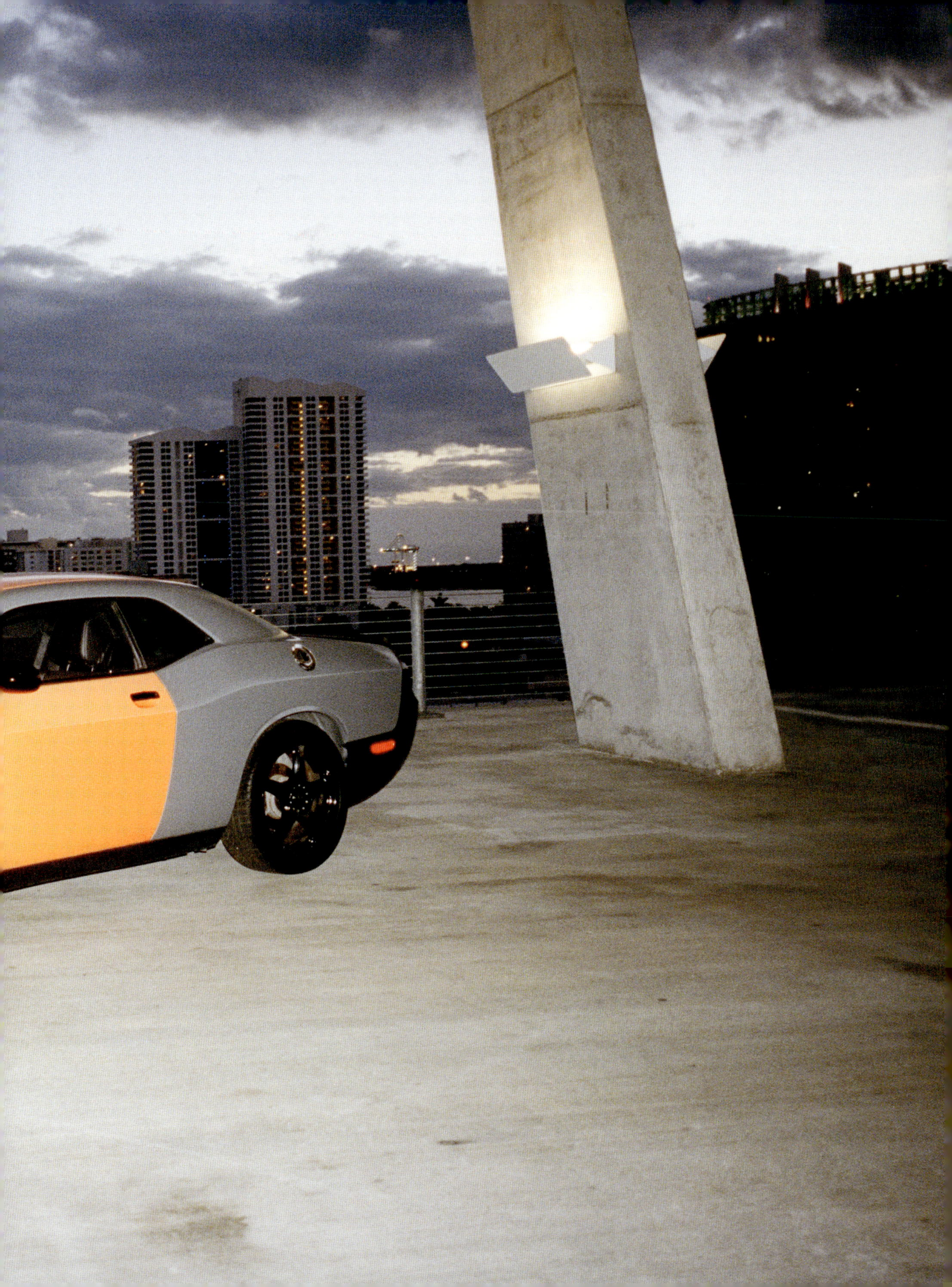

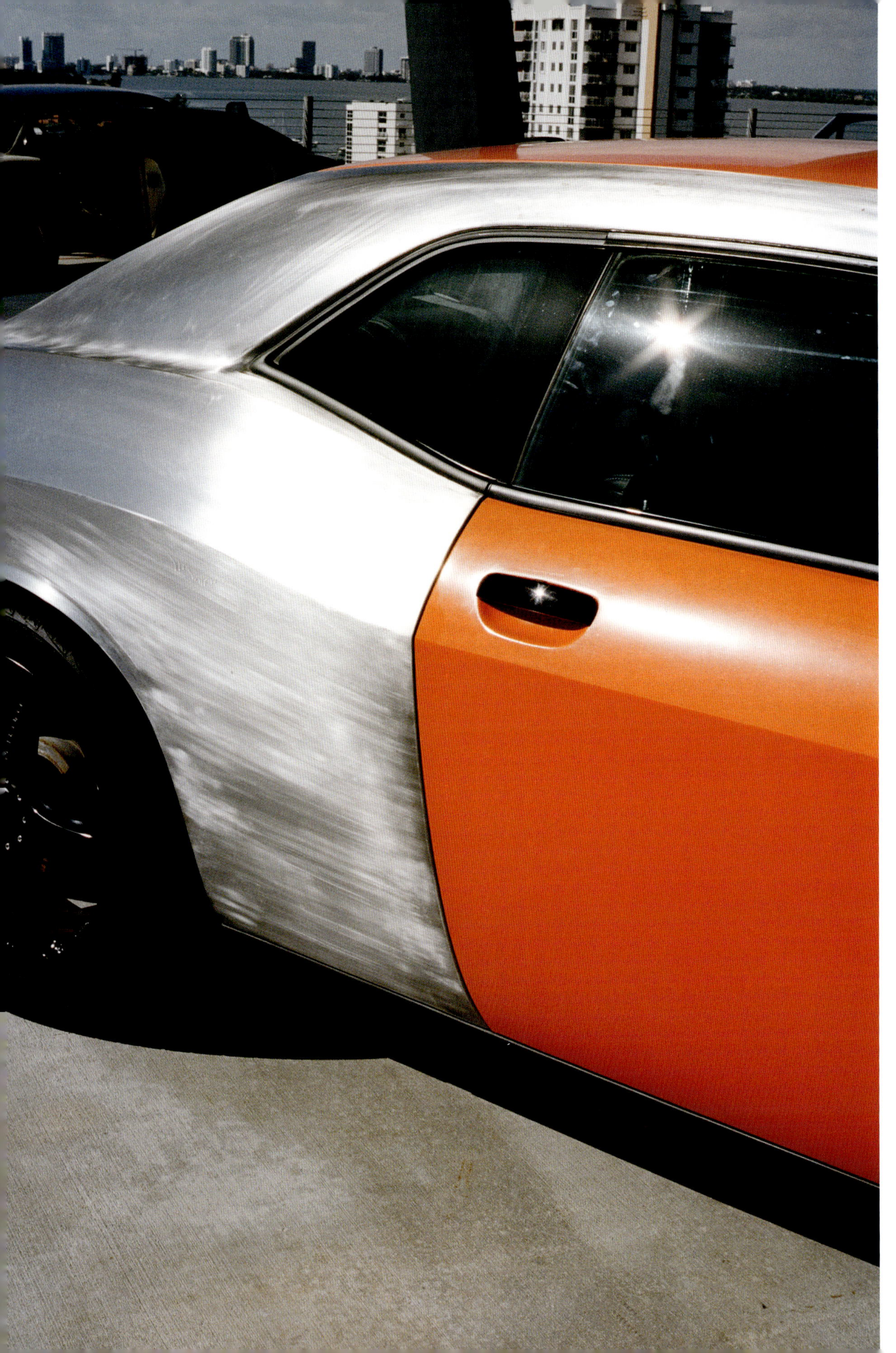

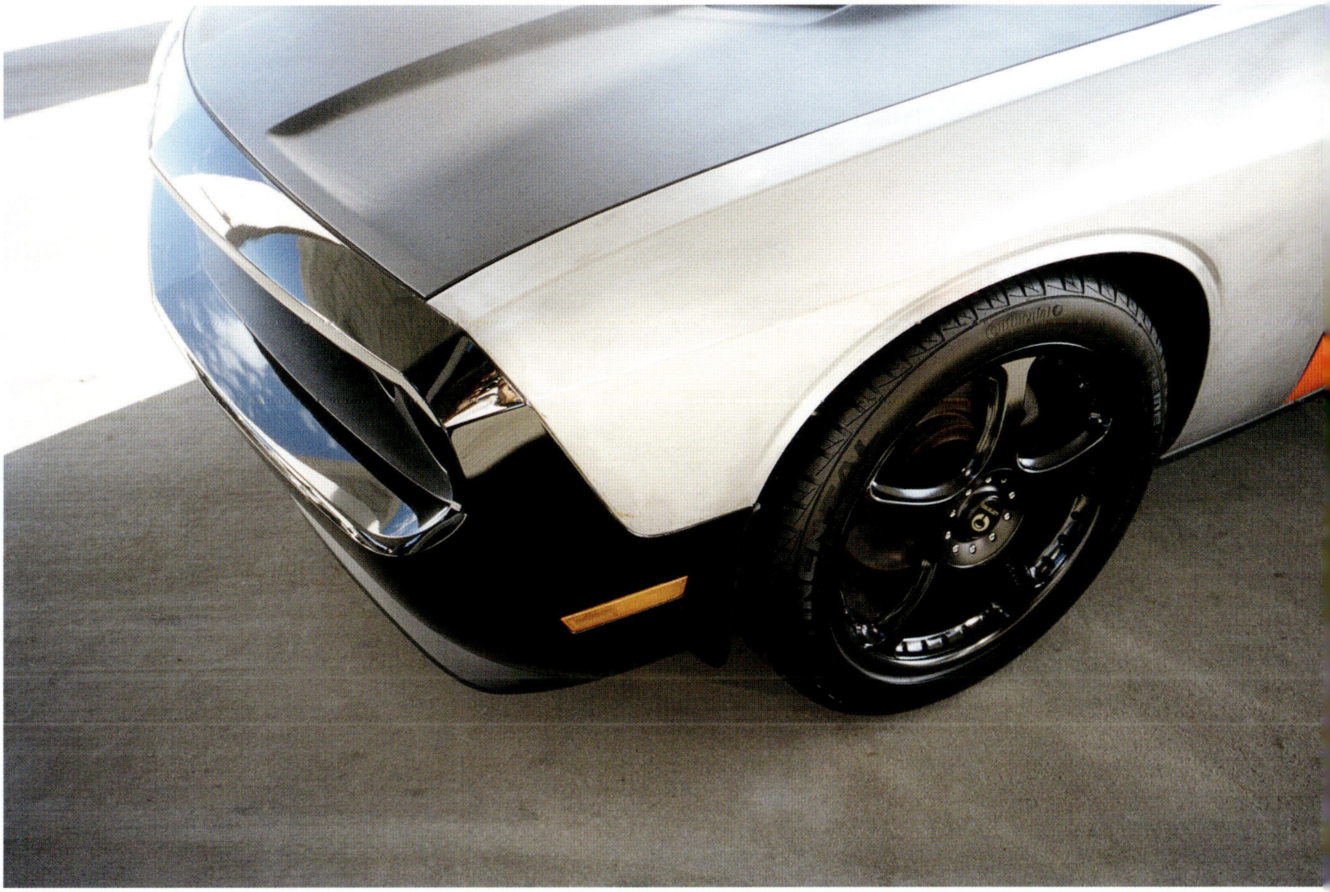

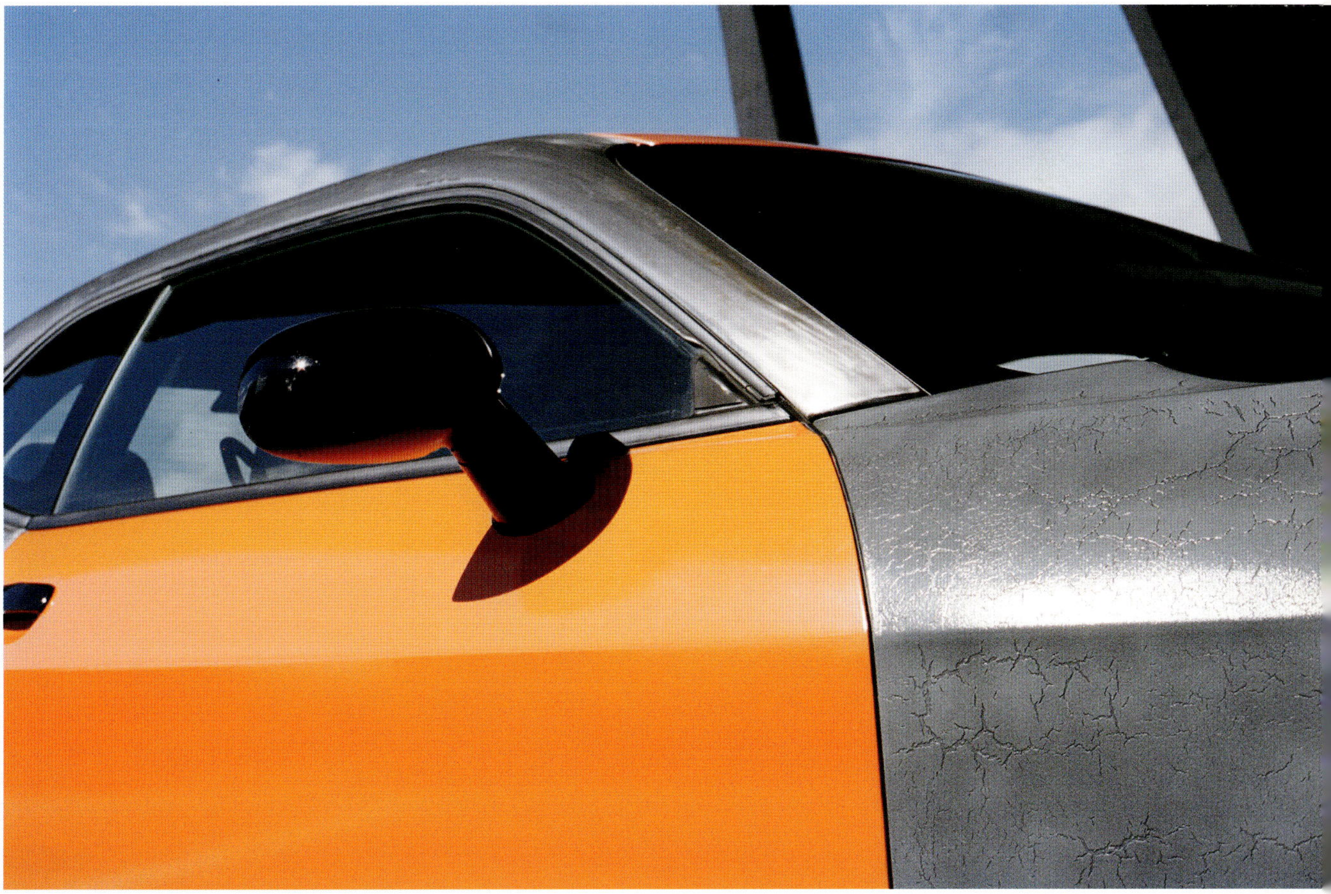

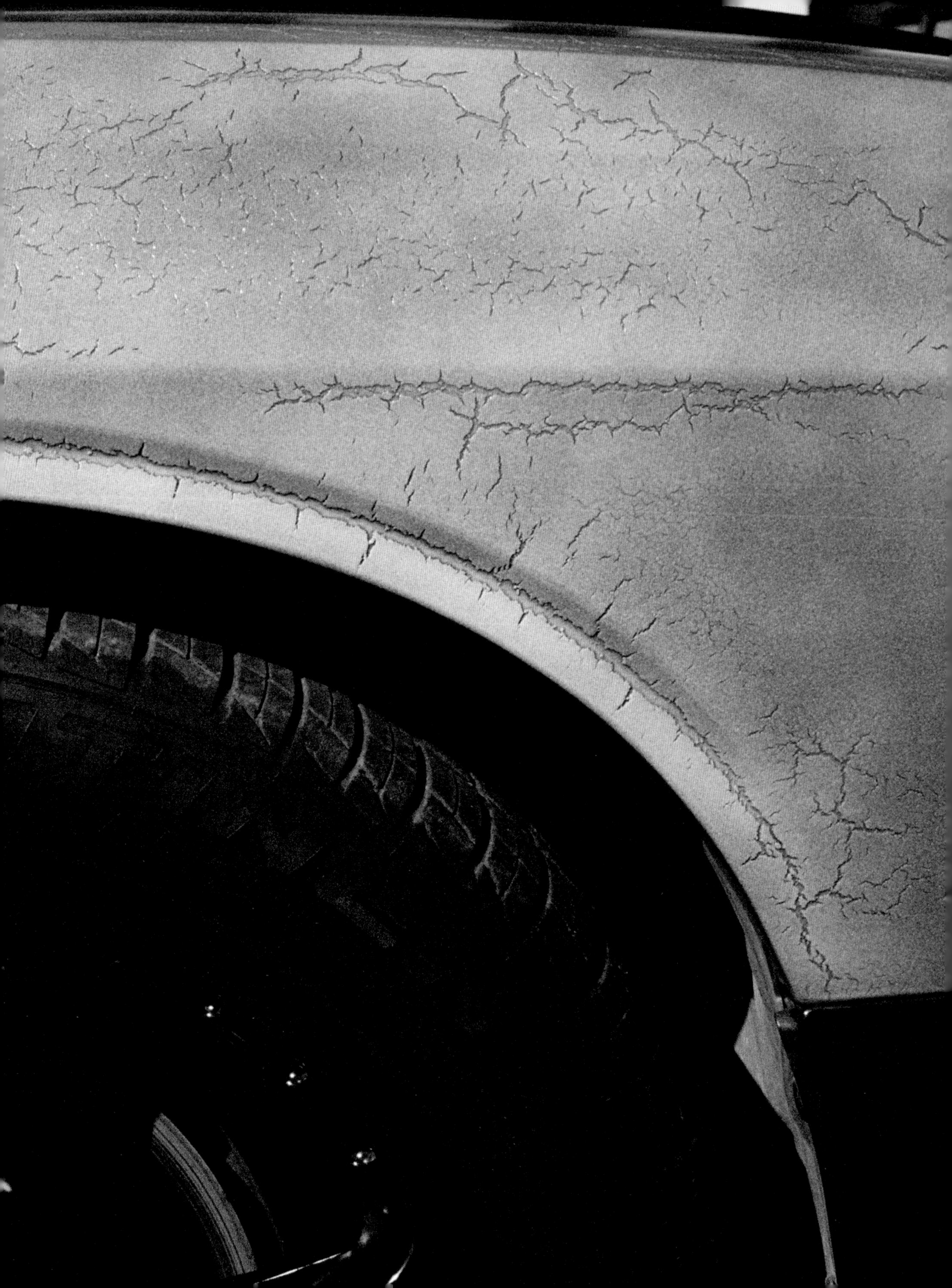

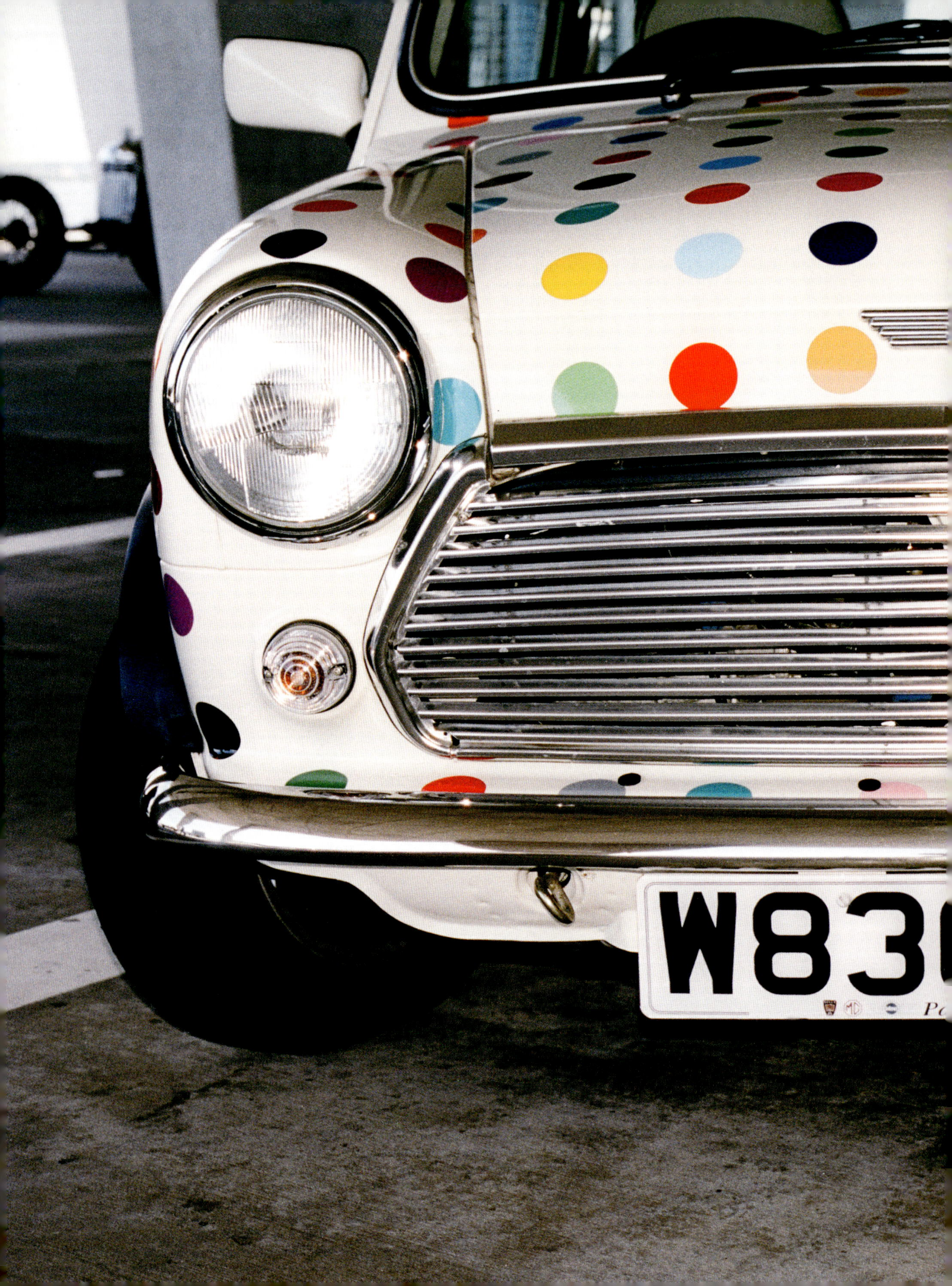
W83

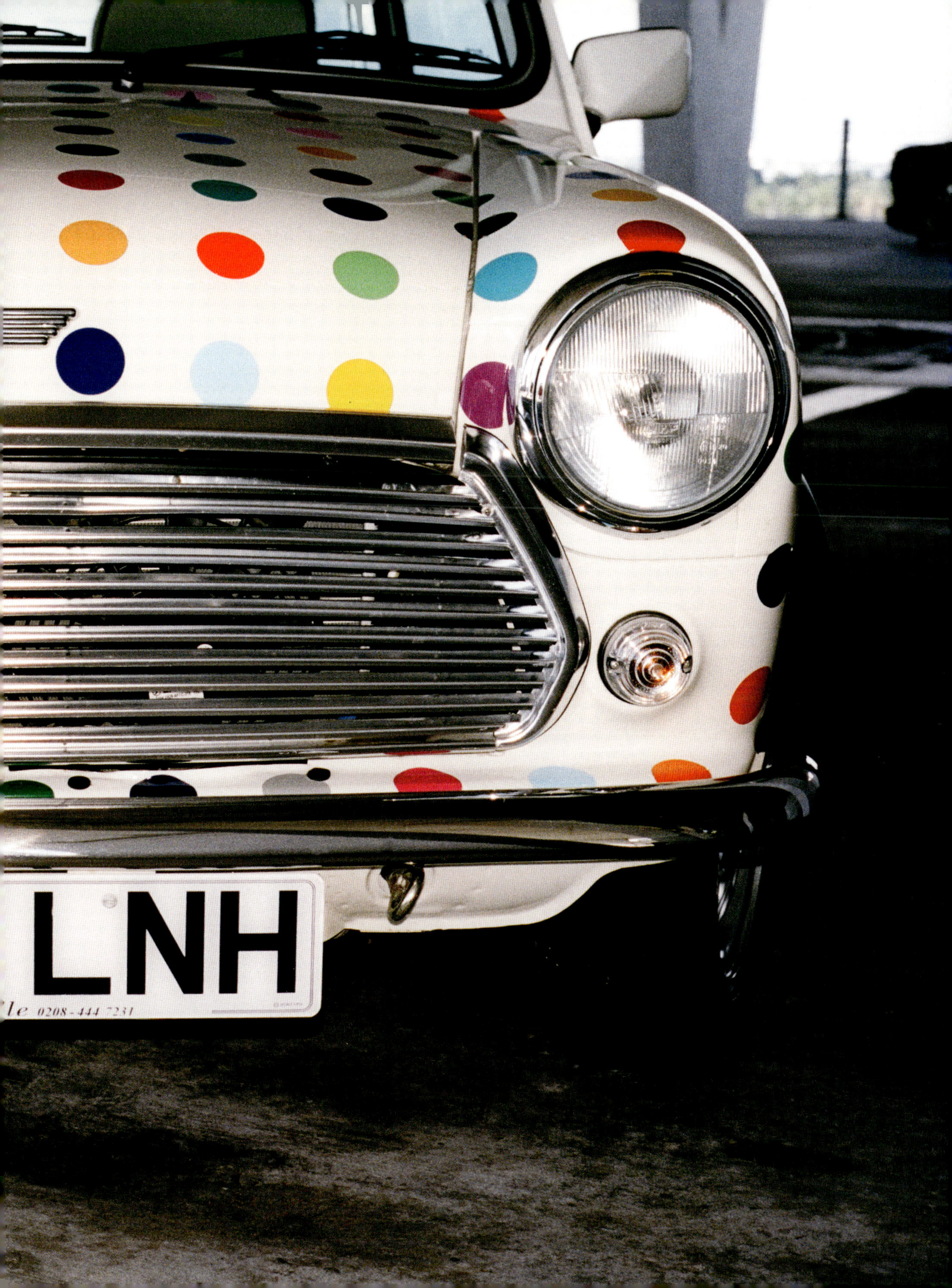
LNH
le 0208-444 7231

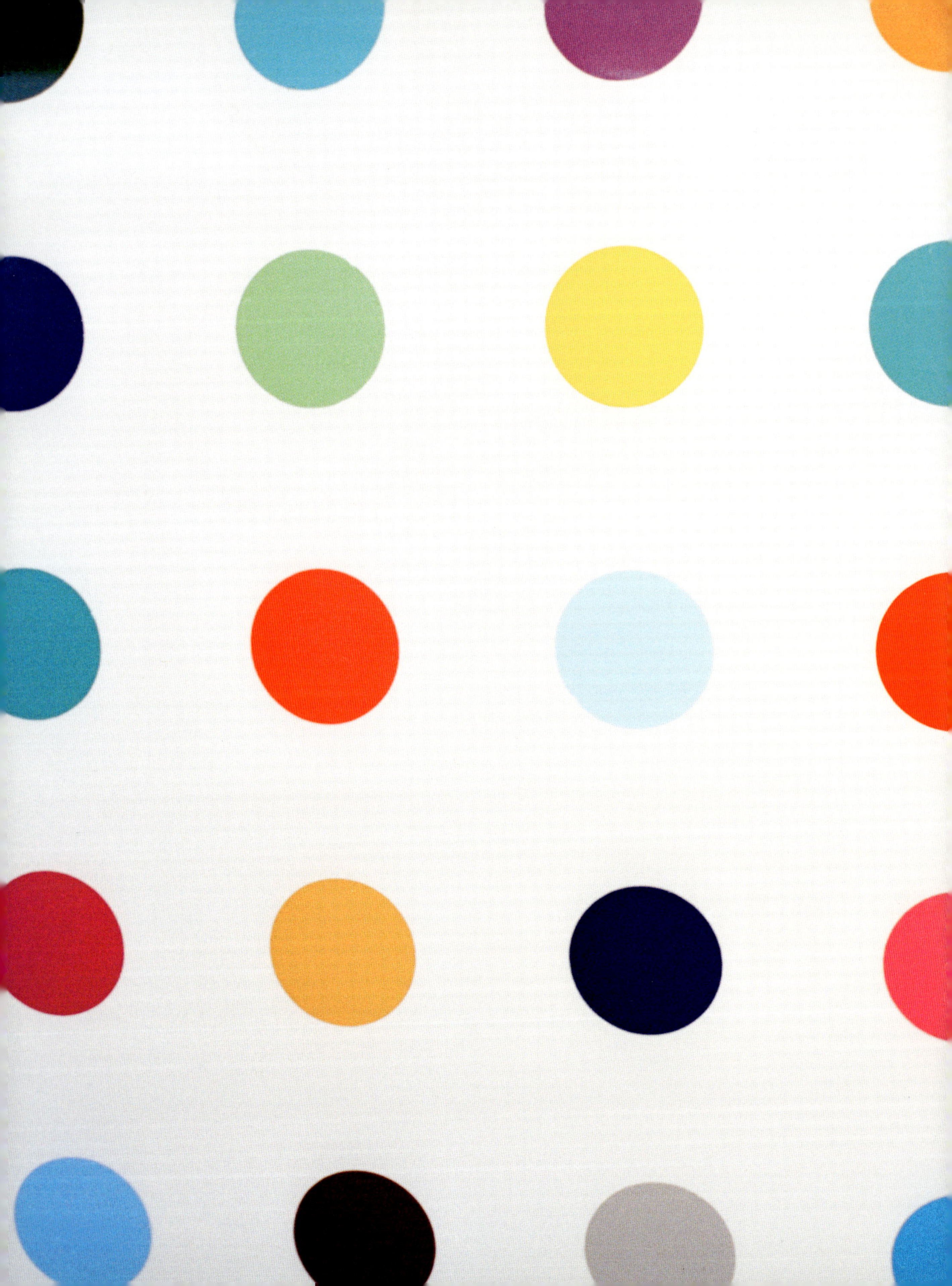

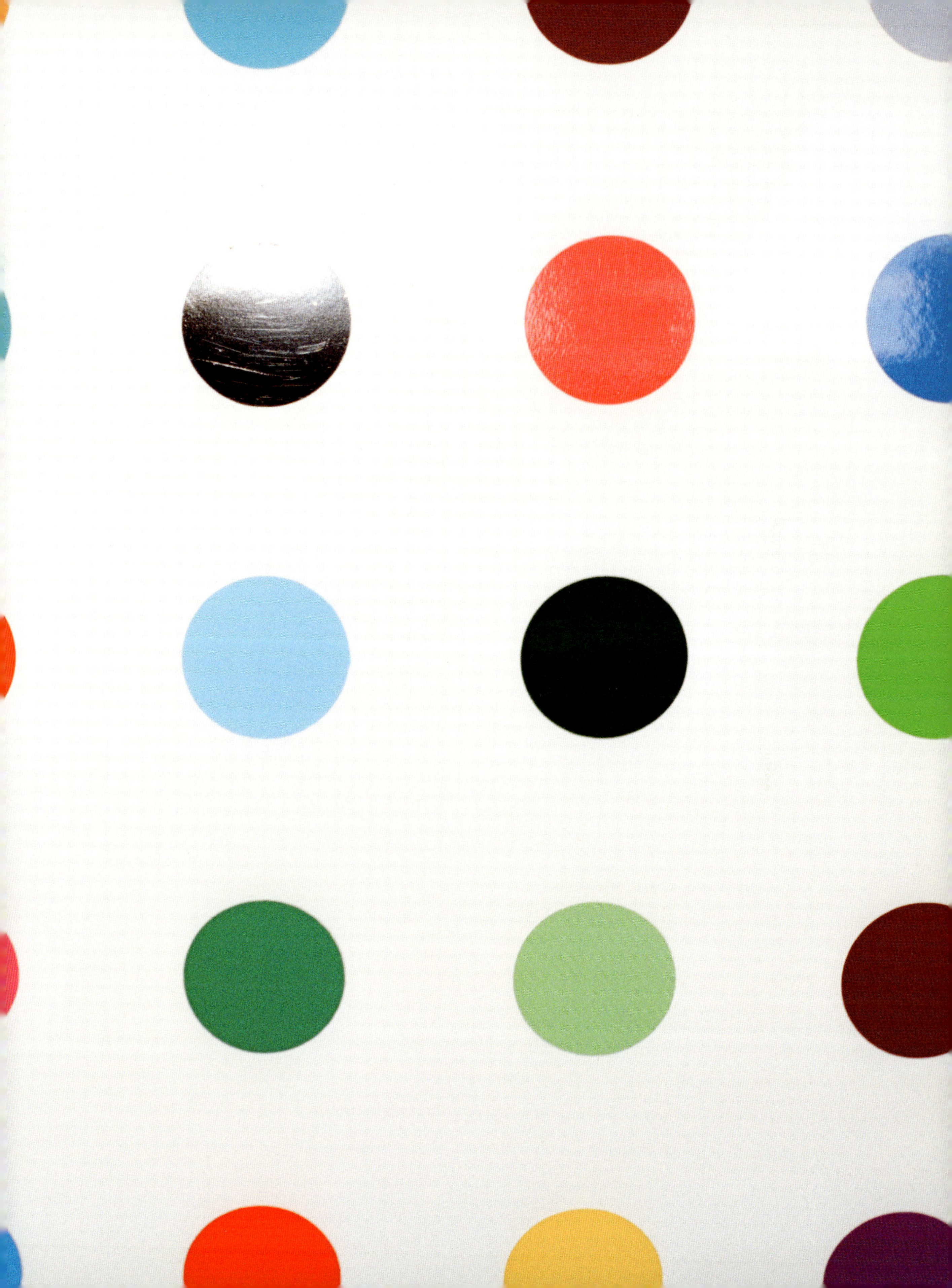

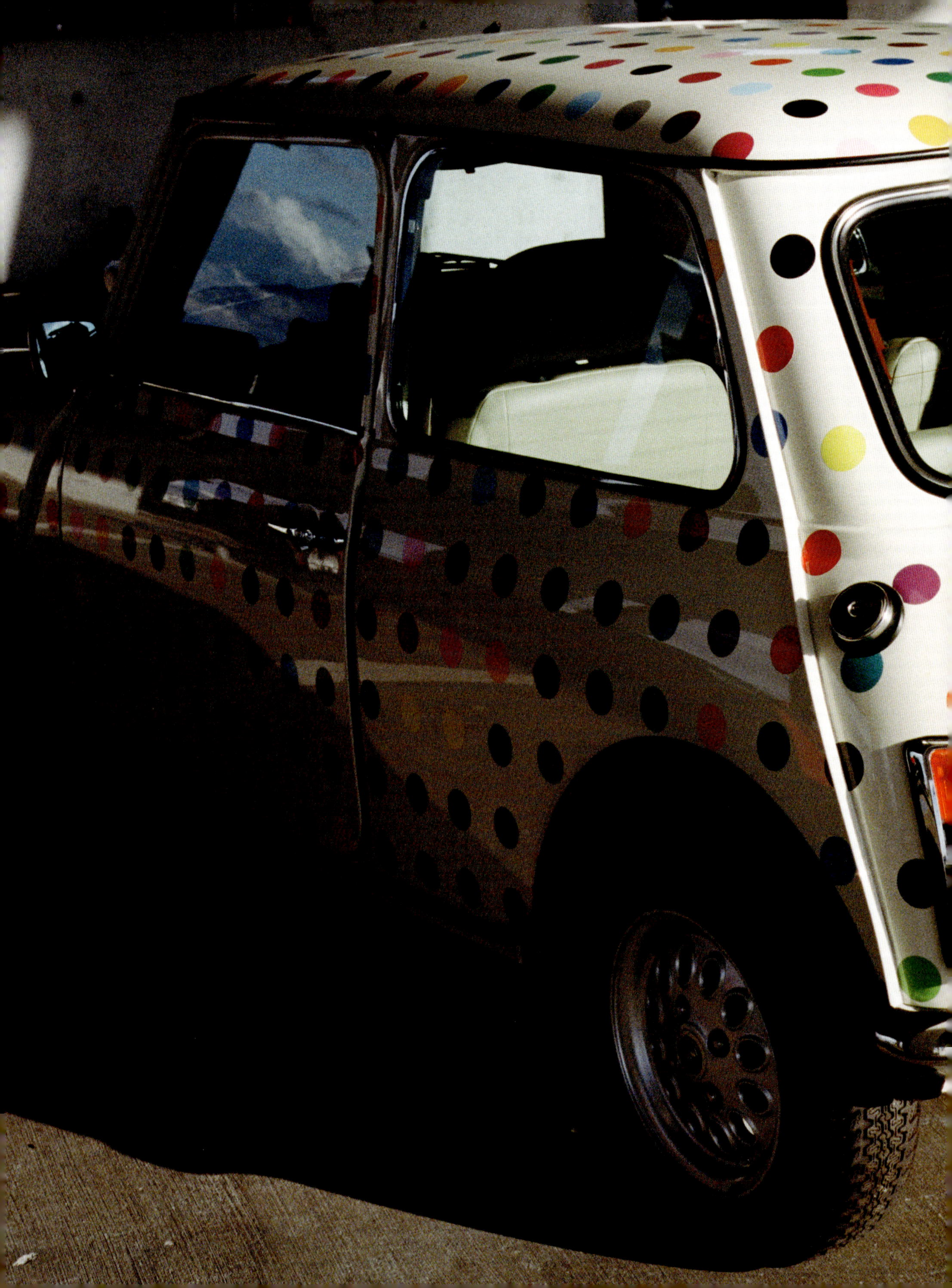

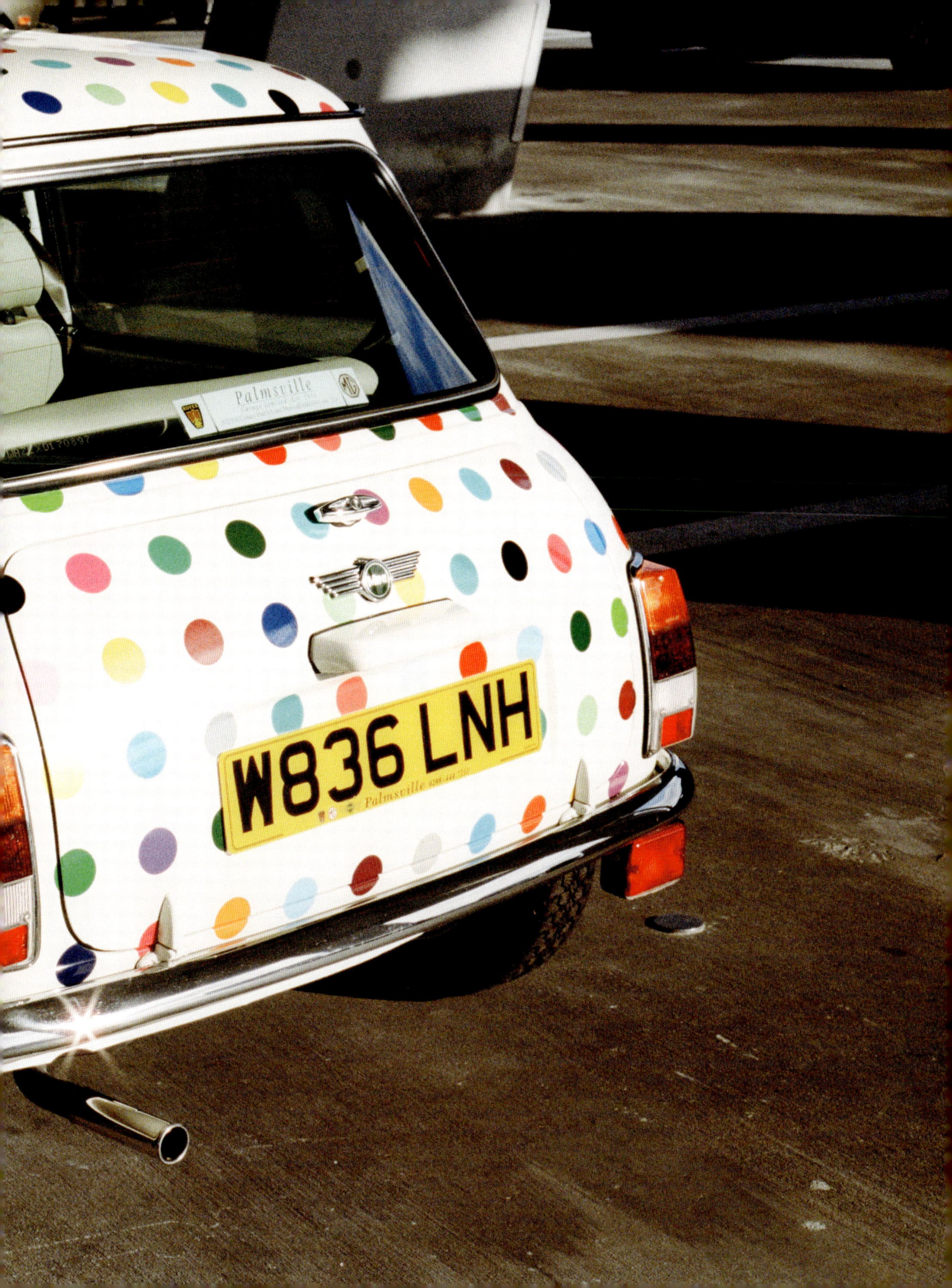
Palmsville
W836 LNH
Palmsville

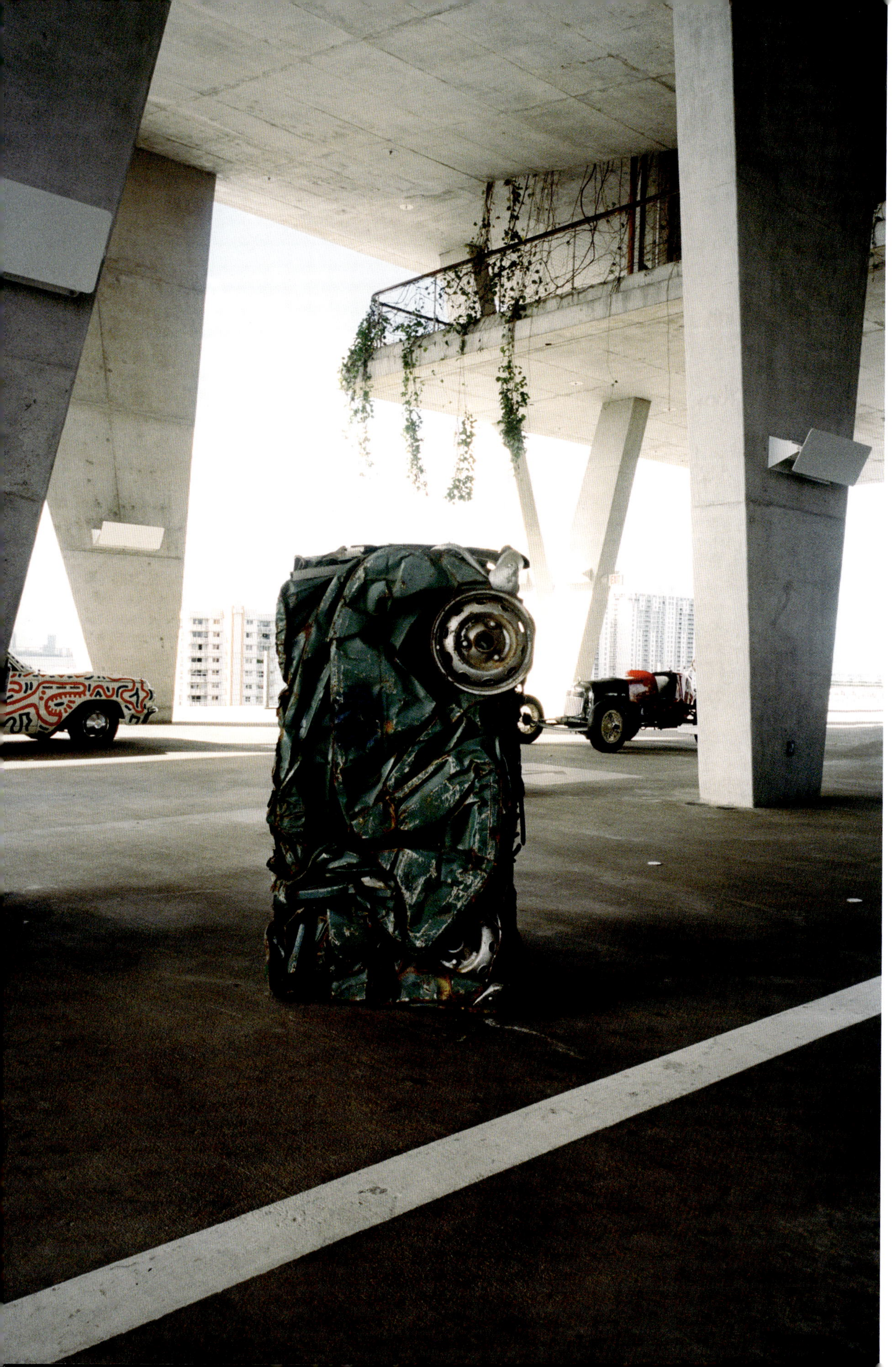

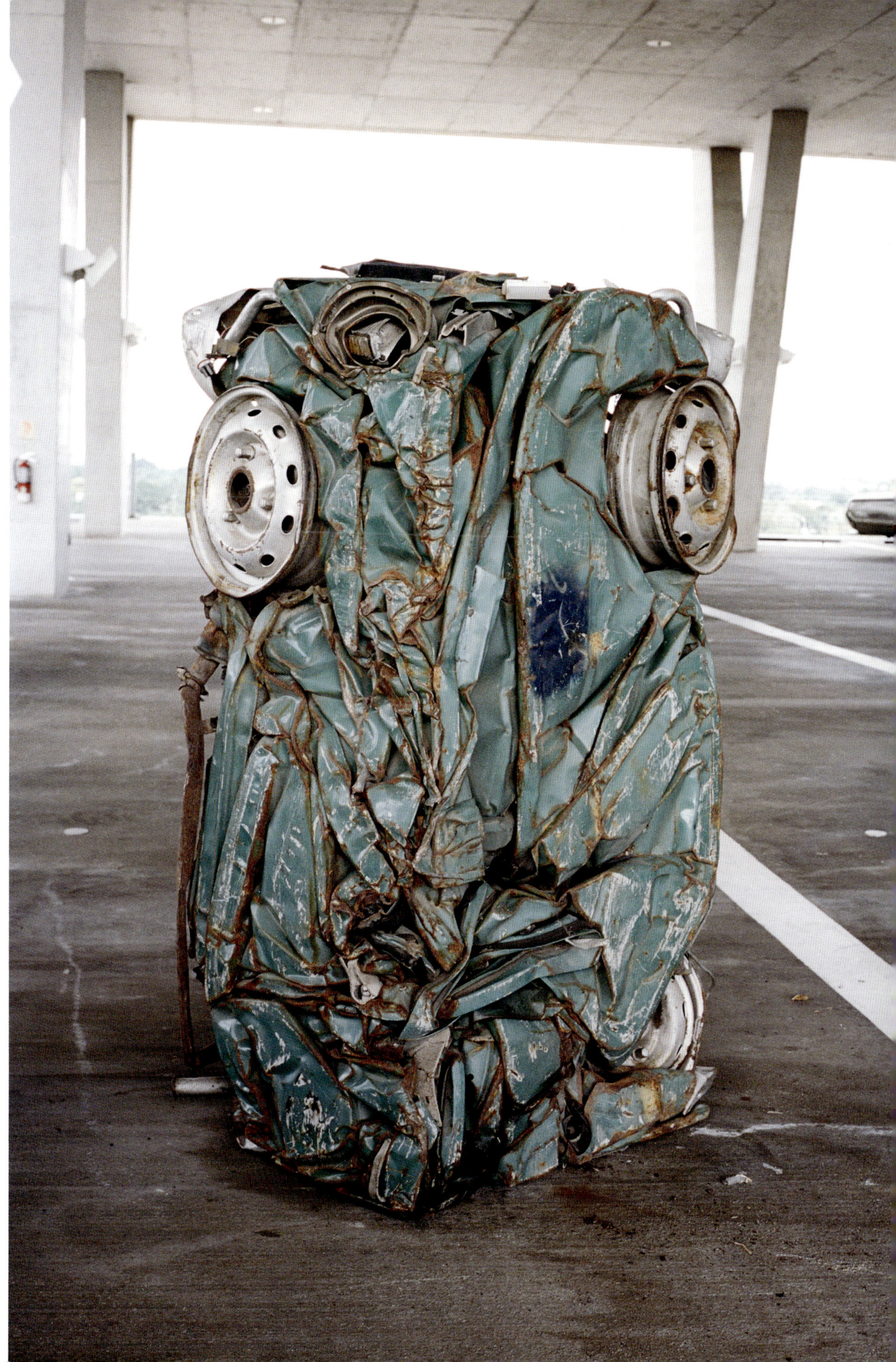

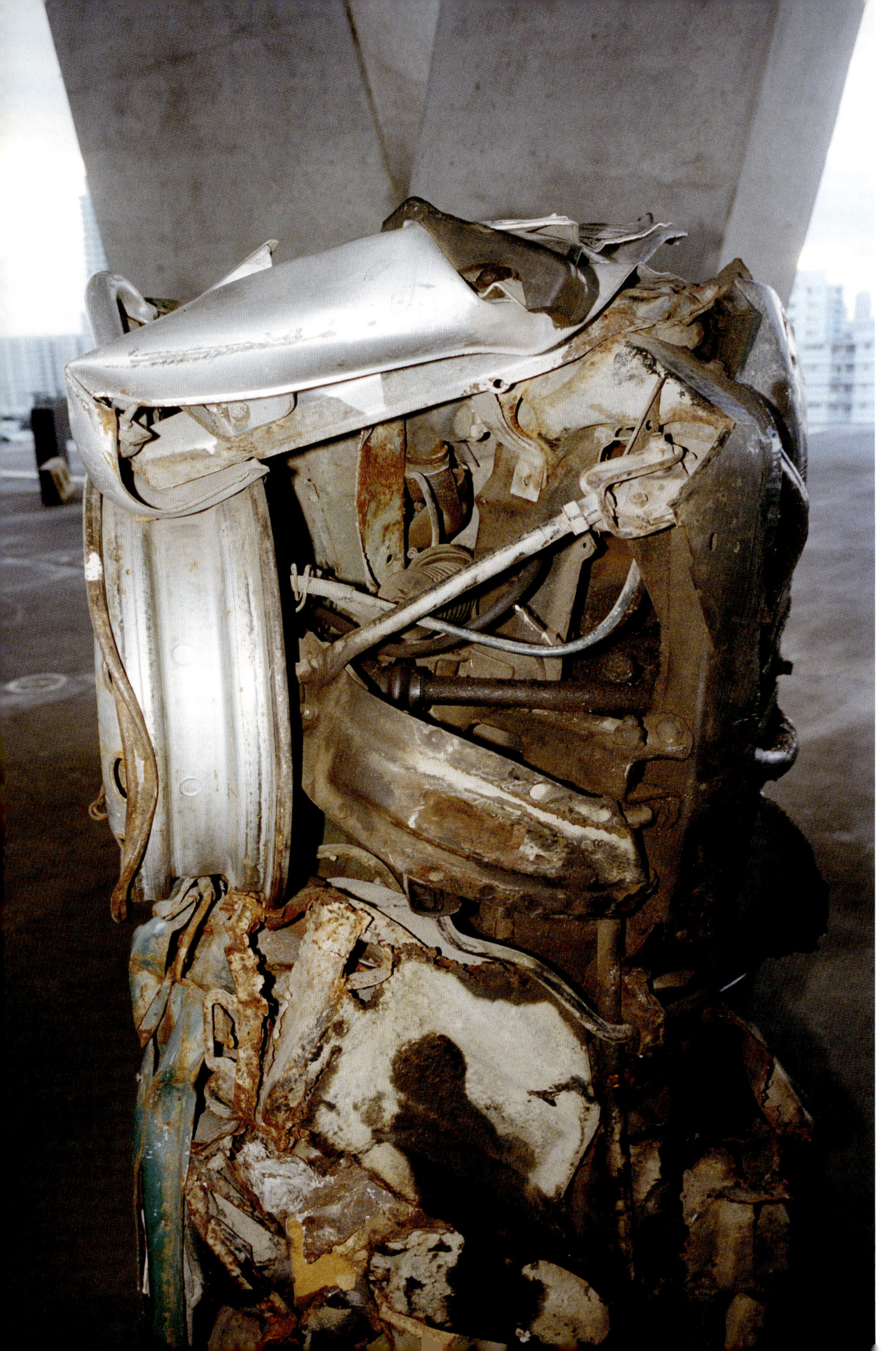

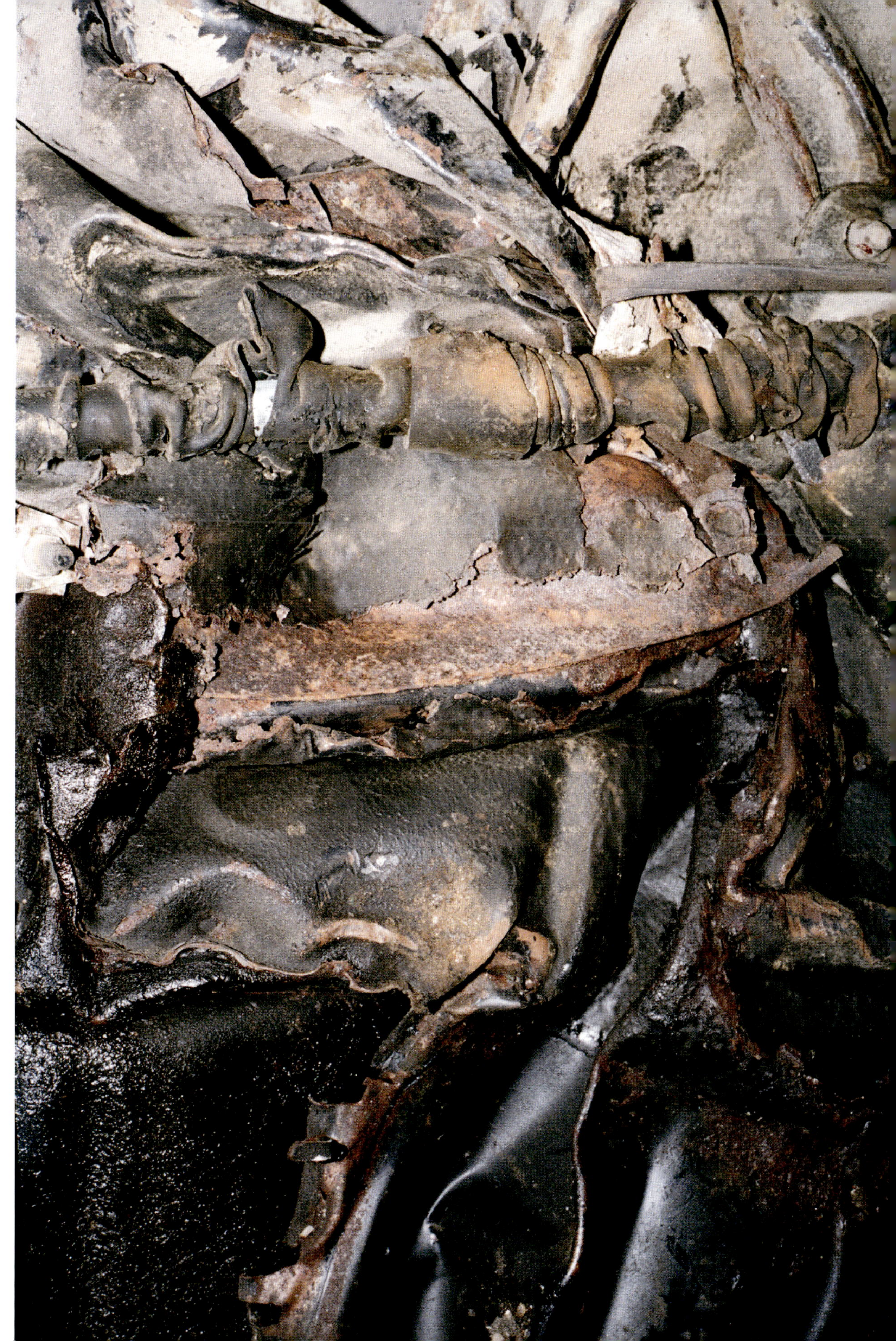

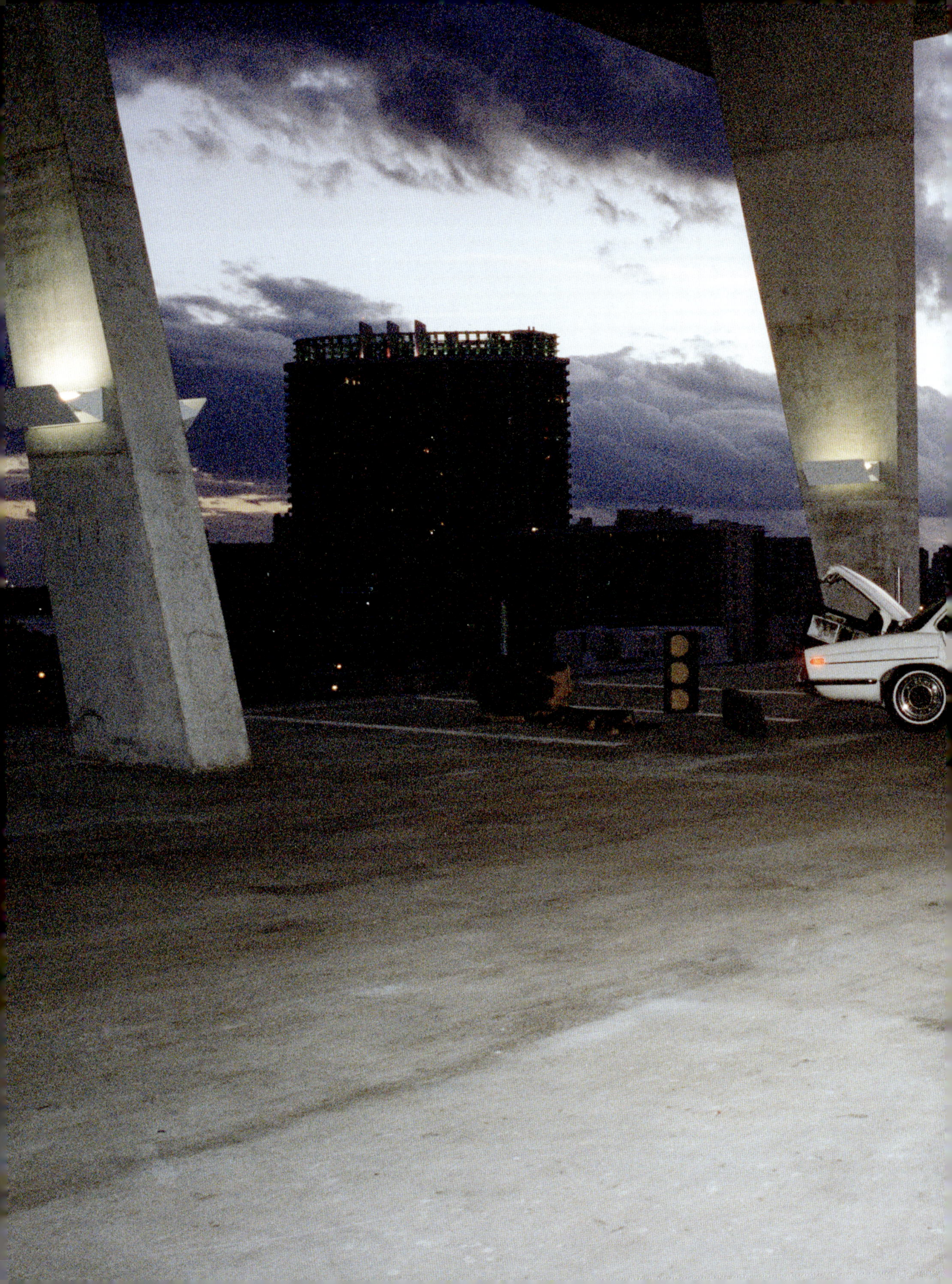

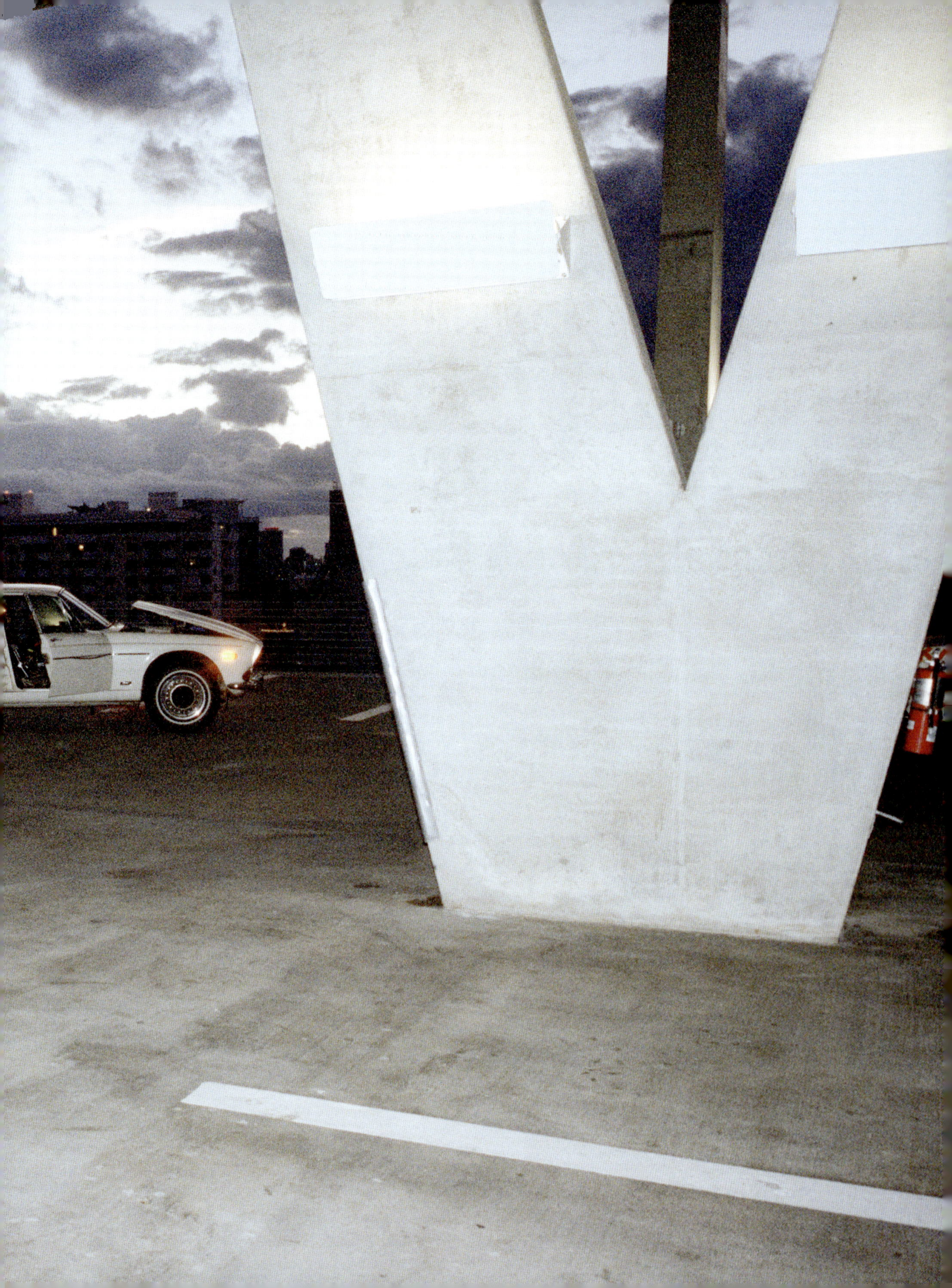

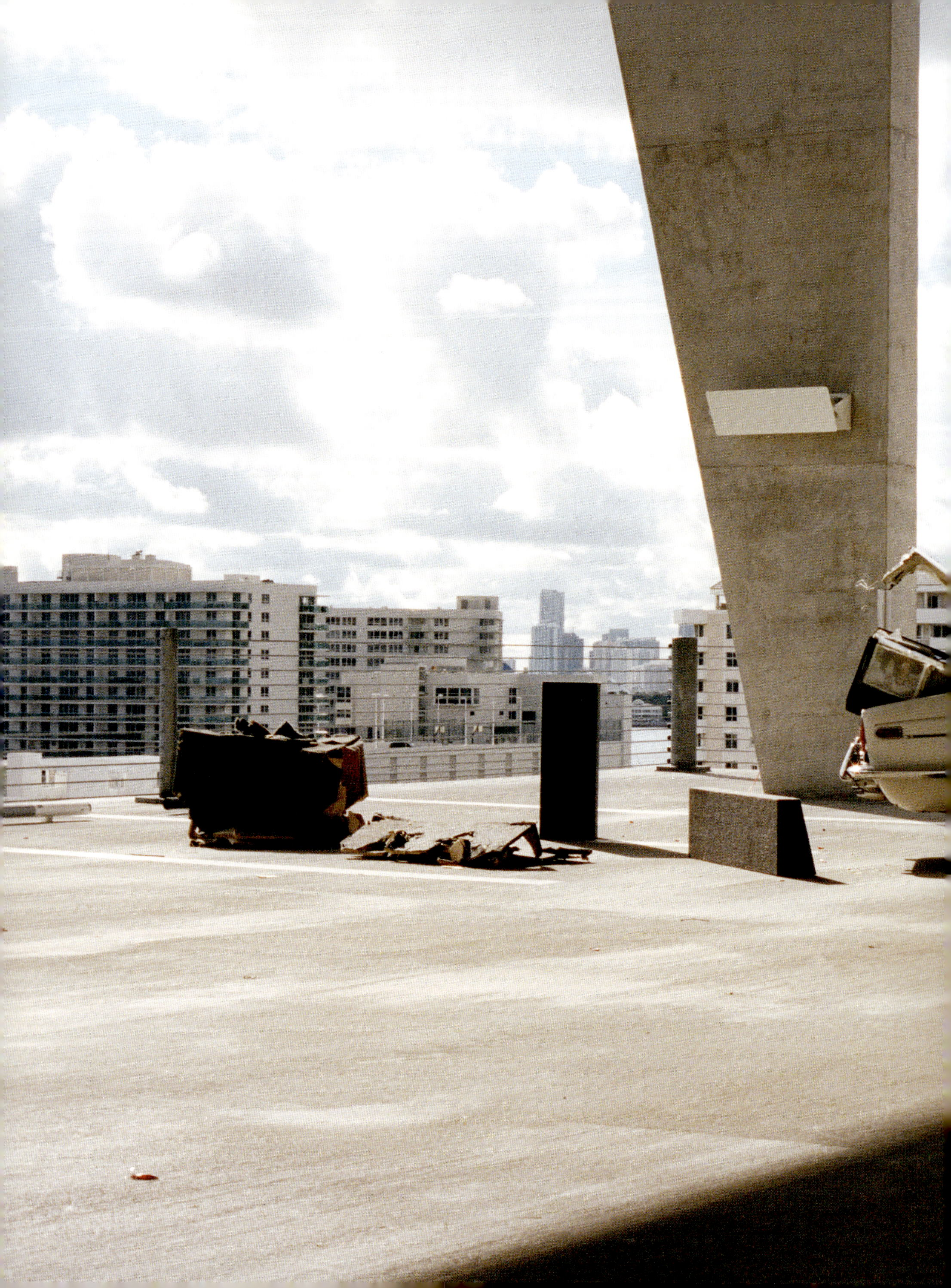

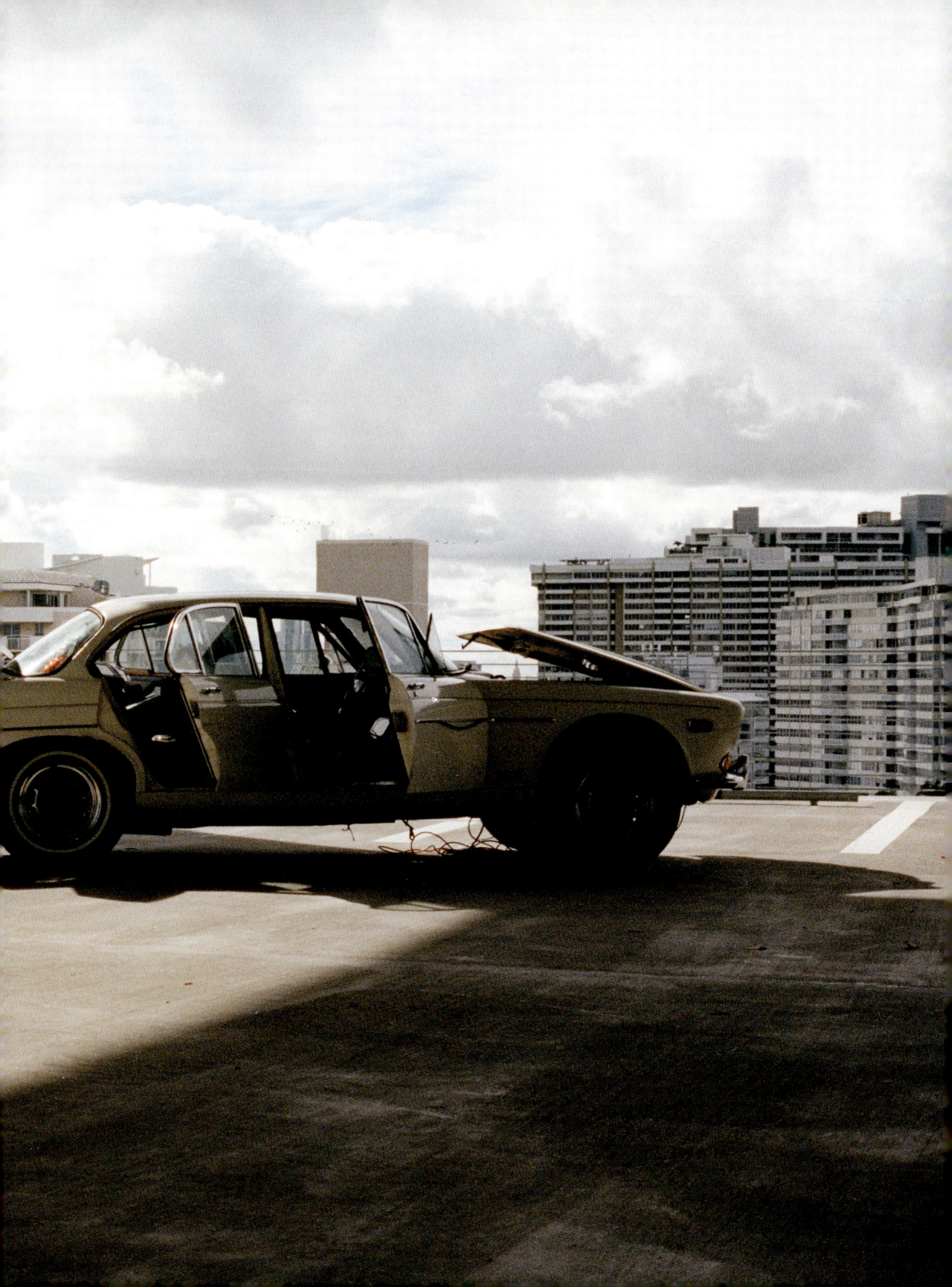

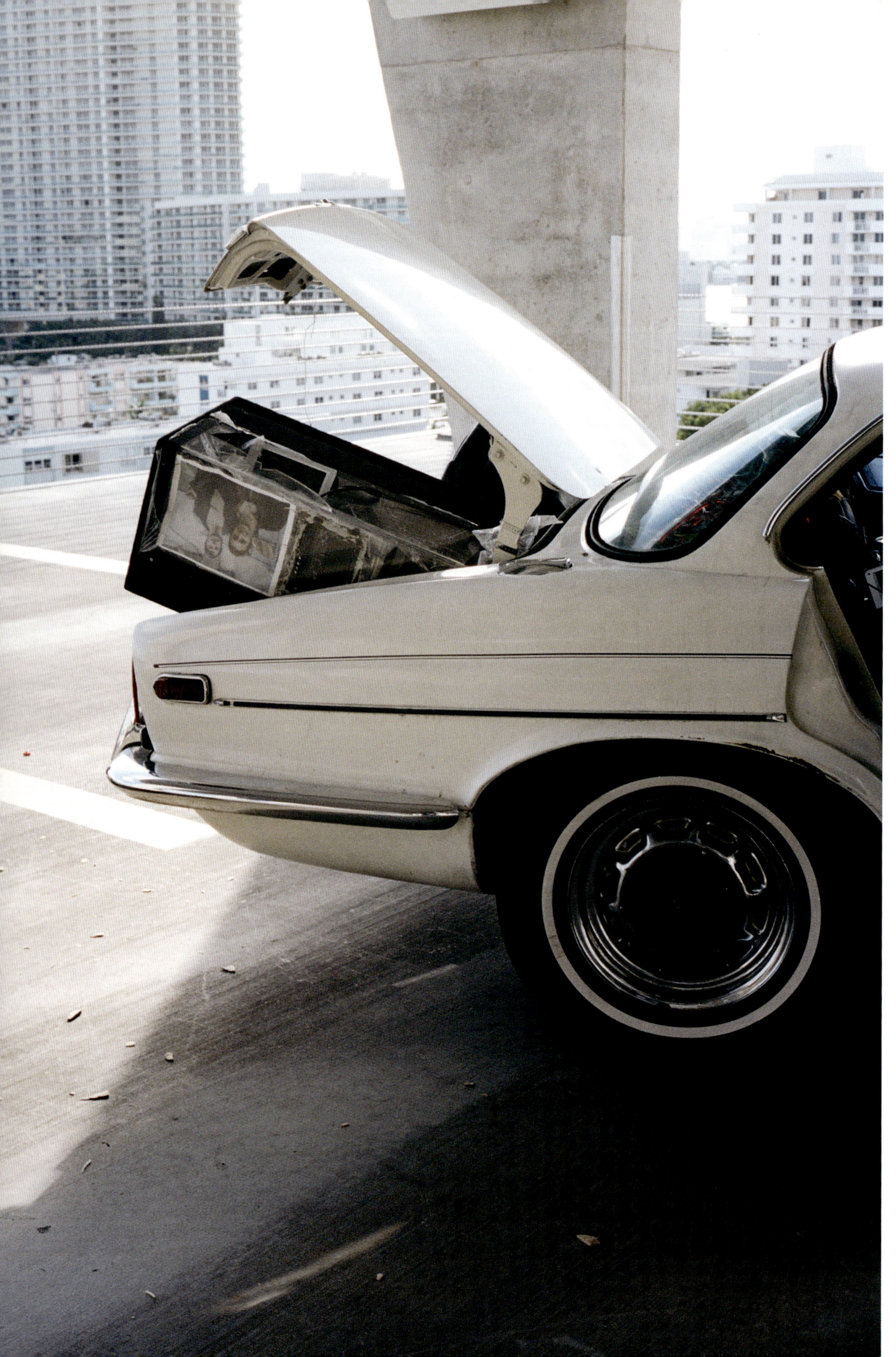

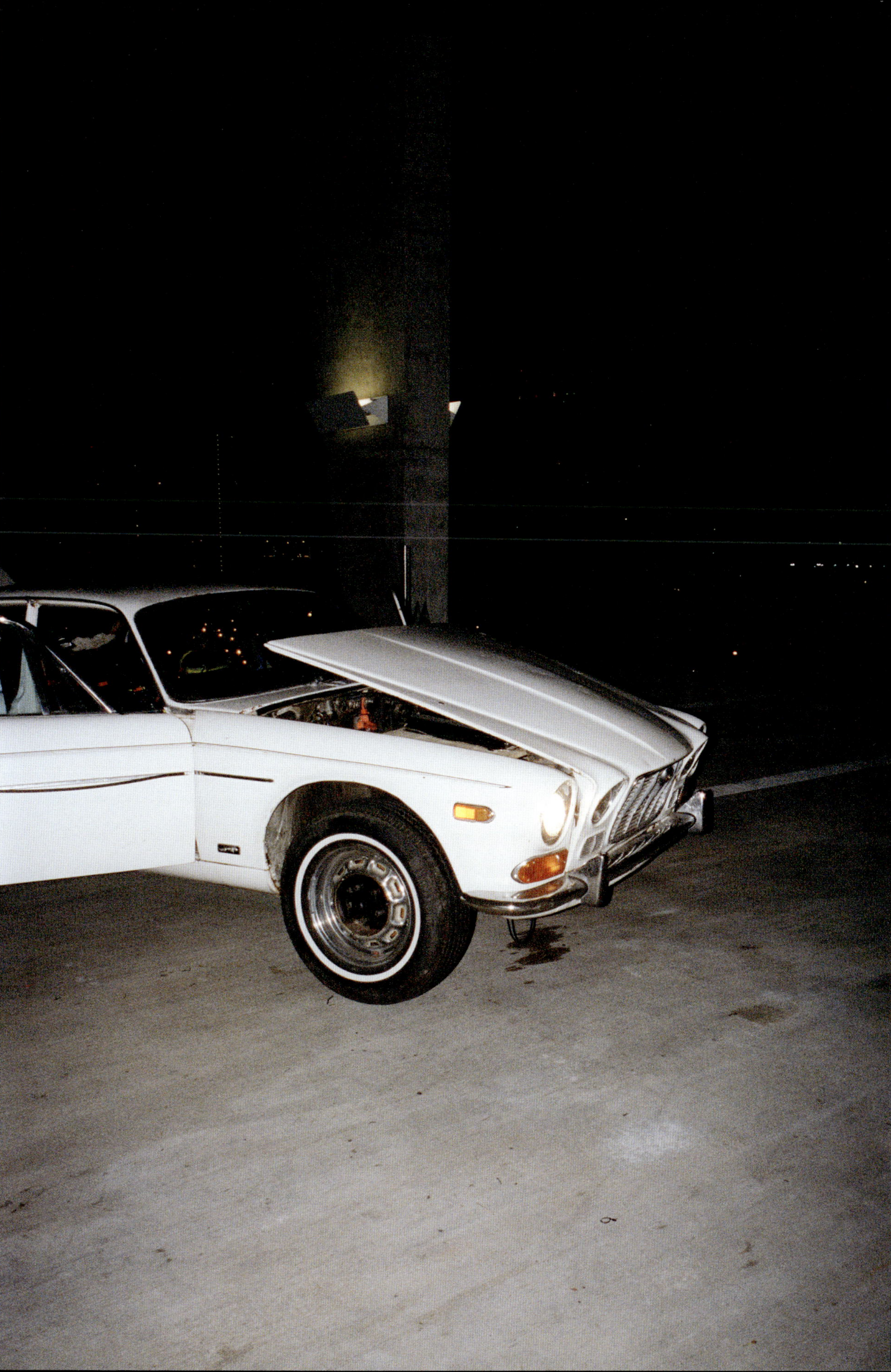

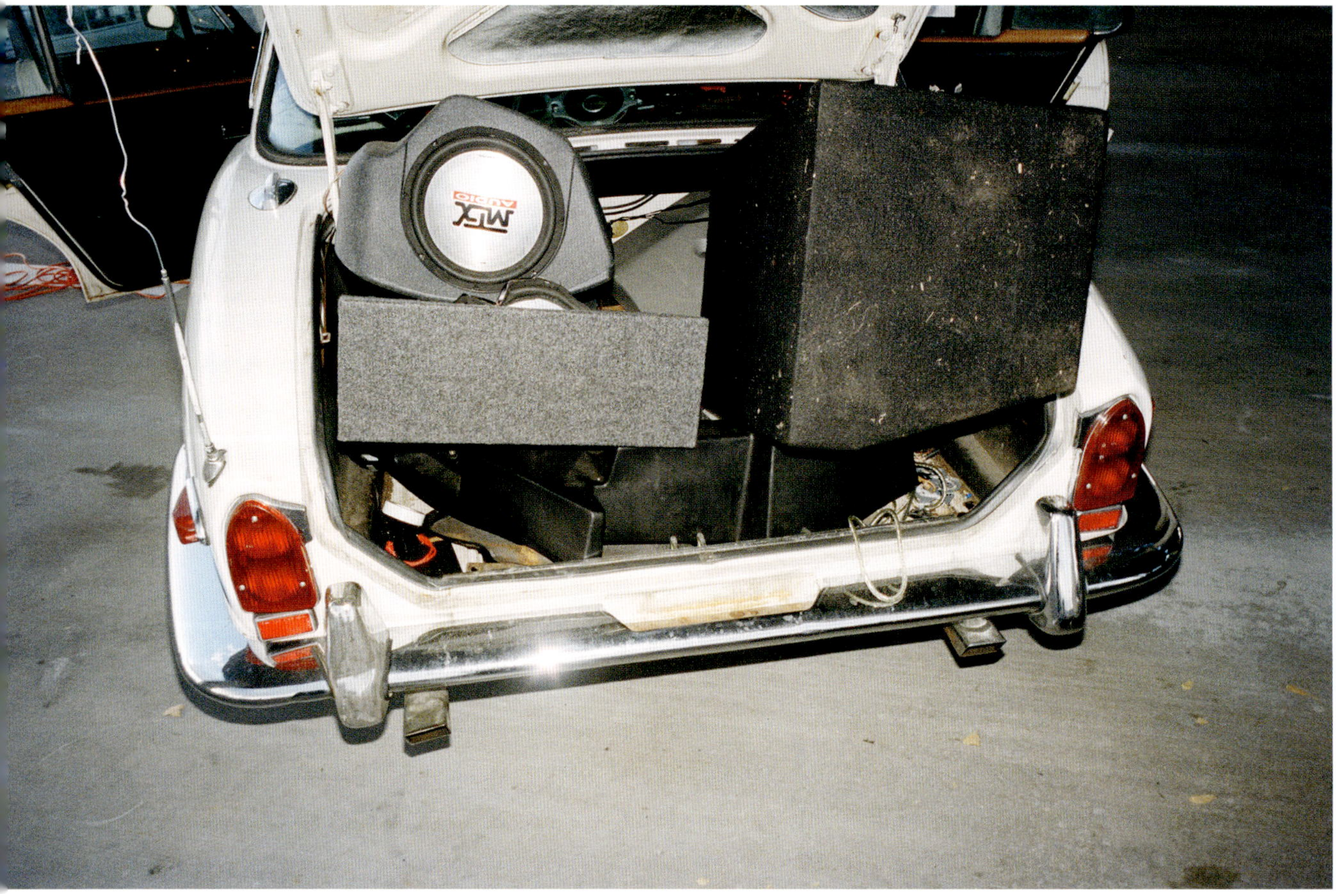

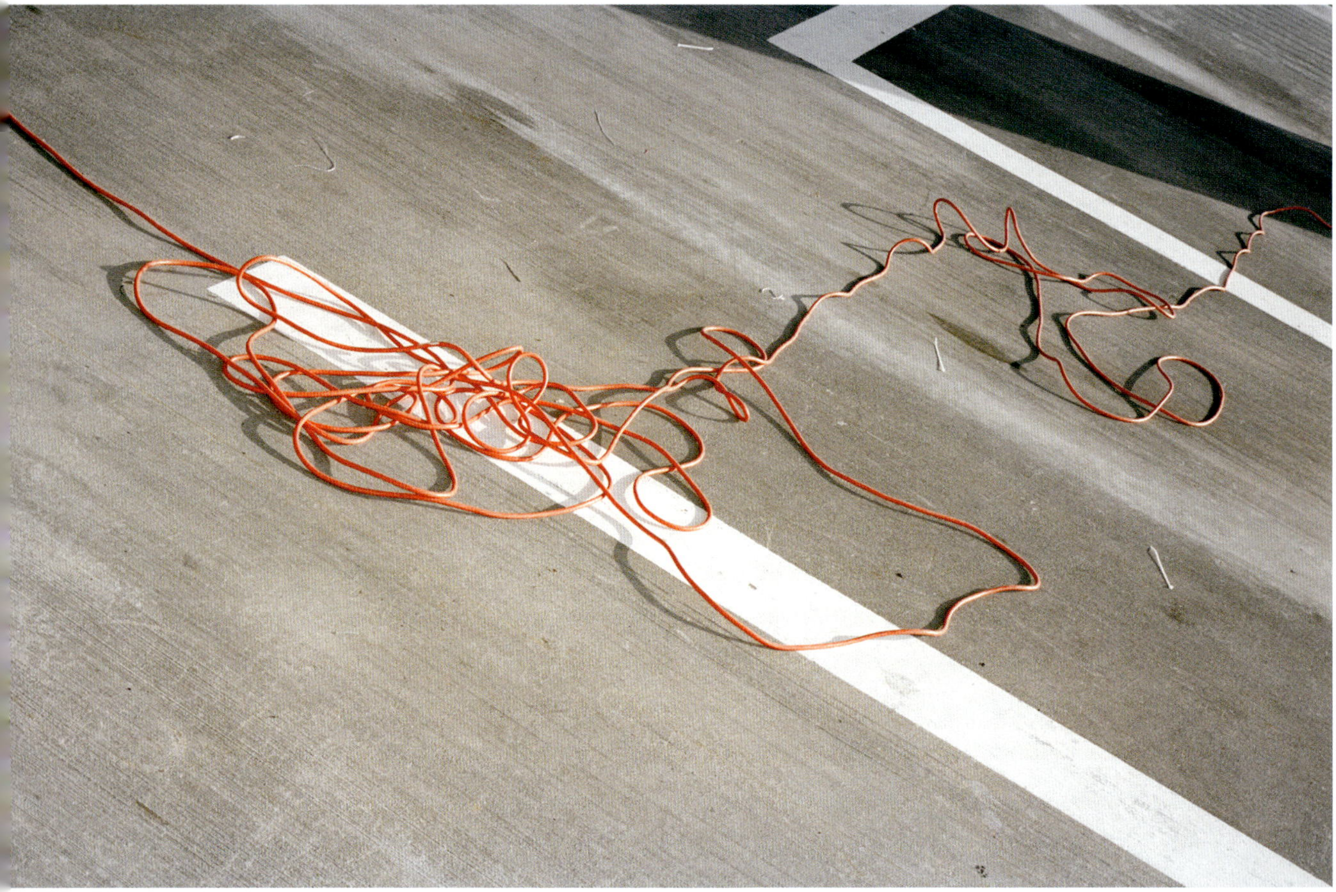

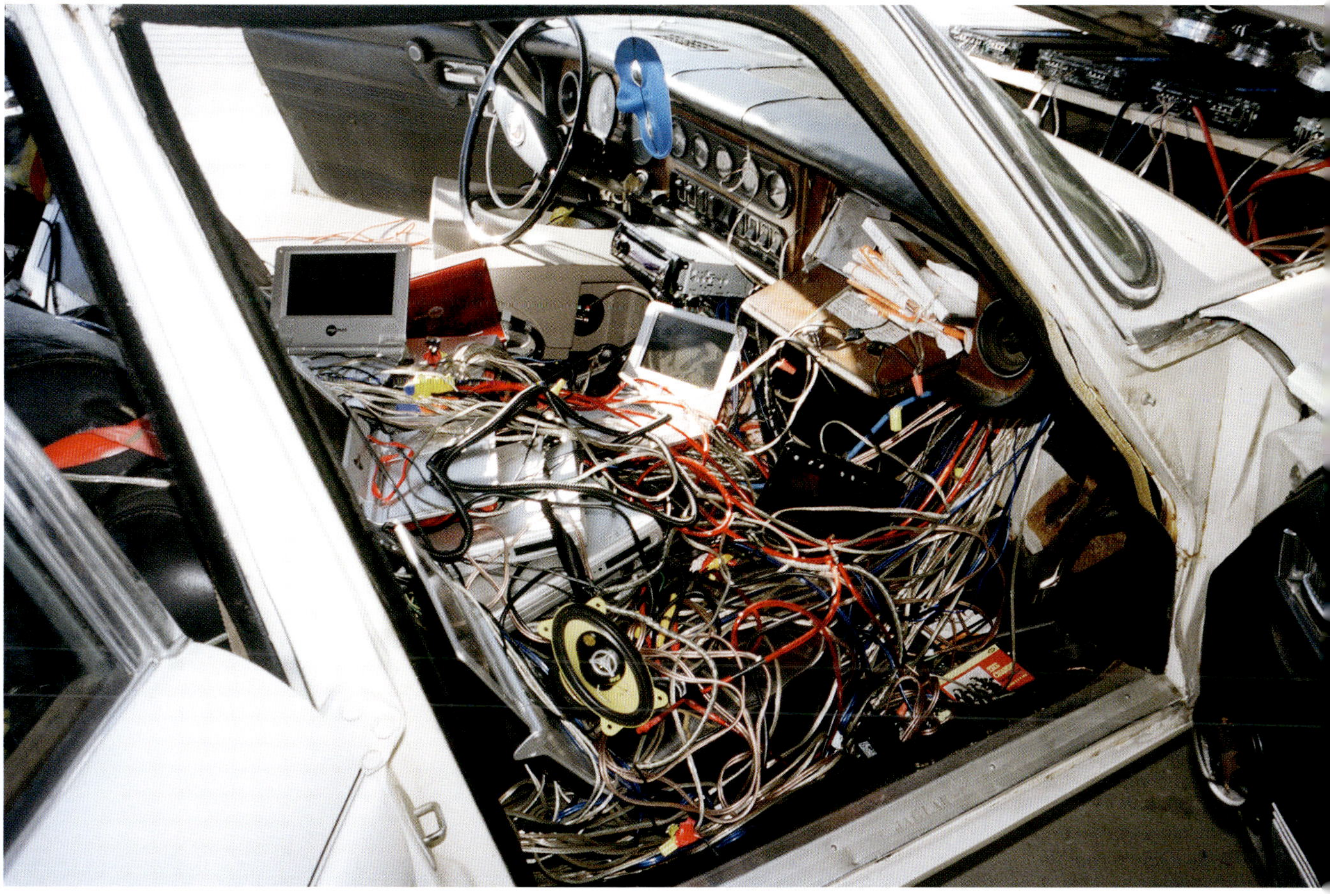

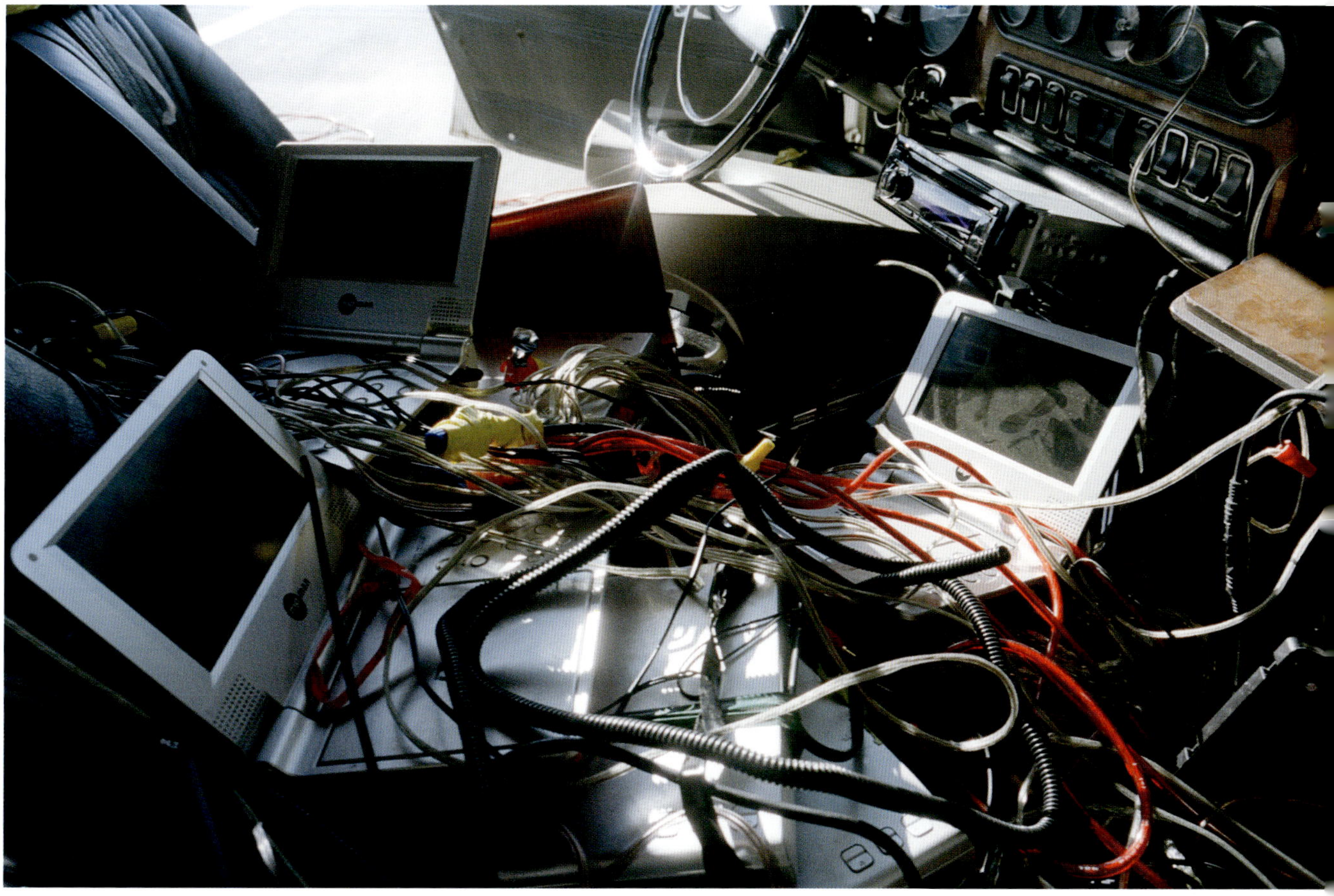

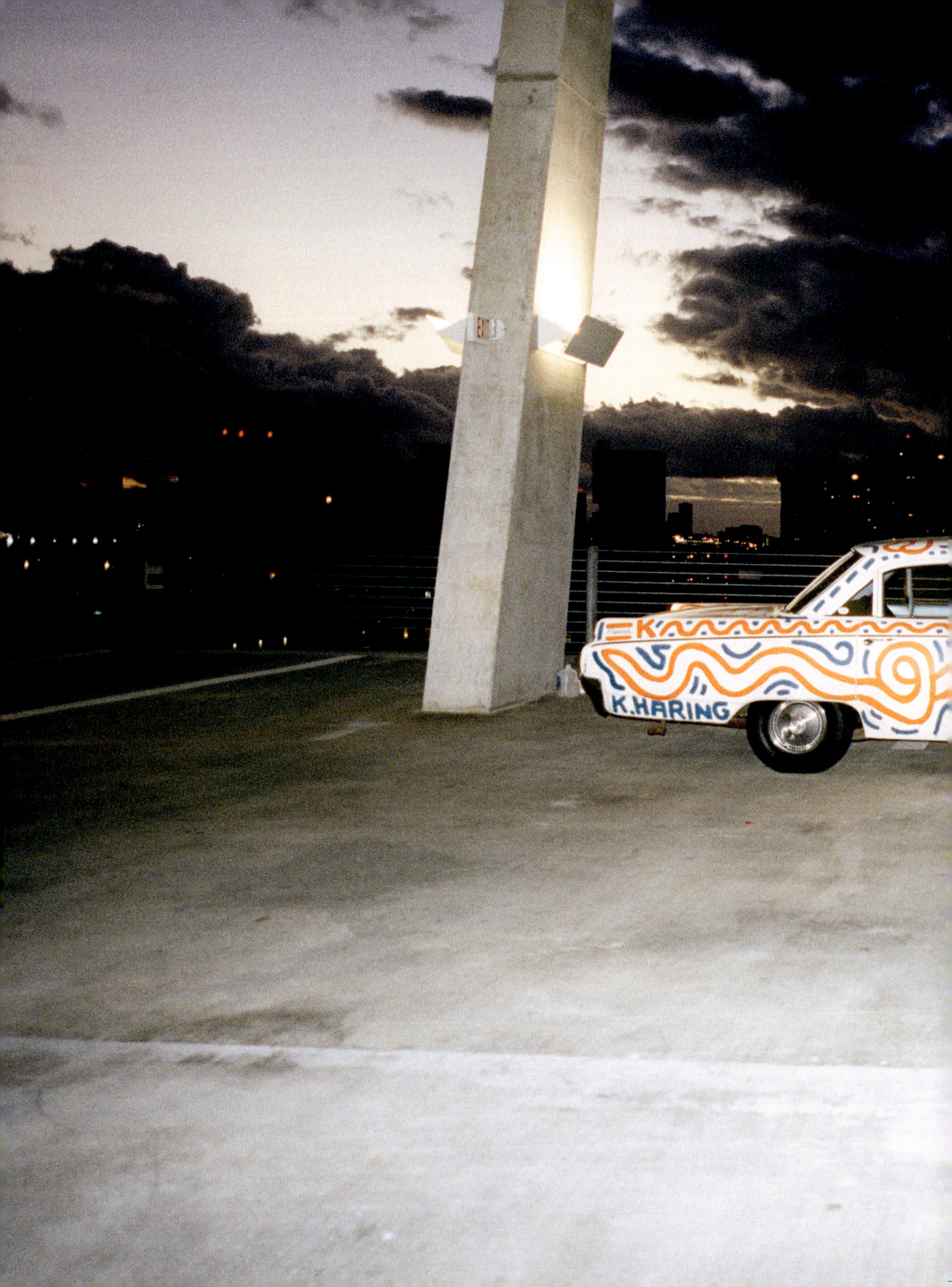
K.HARING

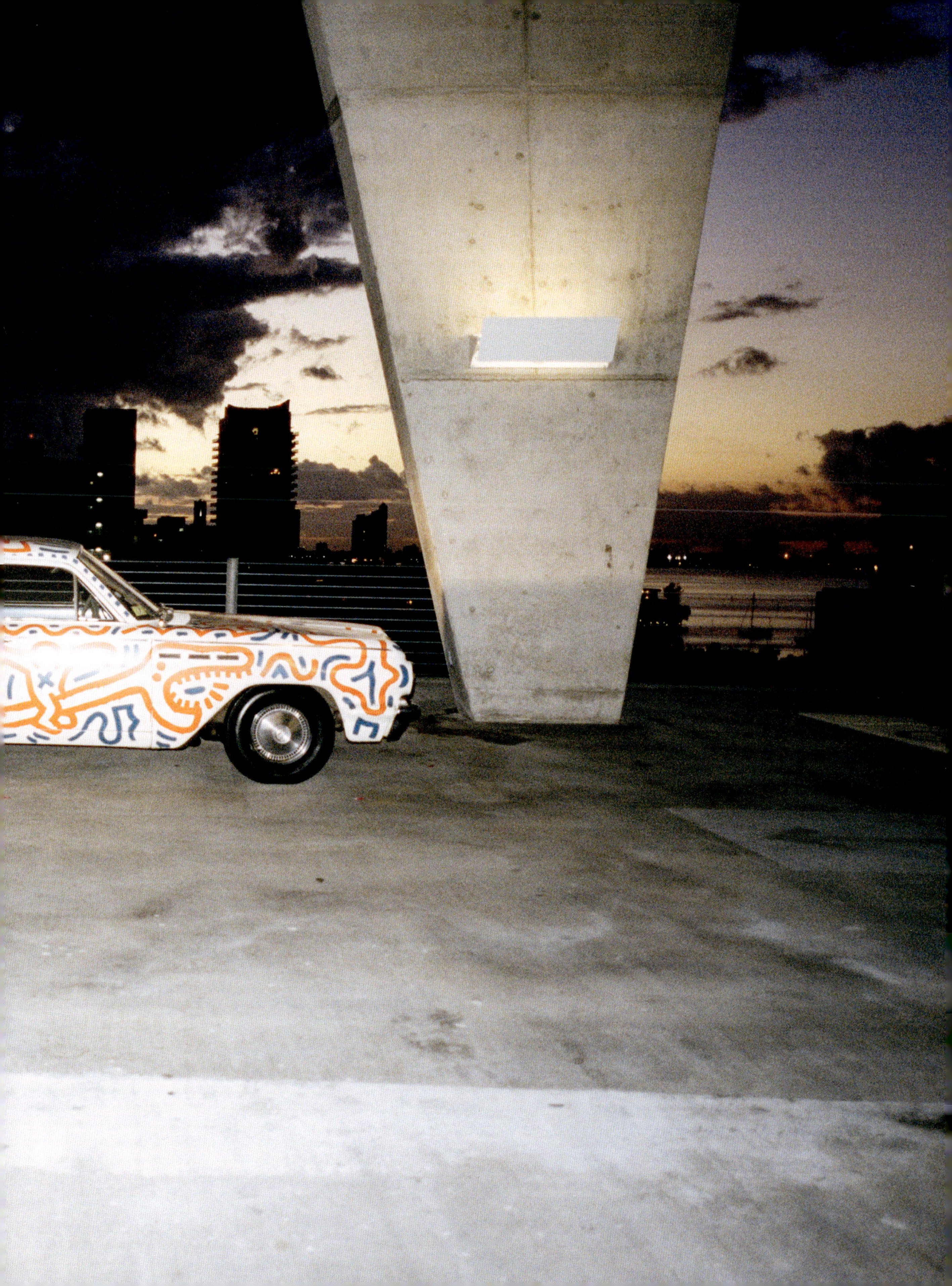

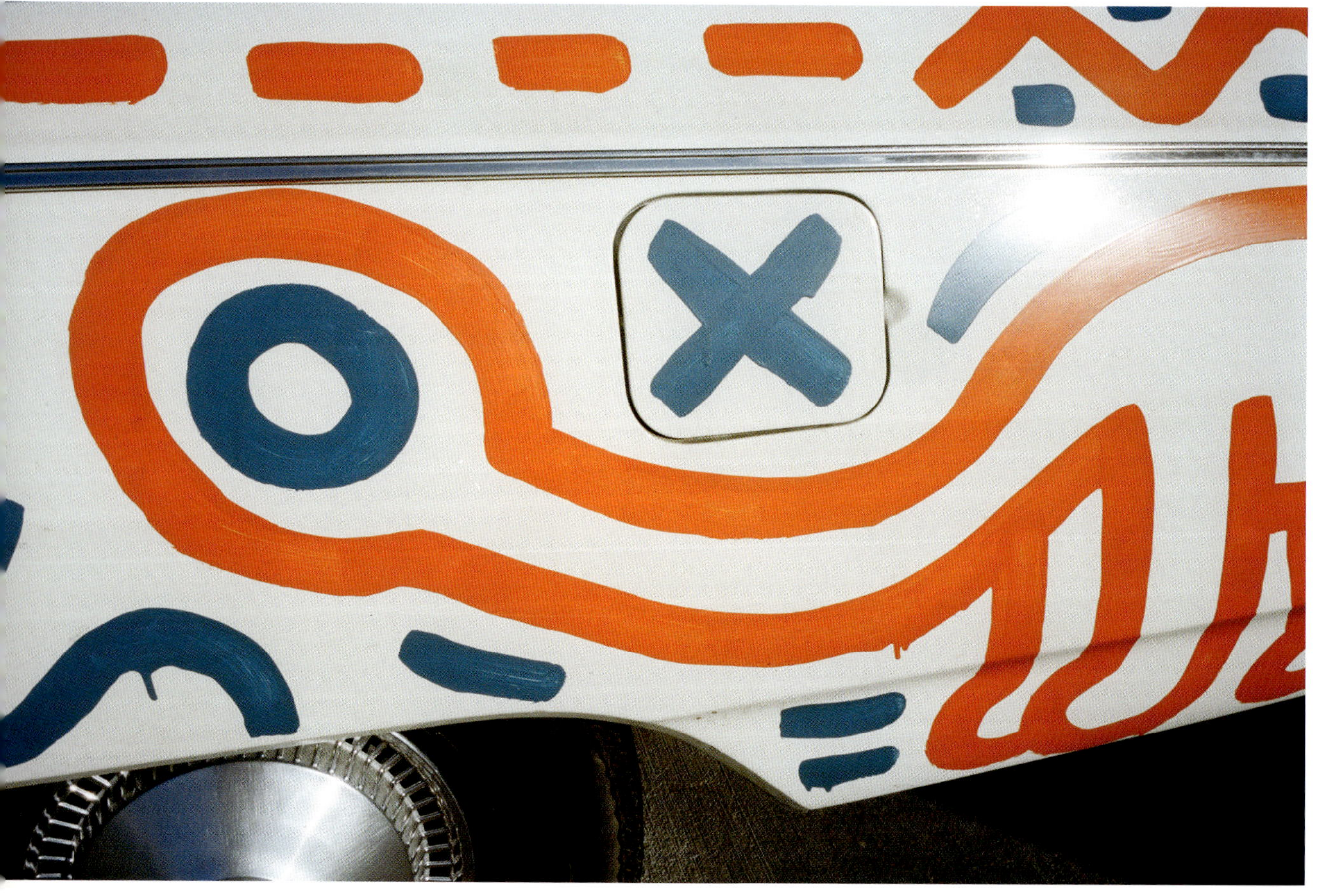

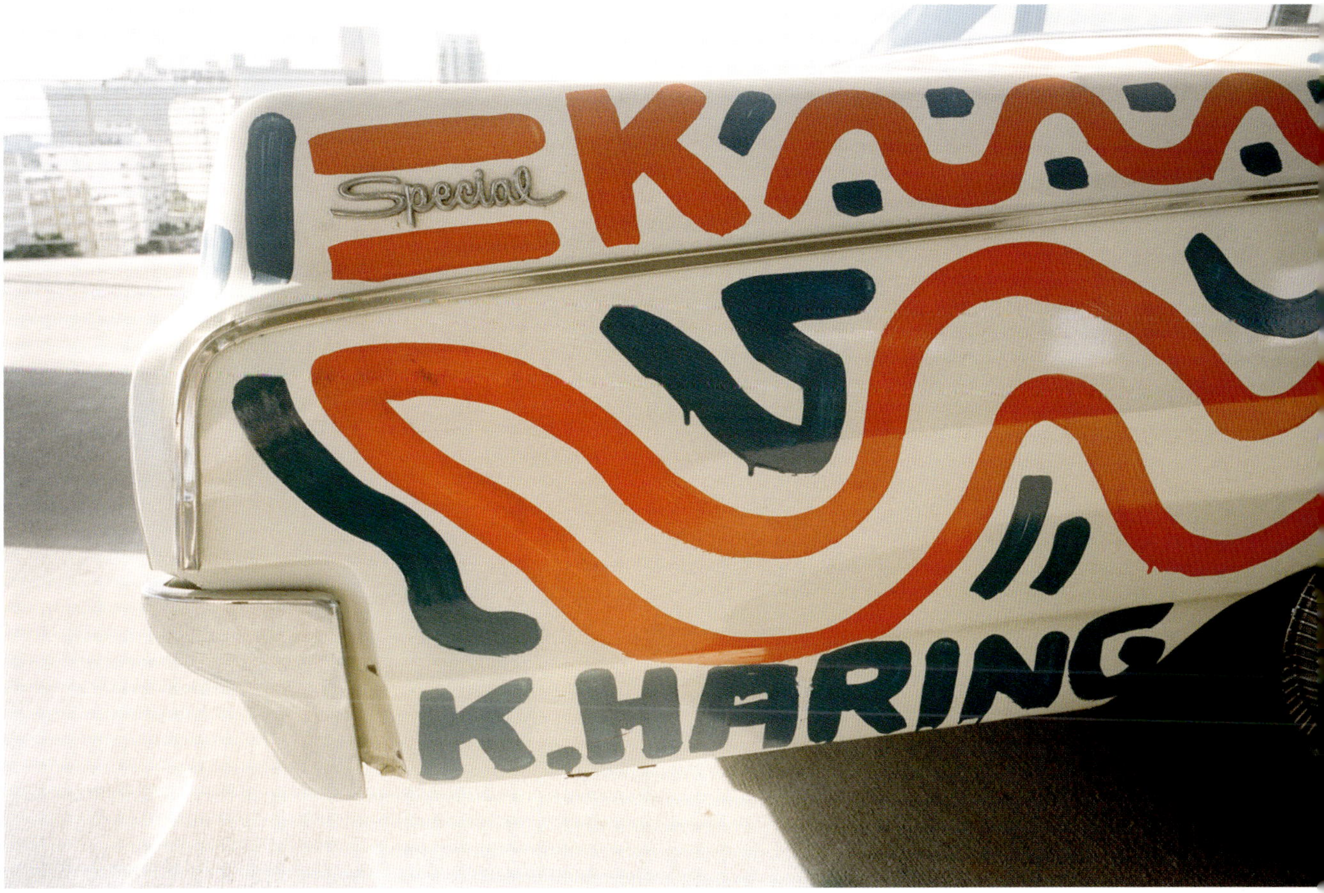

Special
K.HARING

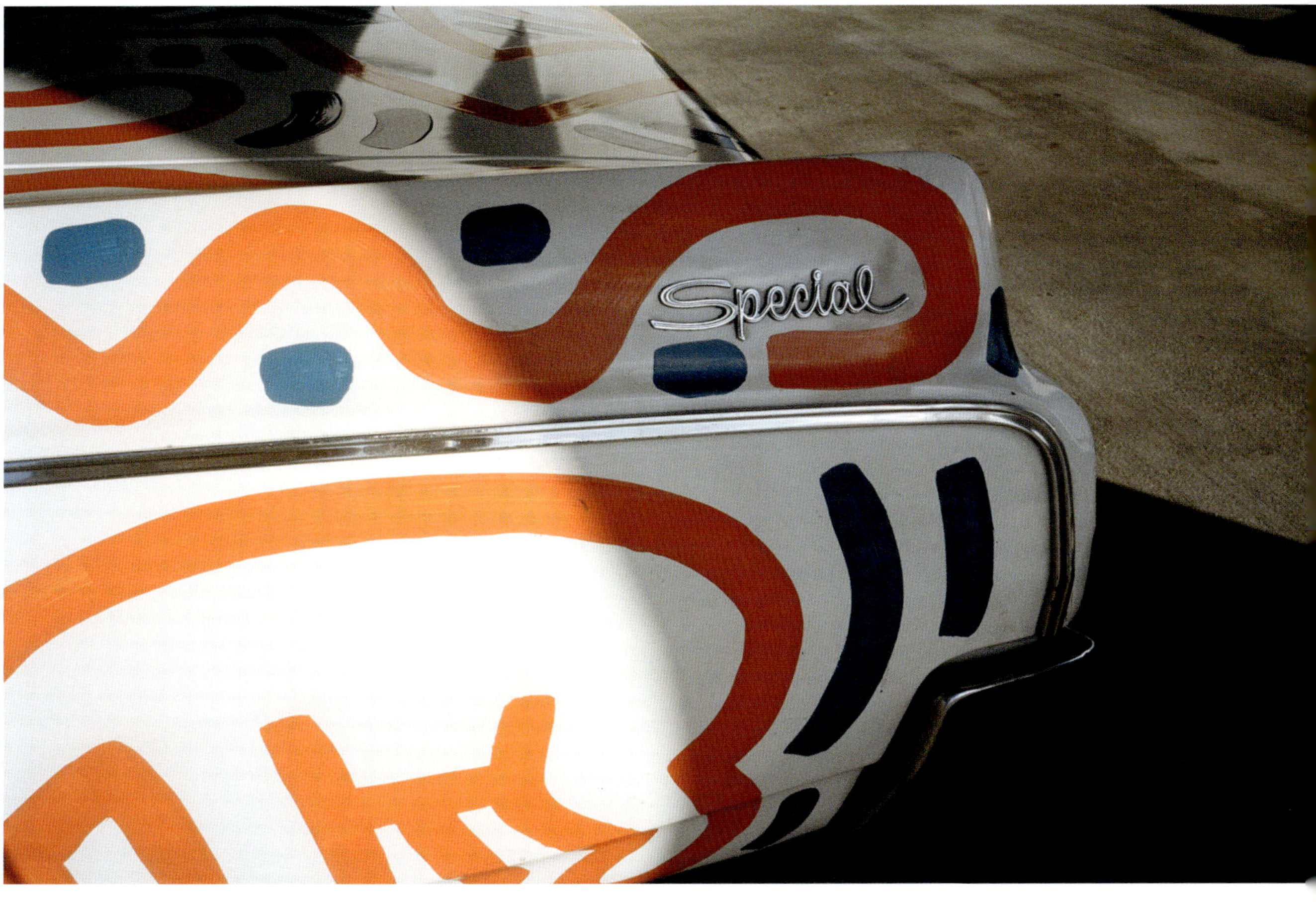

Special

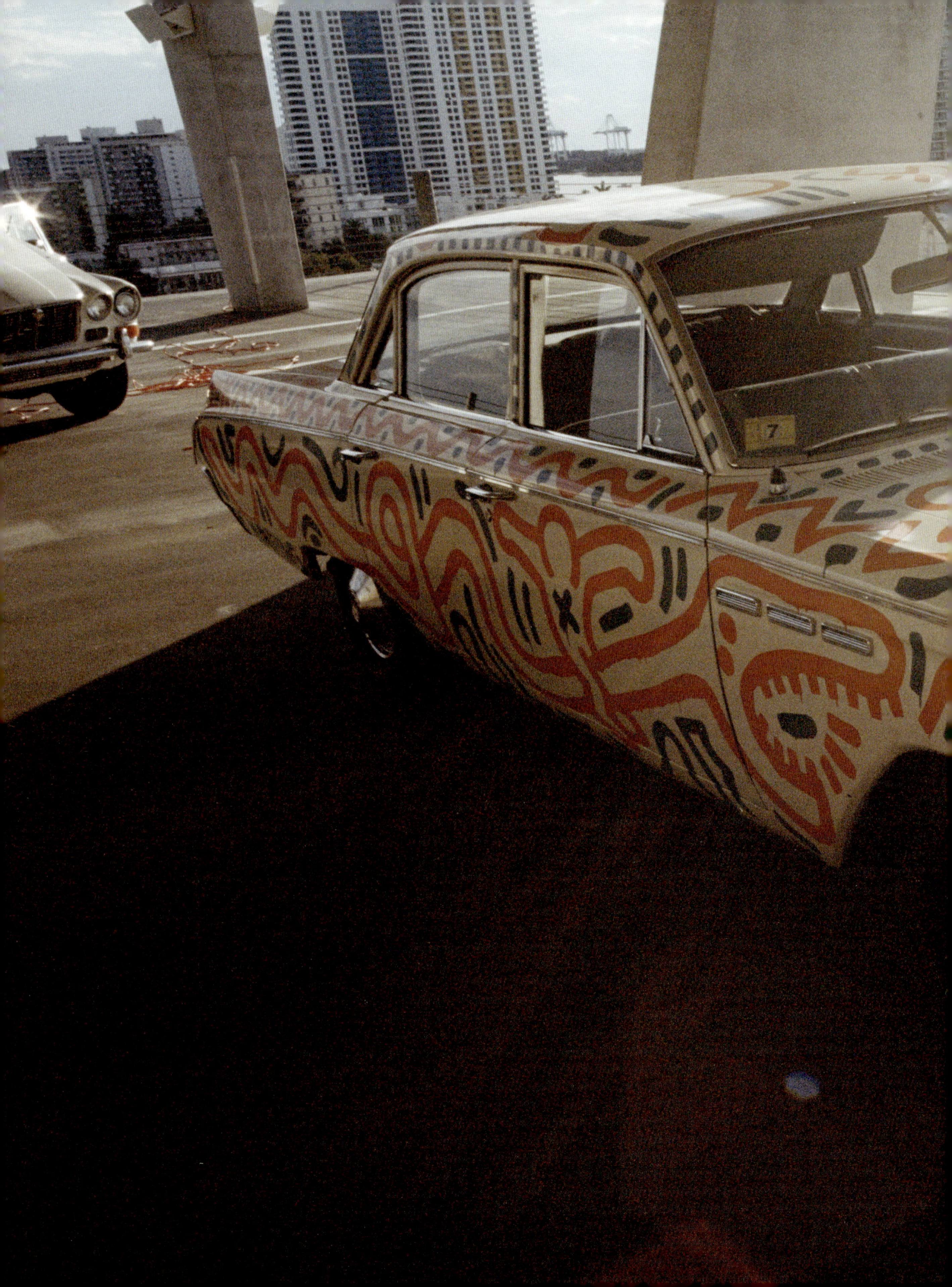
7

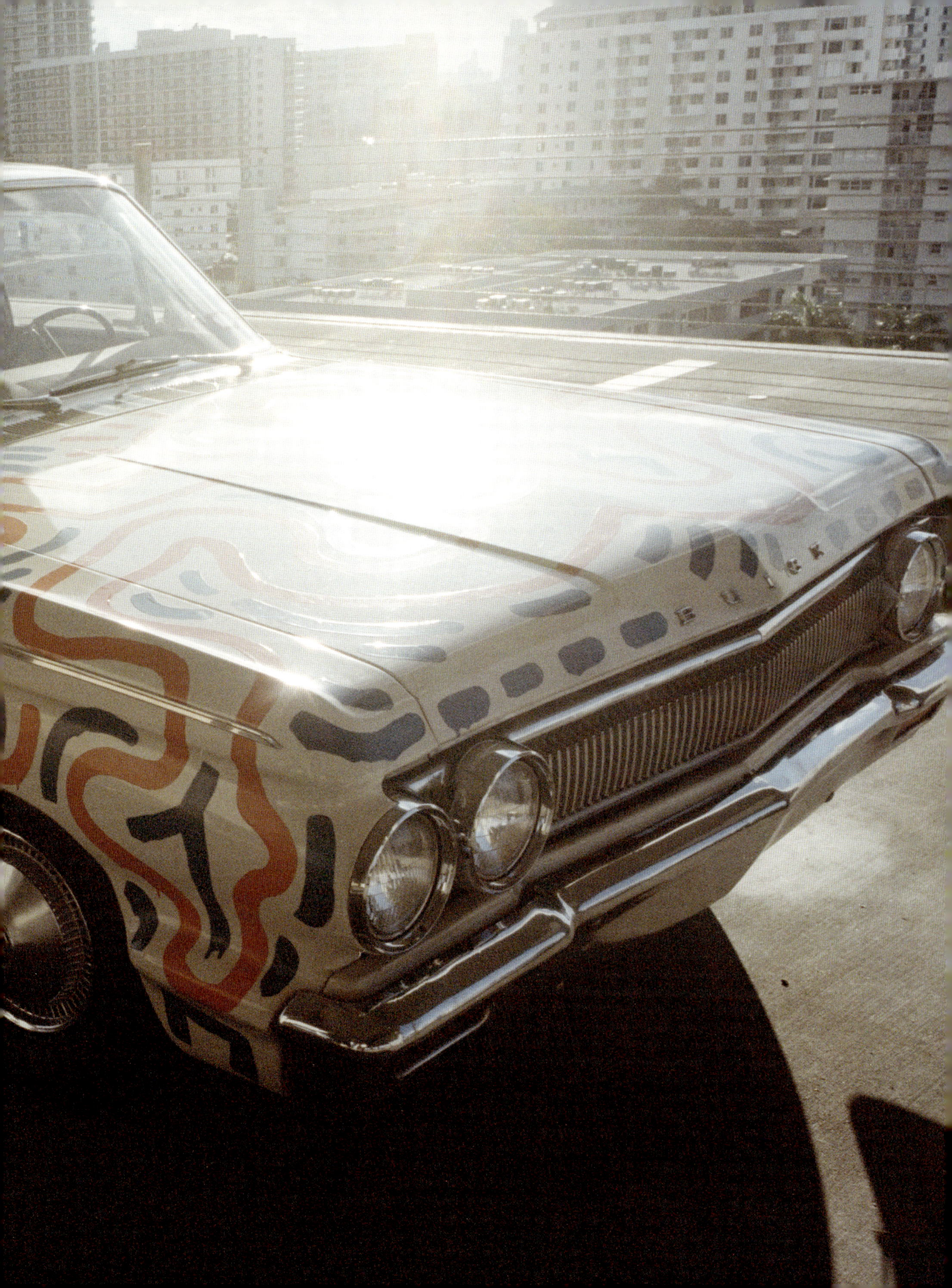
BUICK

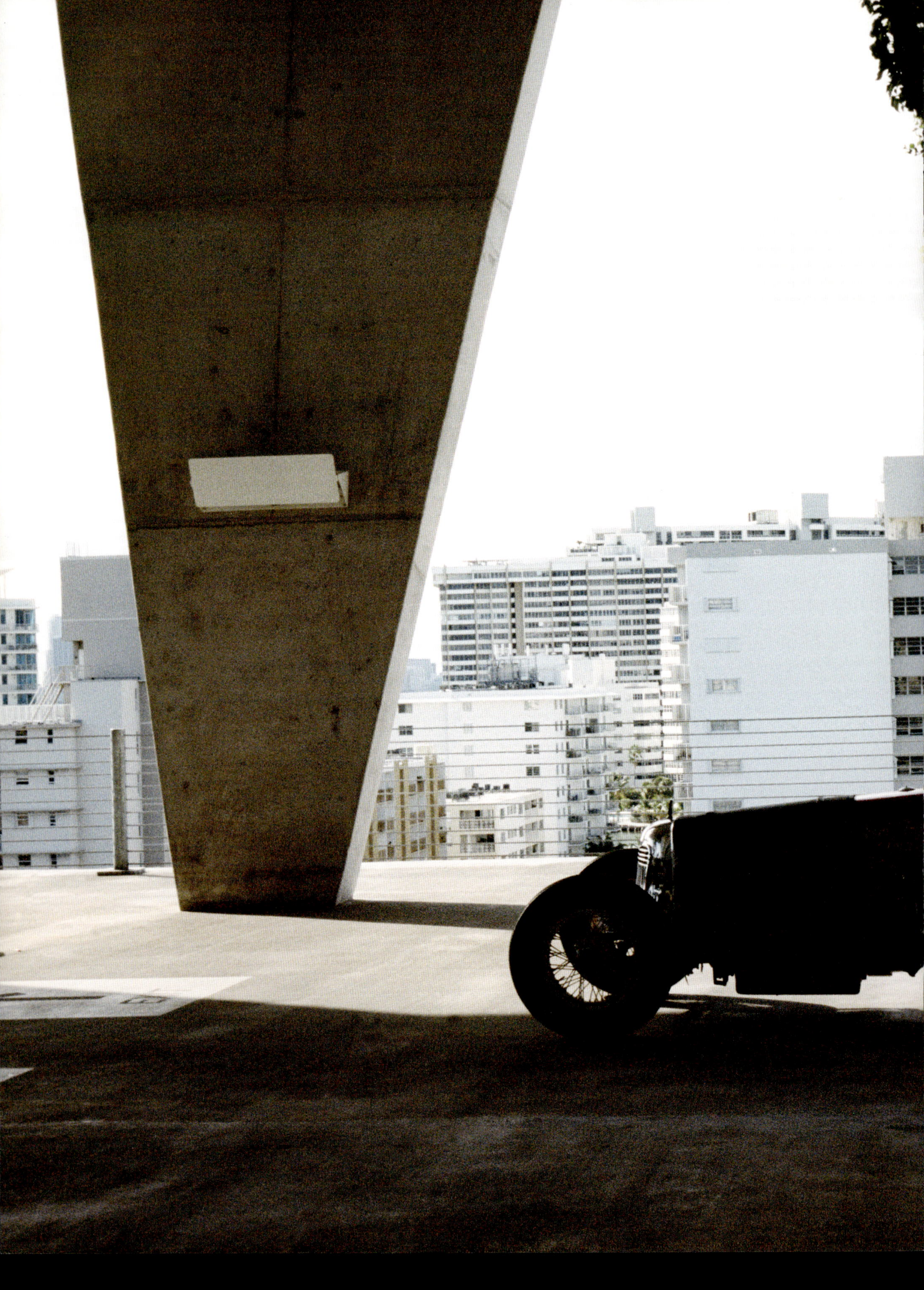

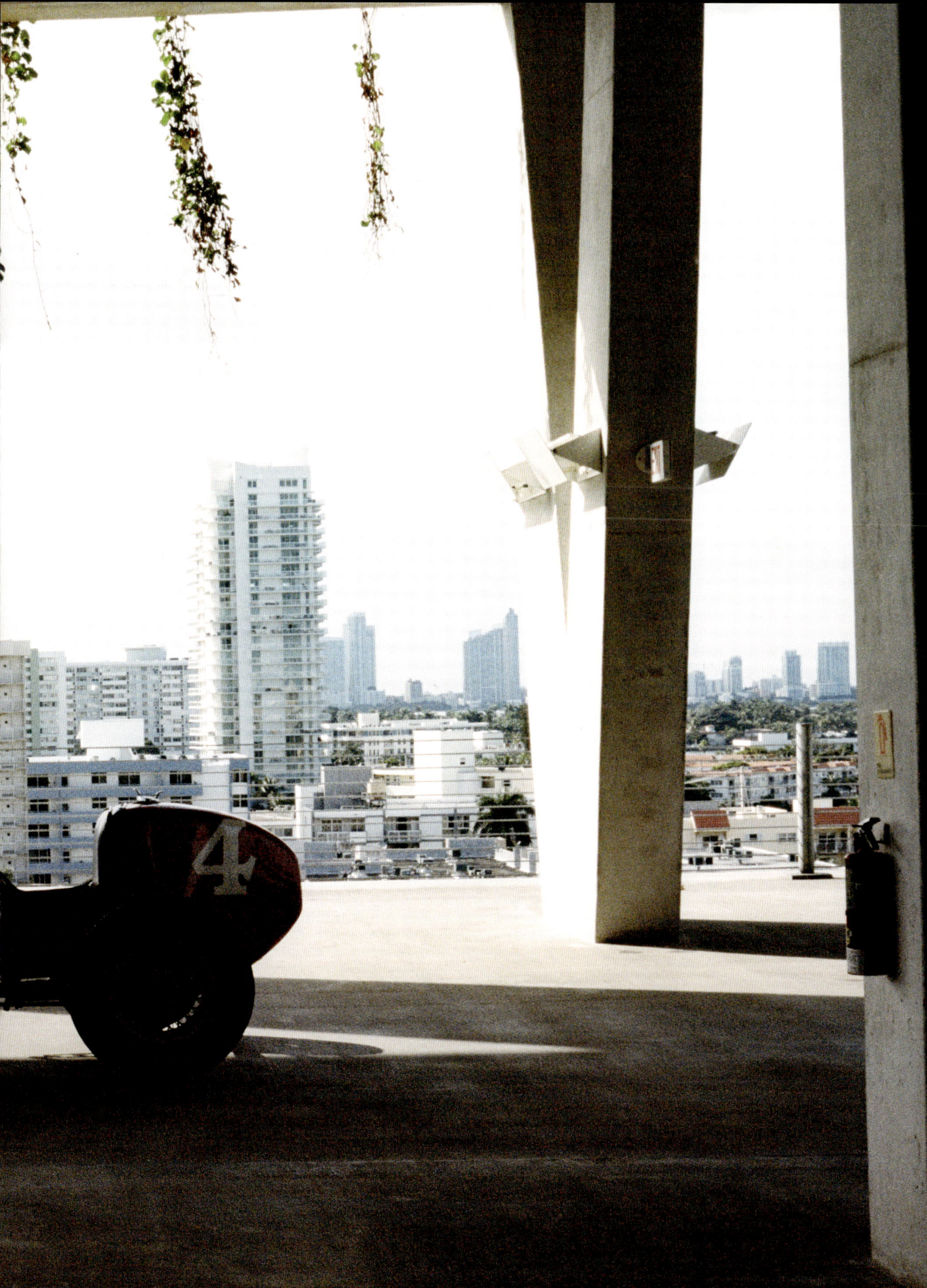

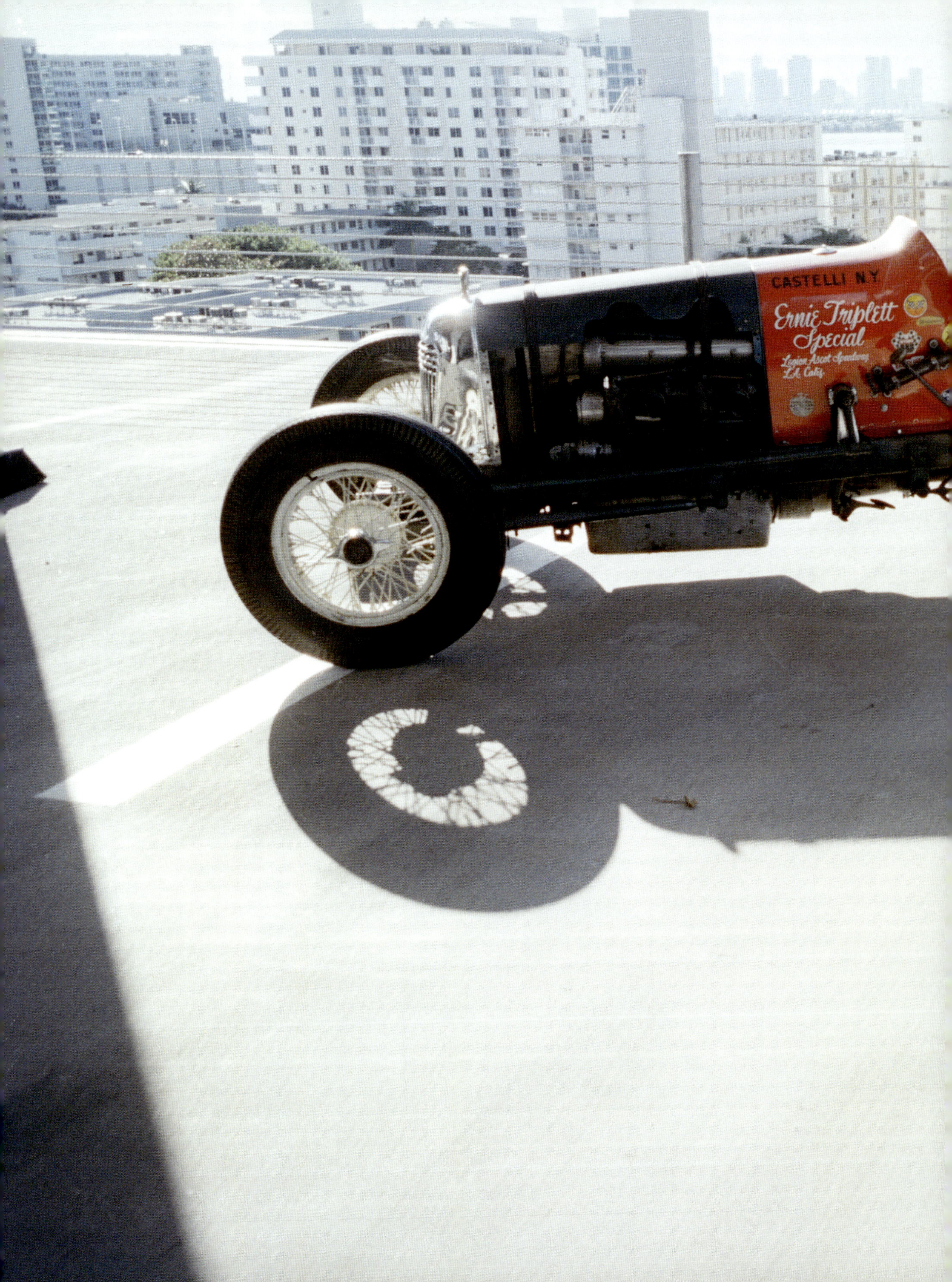
CASTELLI N.Y.
Ernie Triplett Special
Legion Ascot Speedway
L.A. Calif.

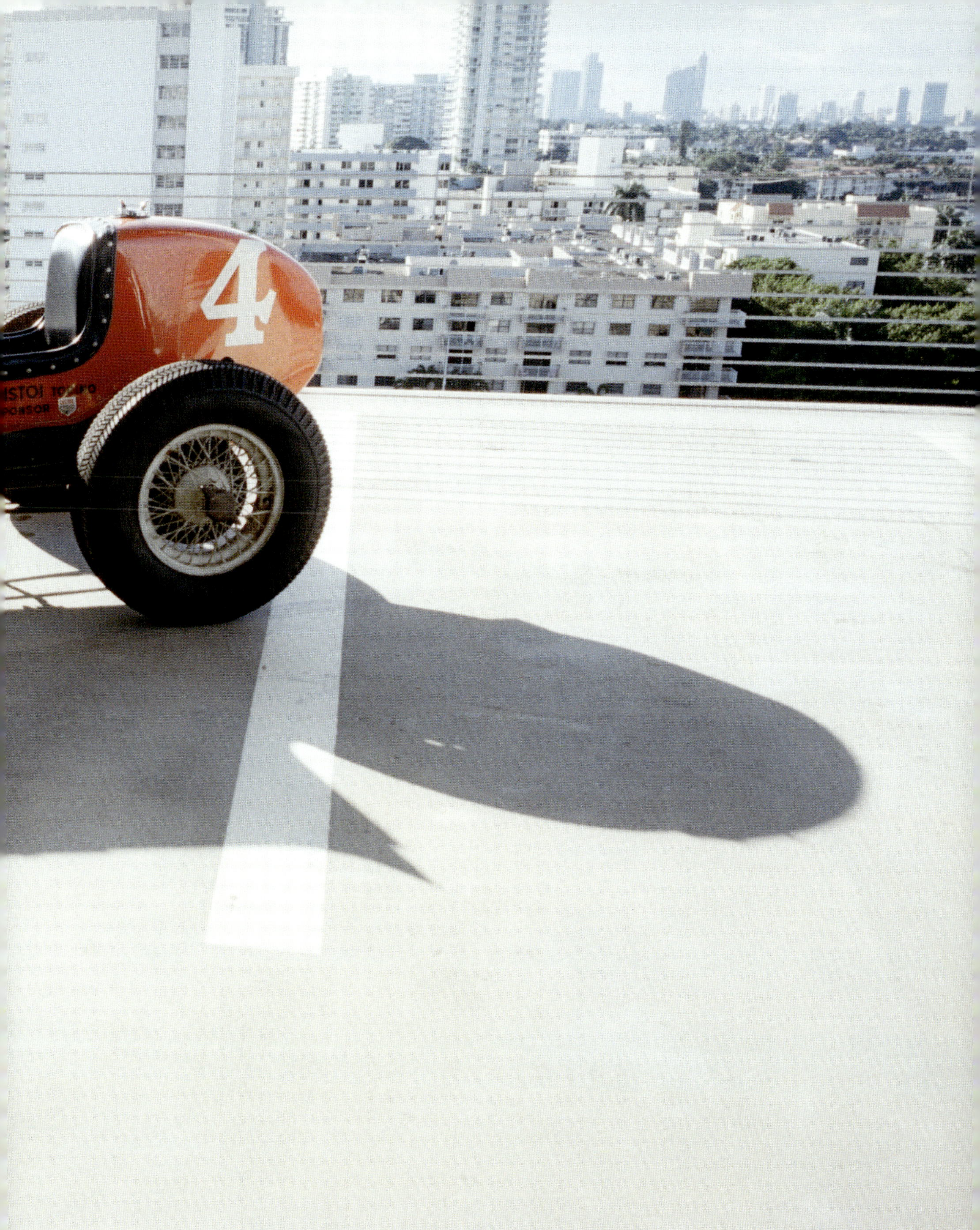
4

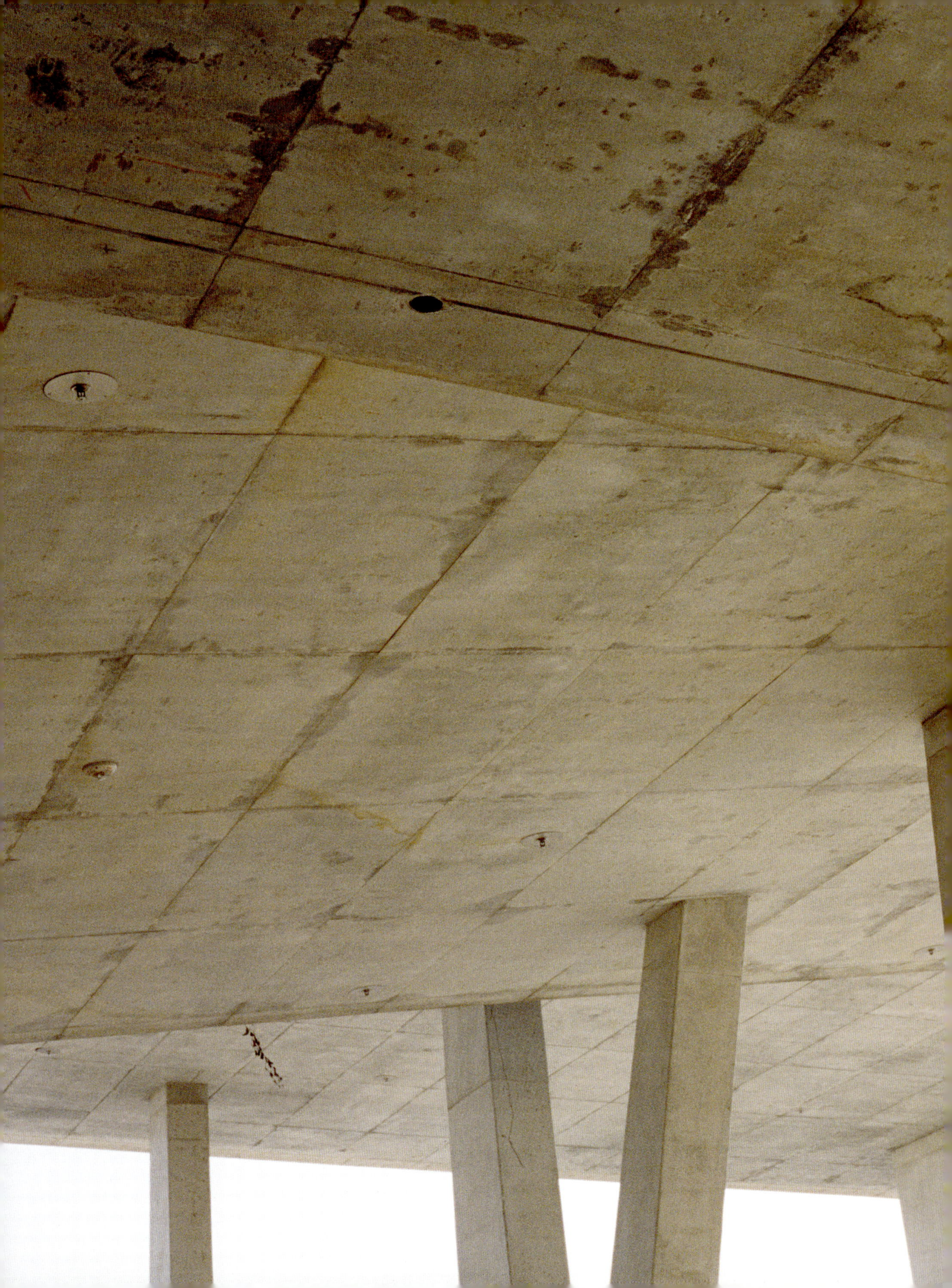

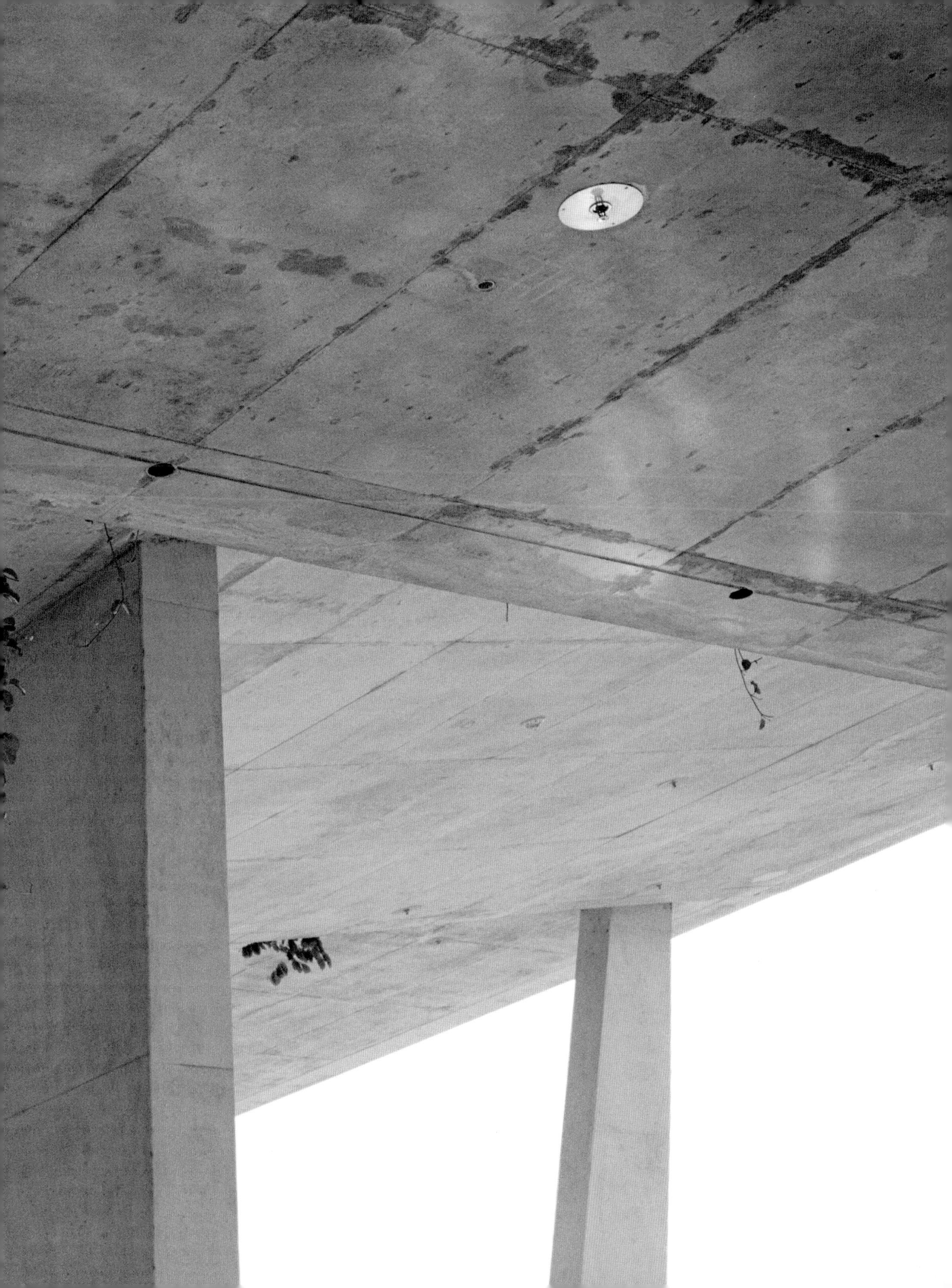

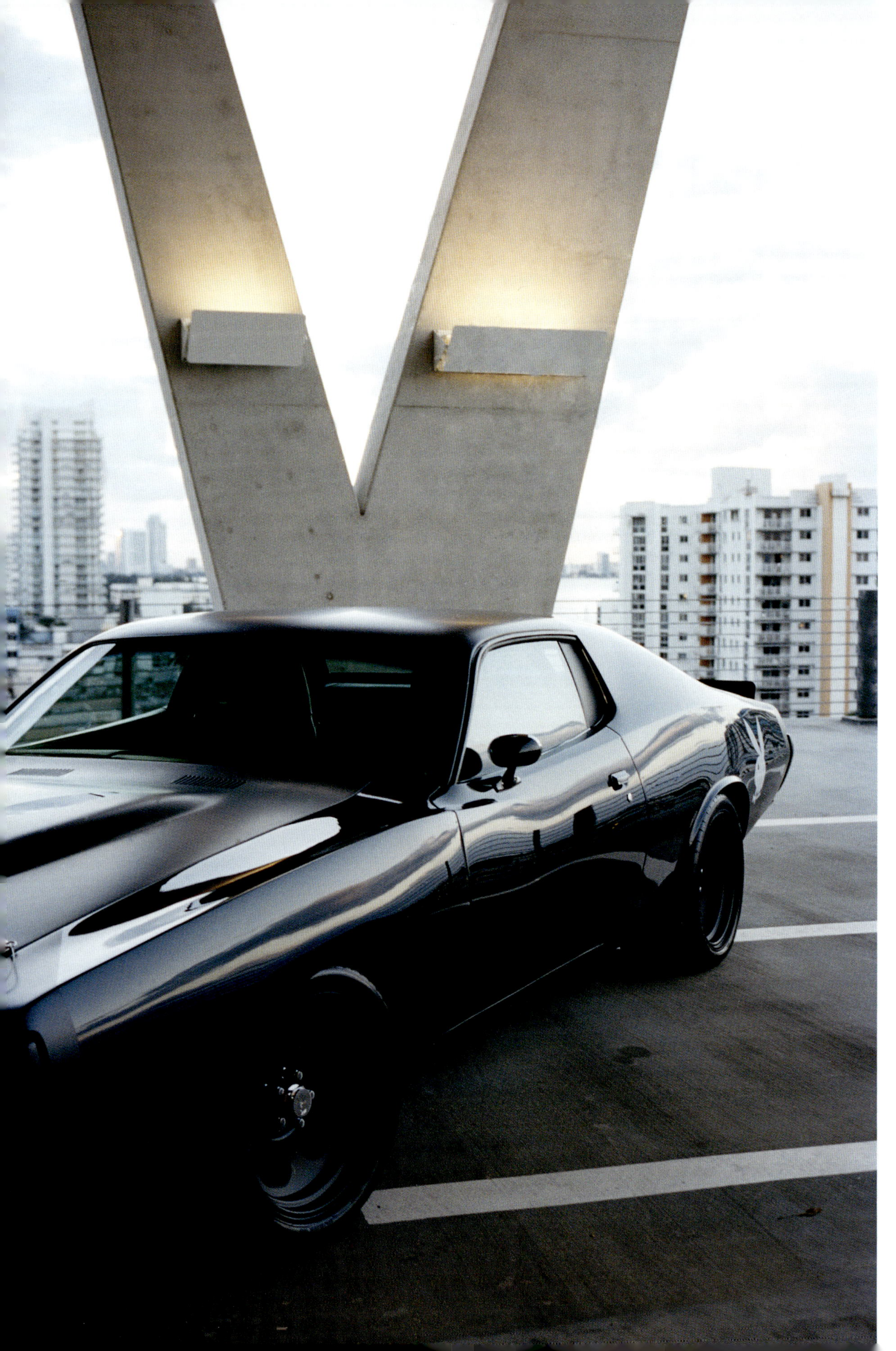

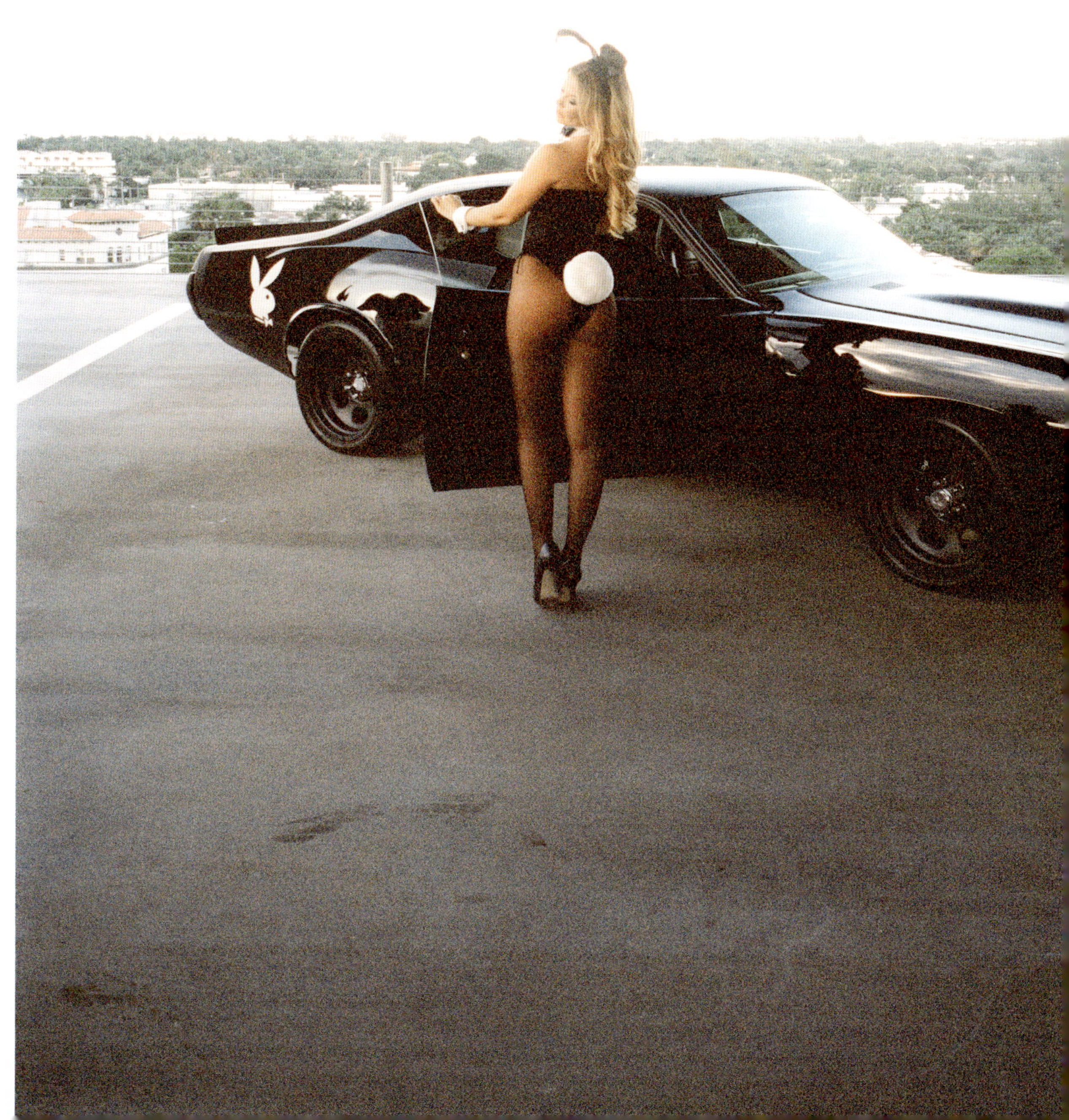

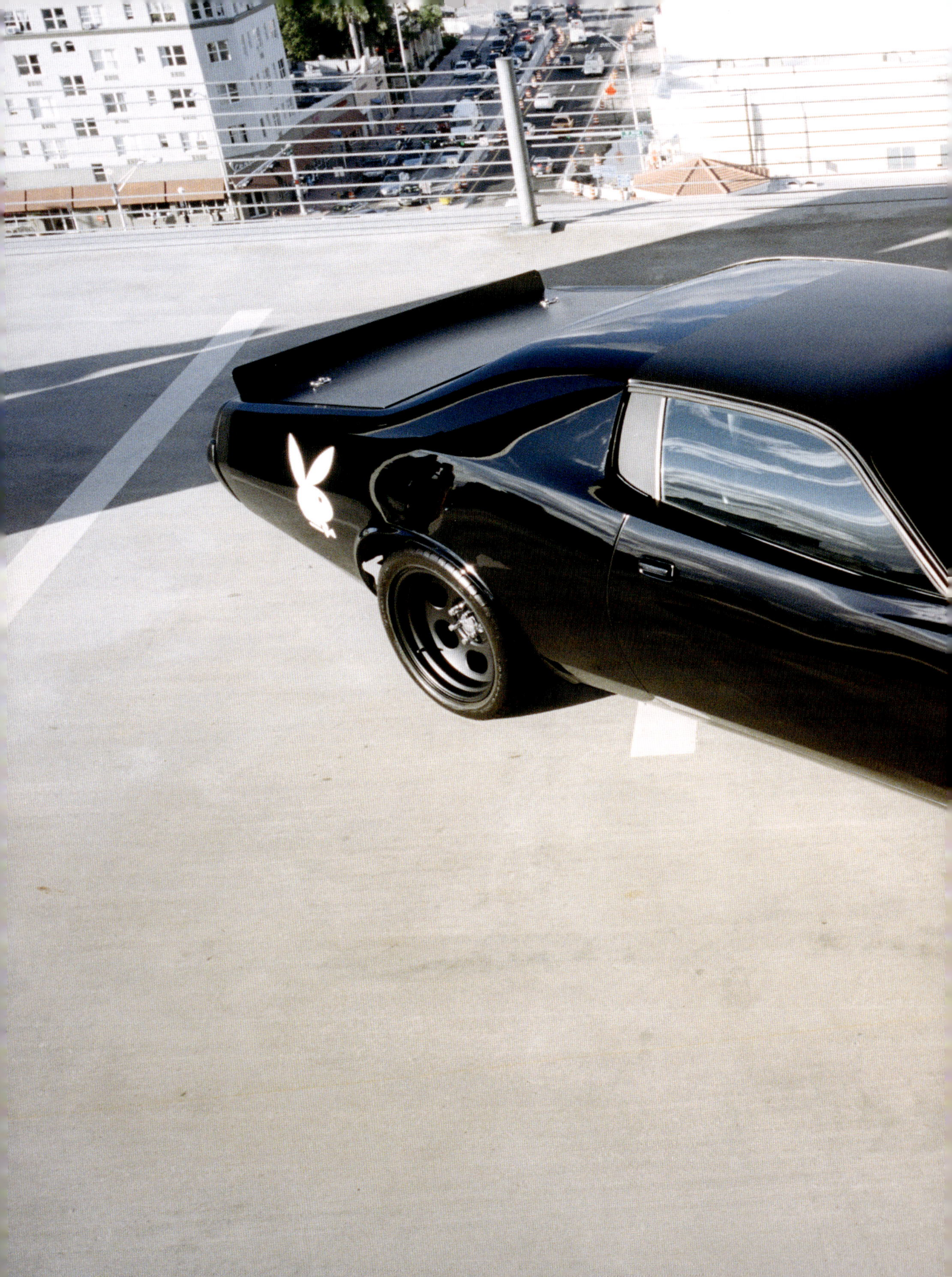

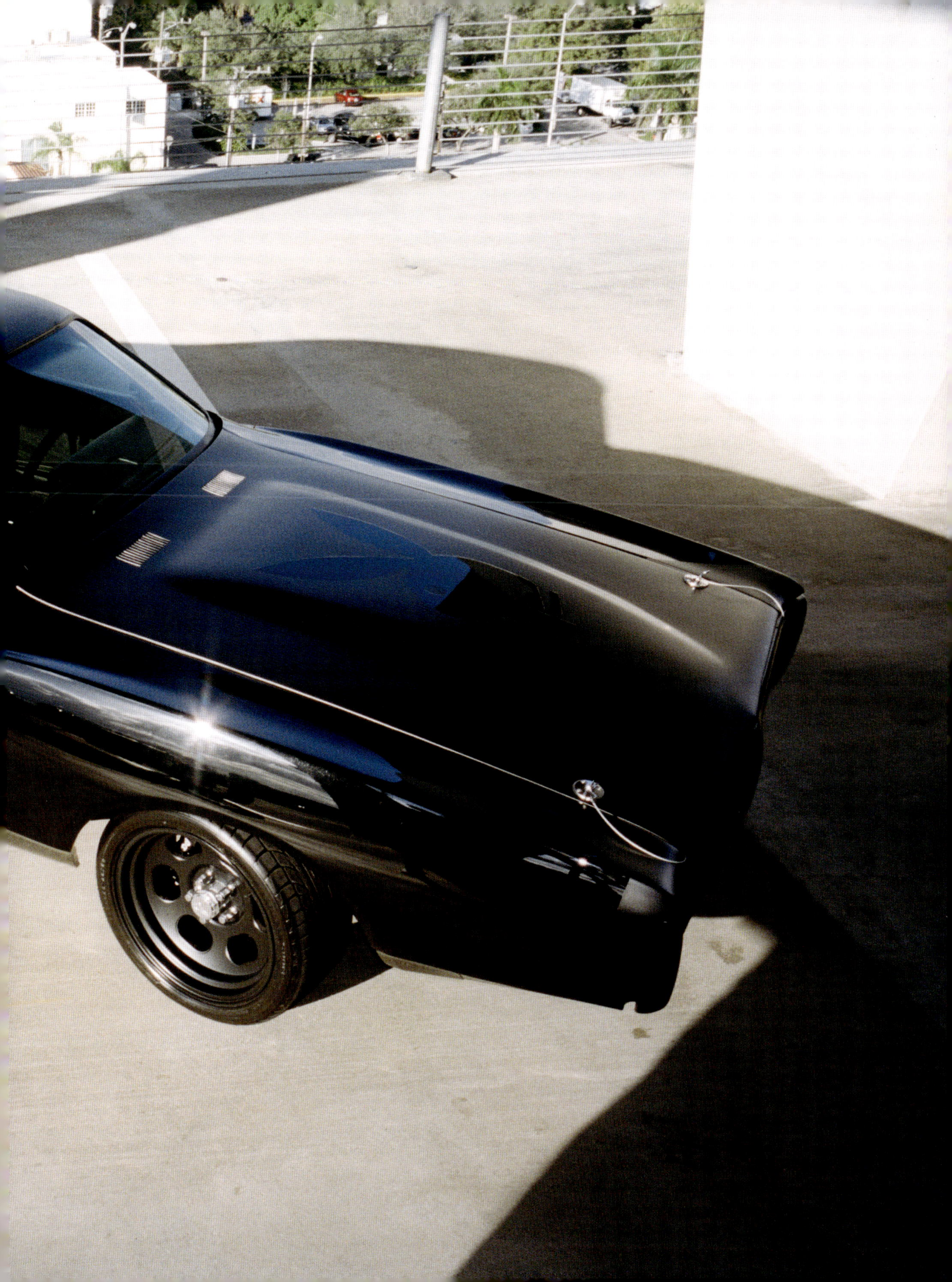

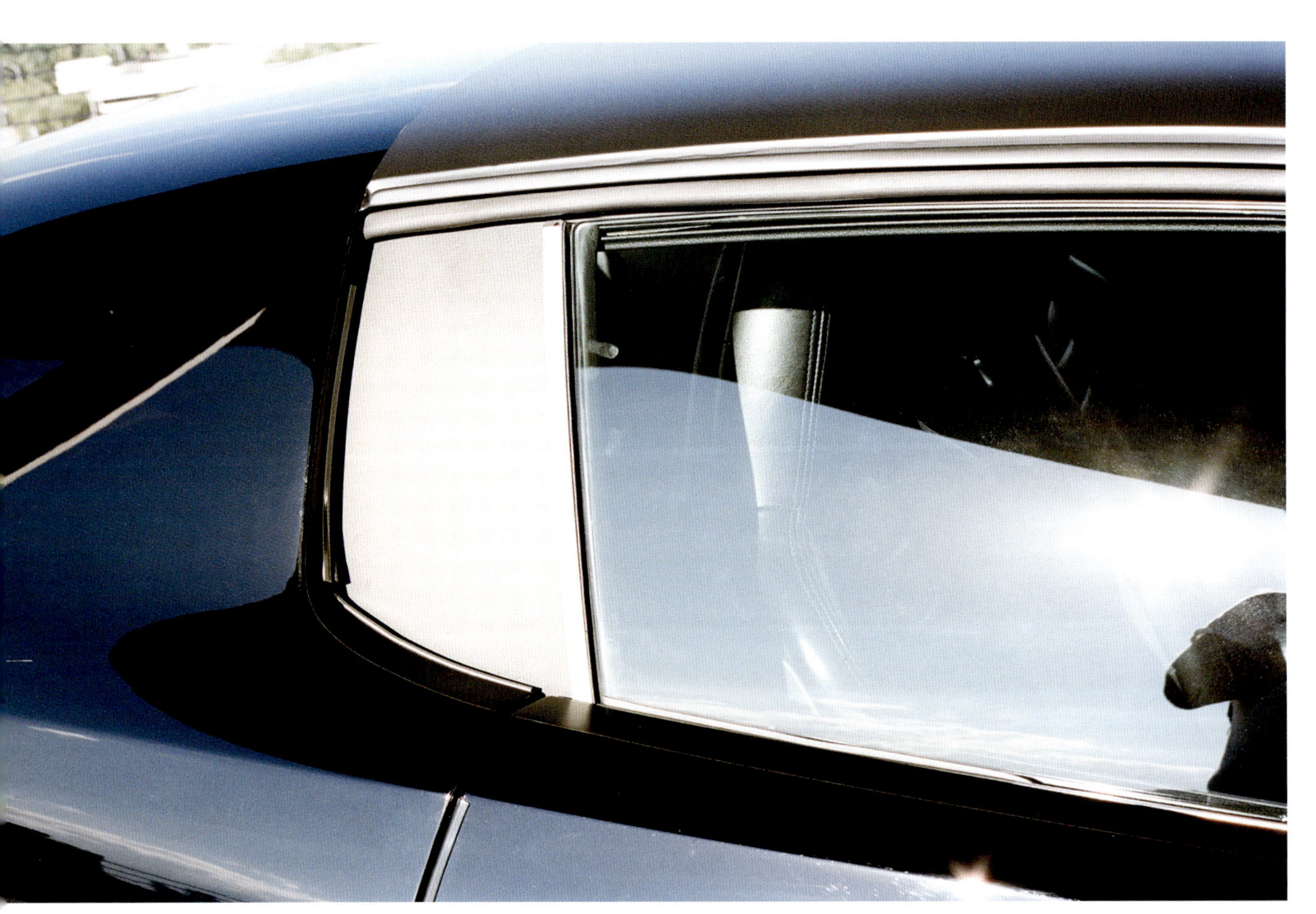

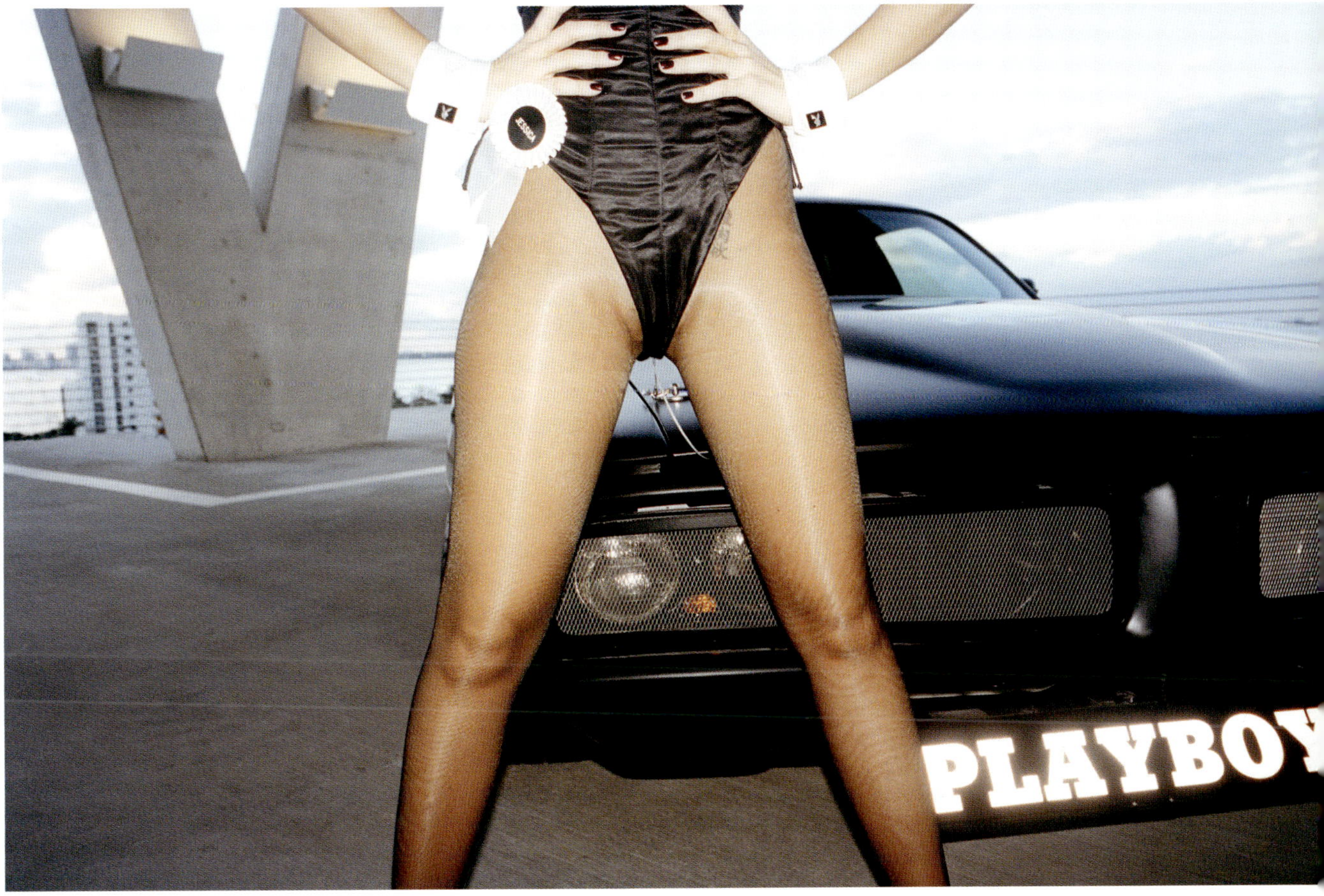

PLAYBOY

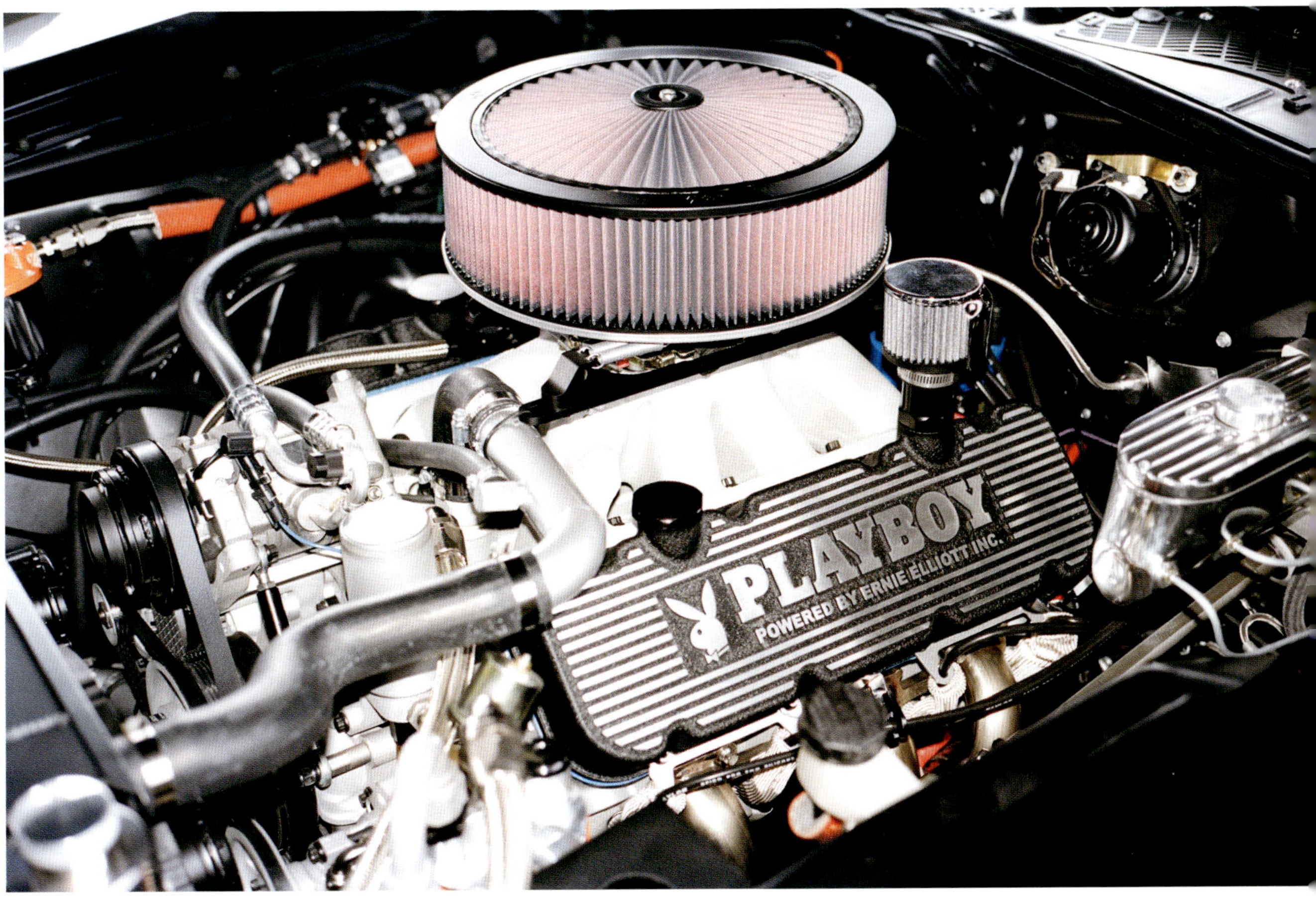

PLAYBOY
PLAYBOY
POWERED BY ERNIE ELLIOTT INC.

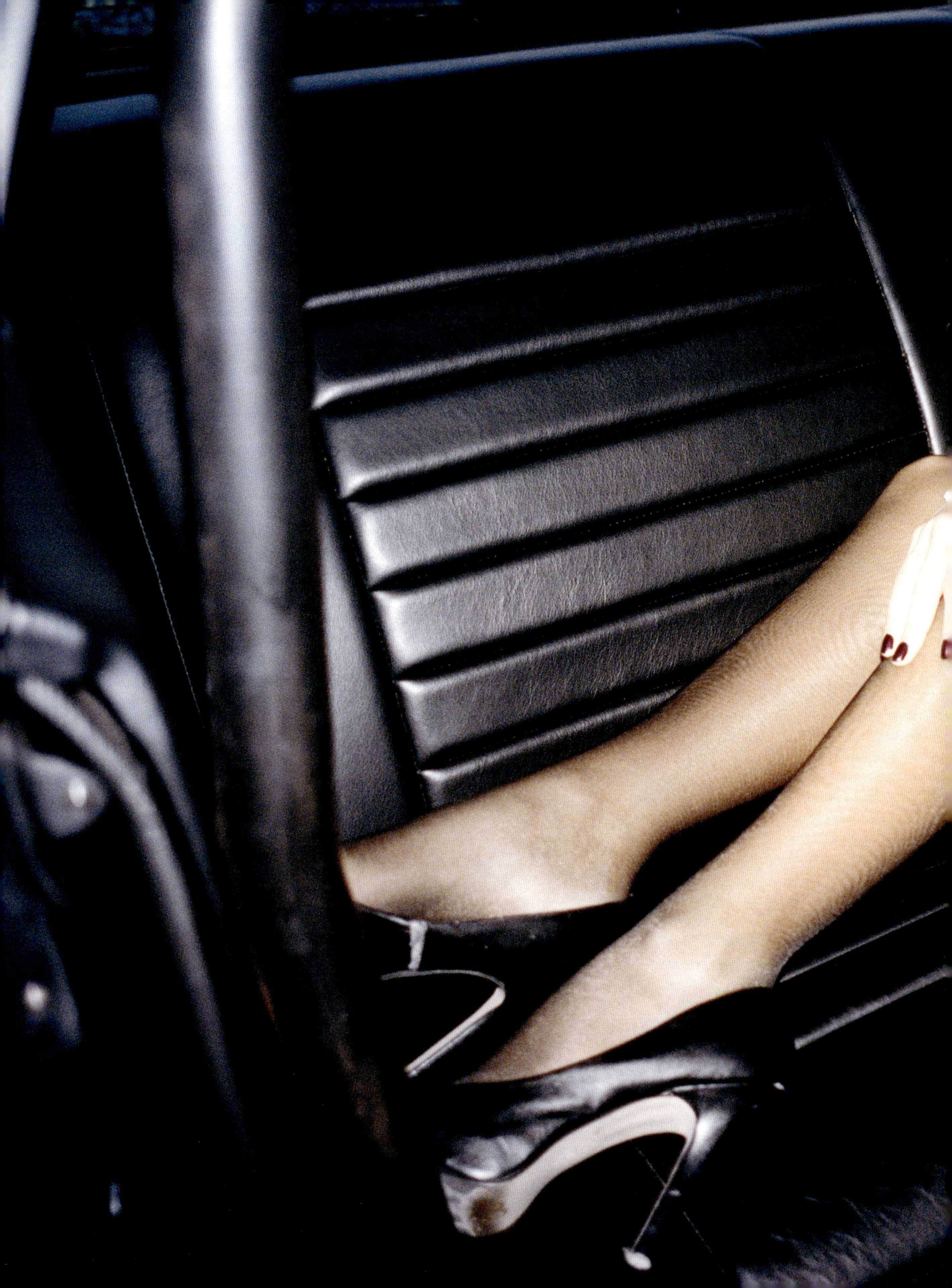

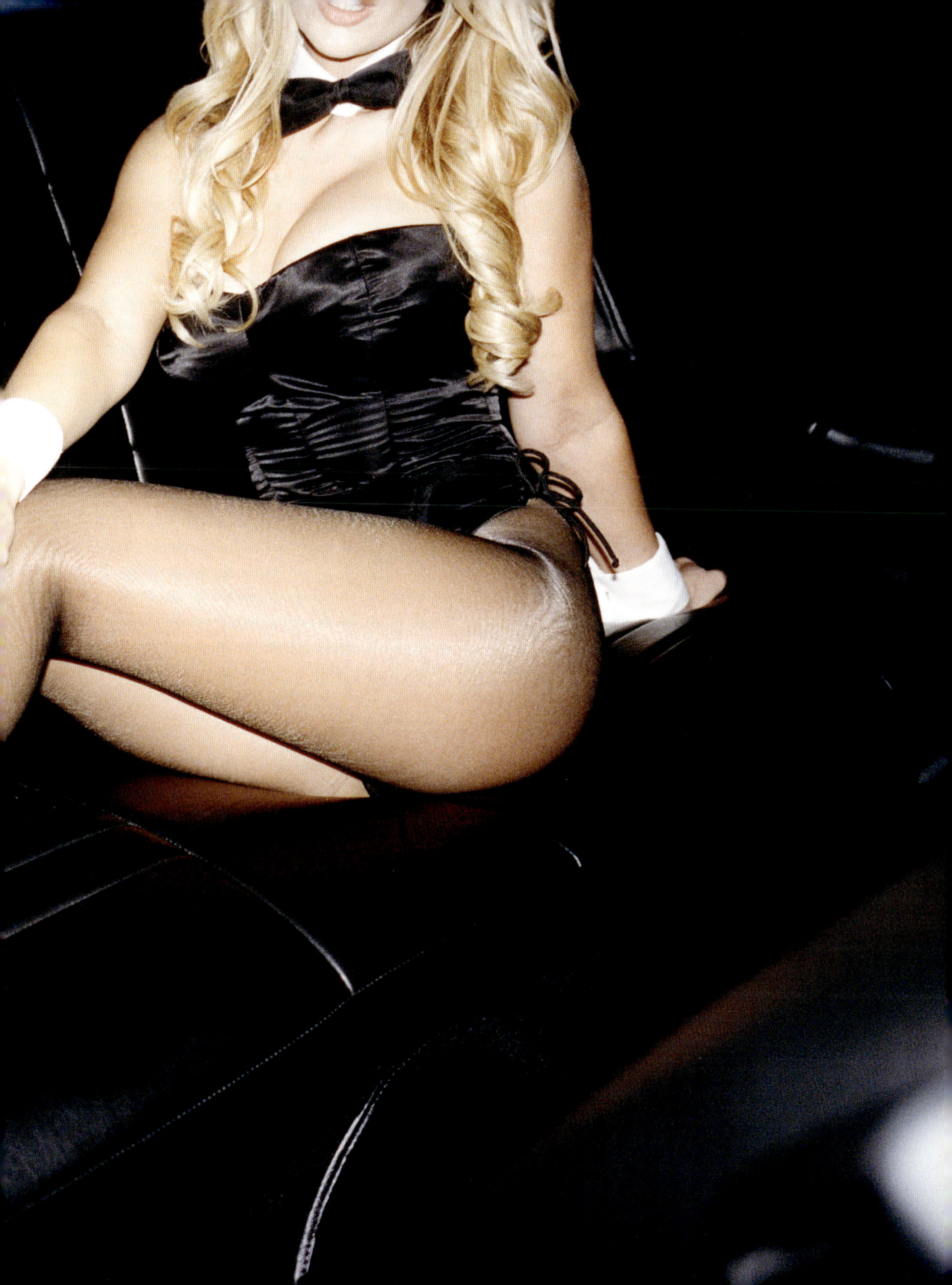

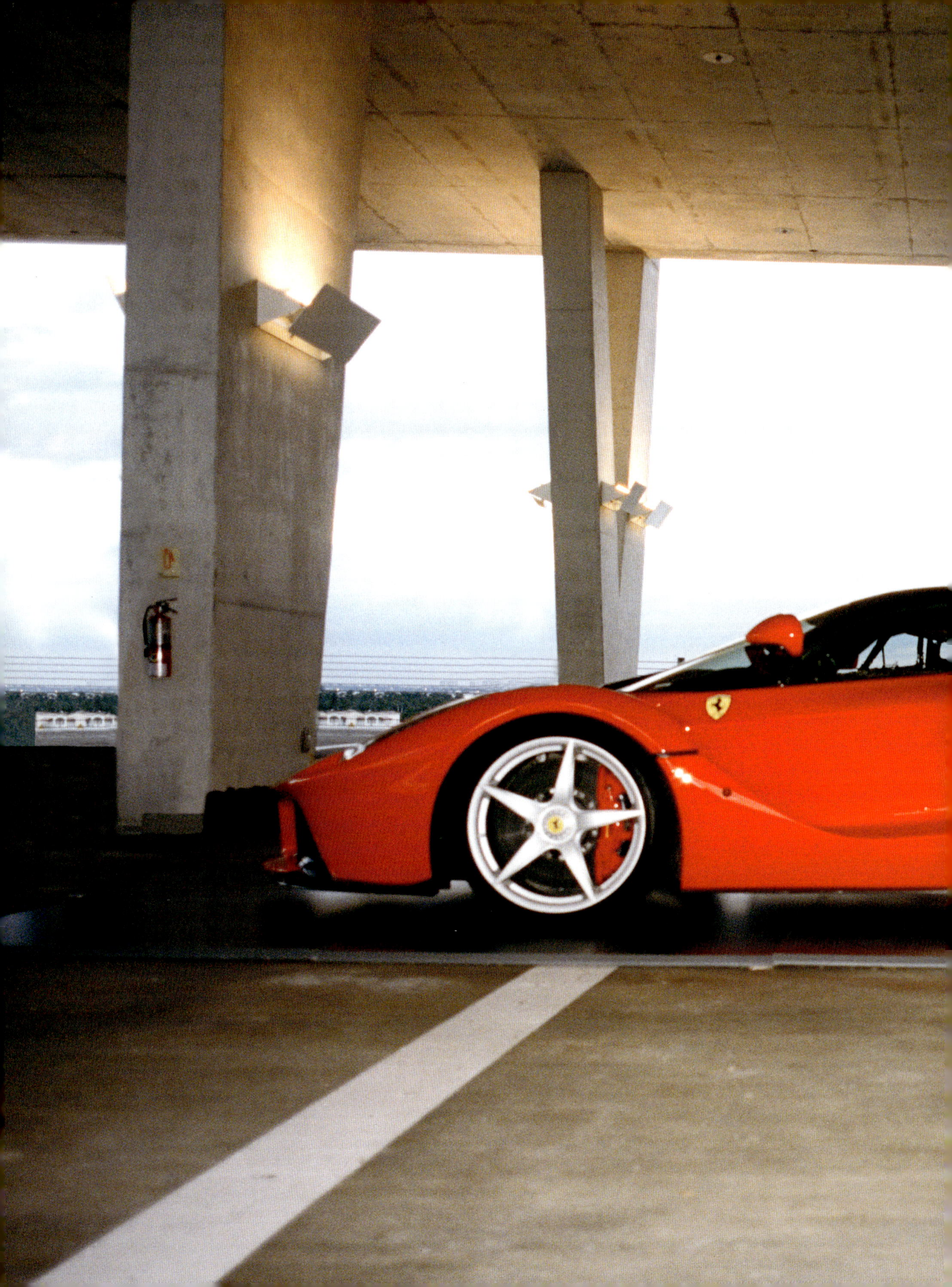

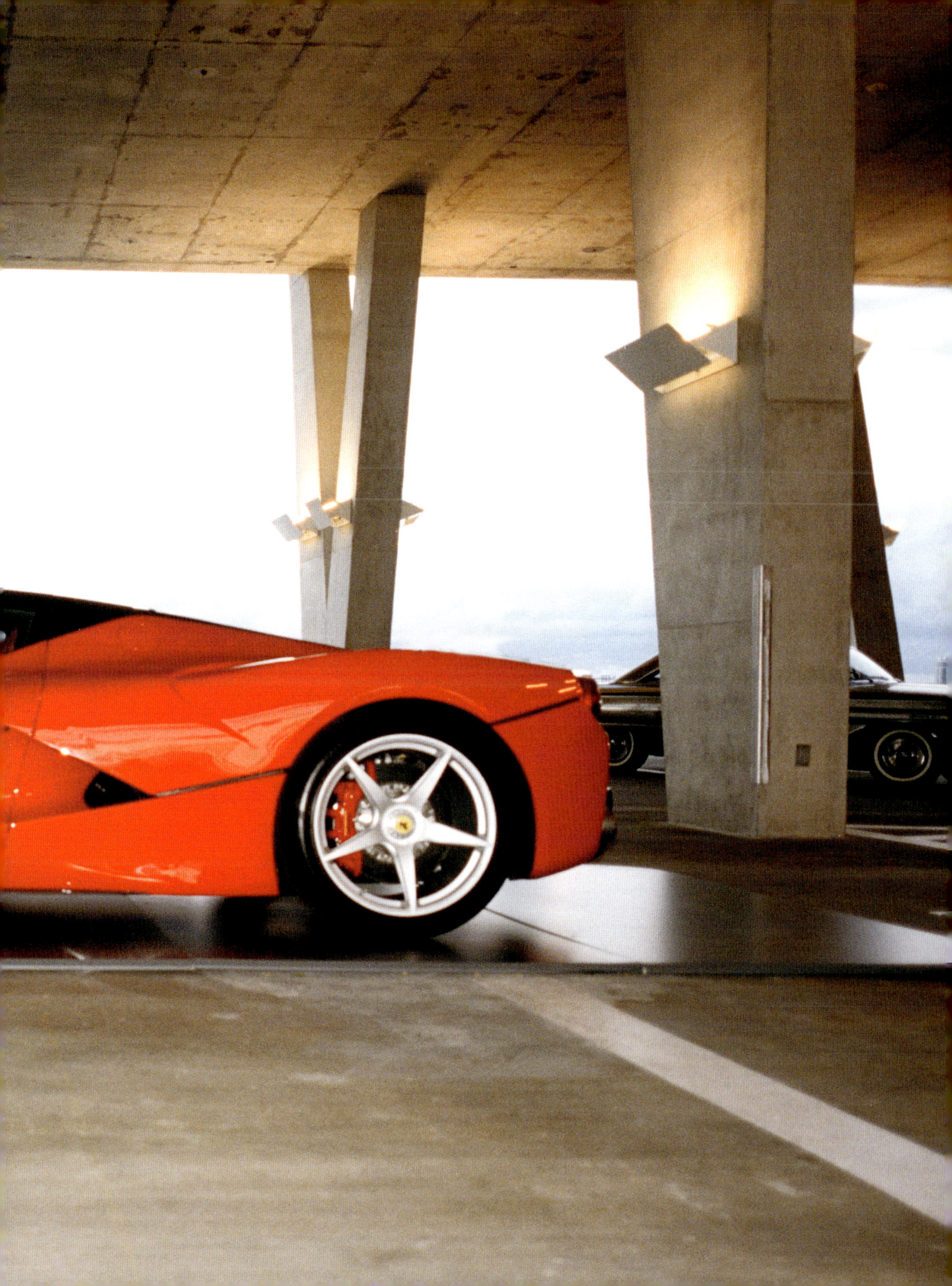

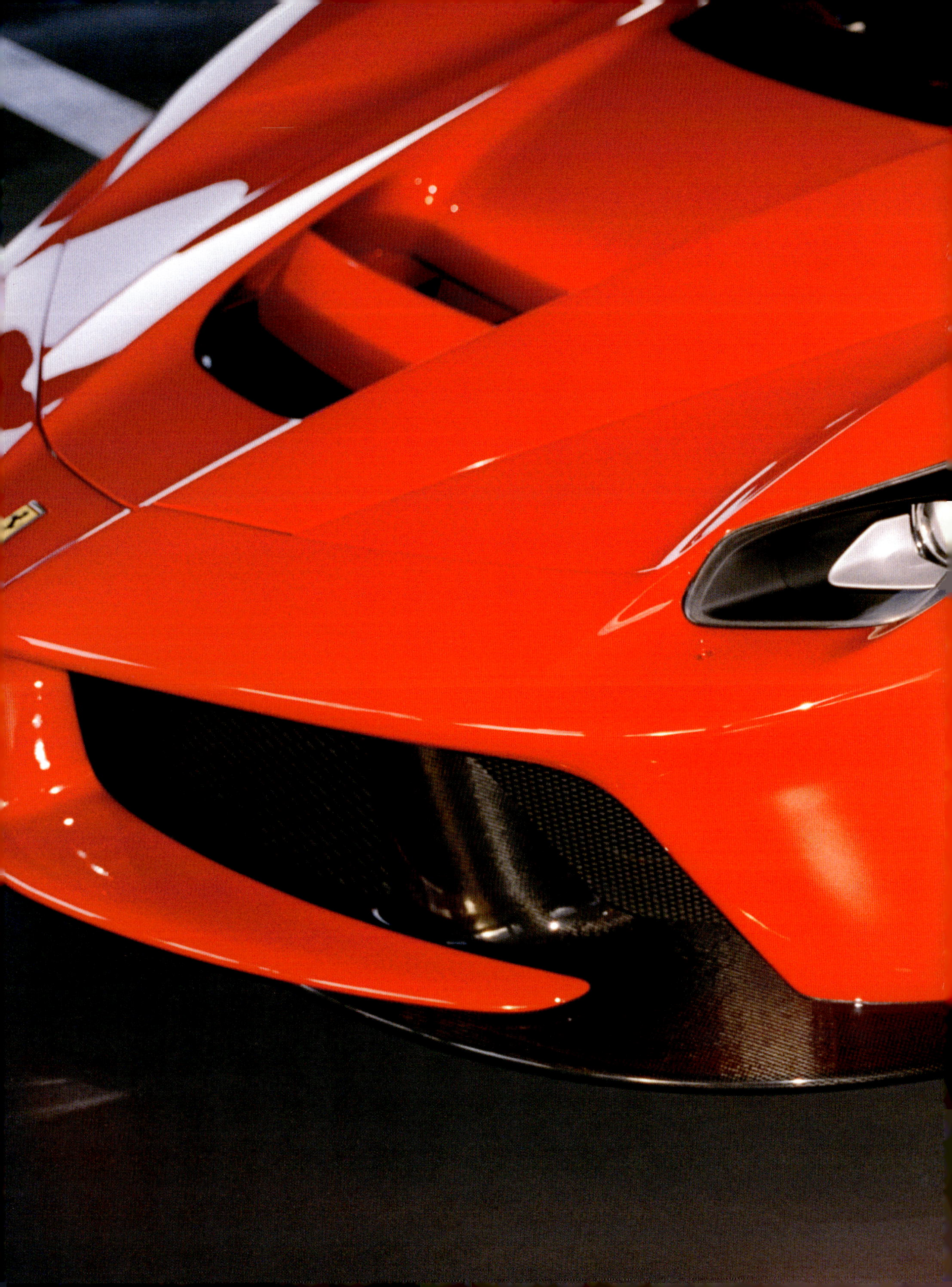

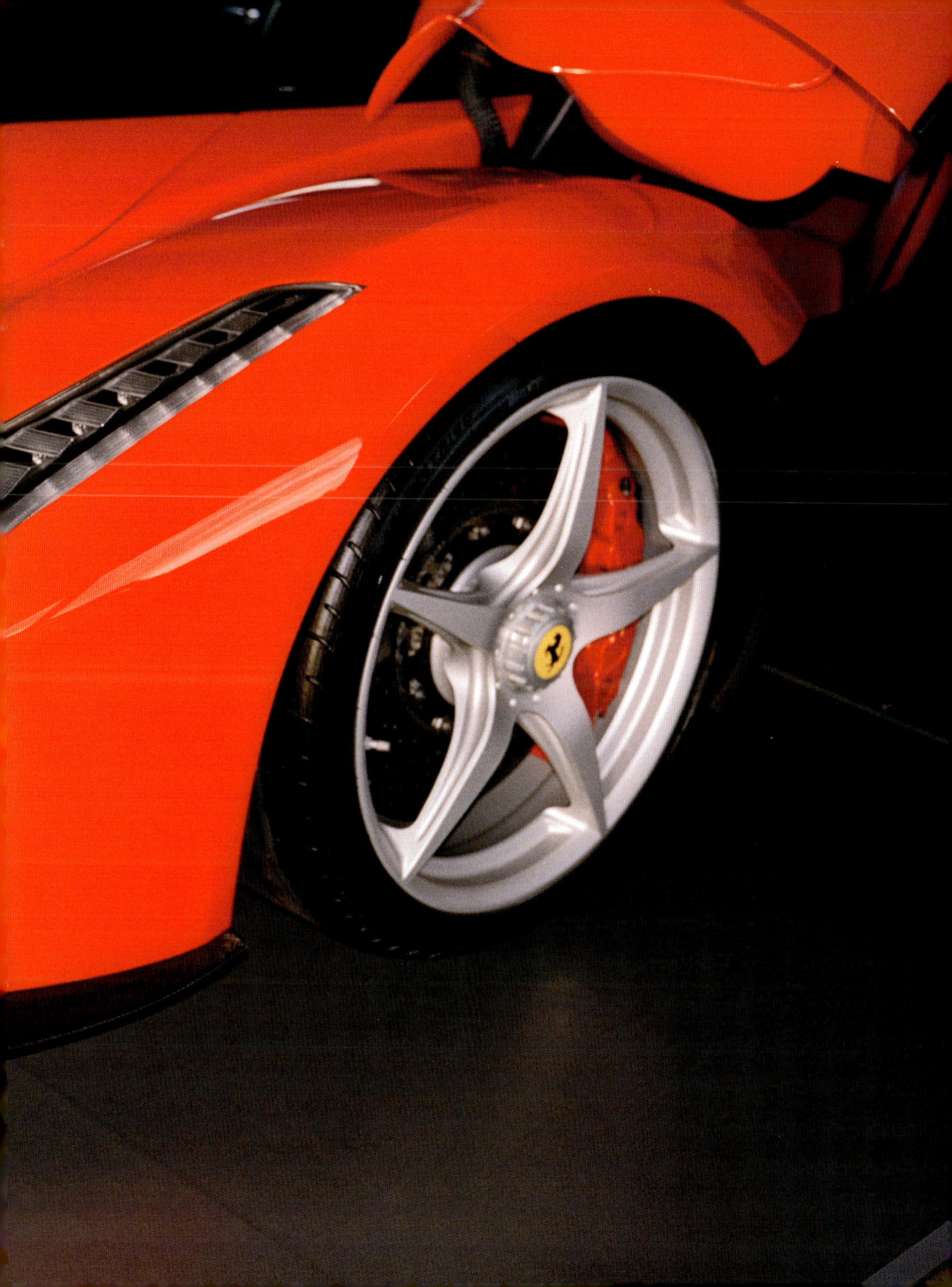

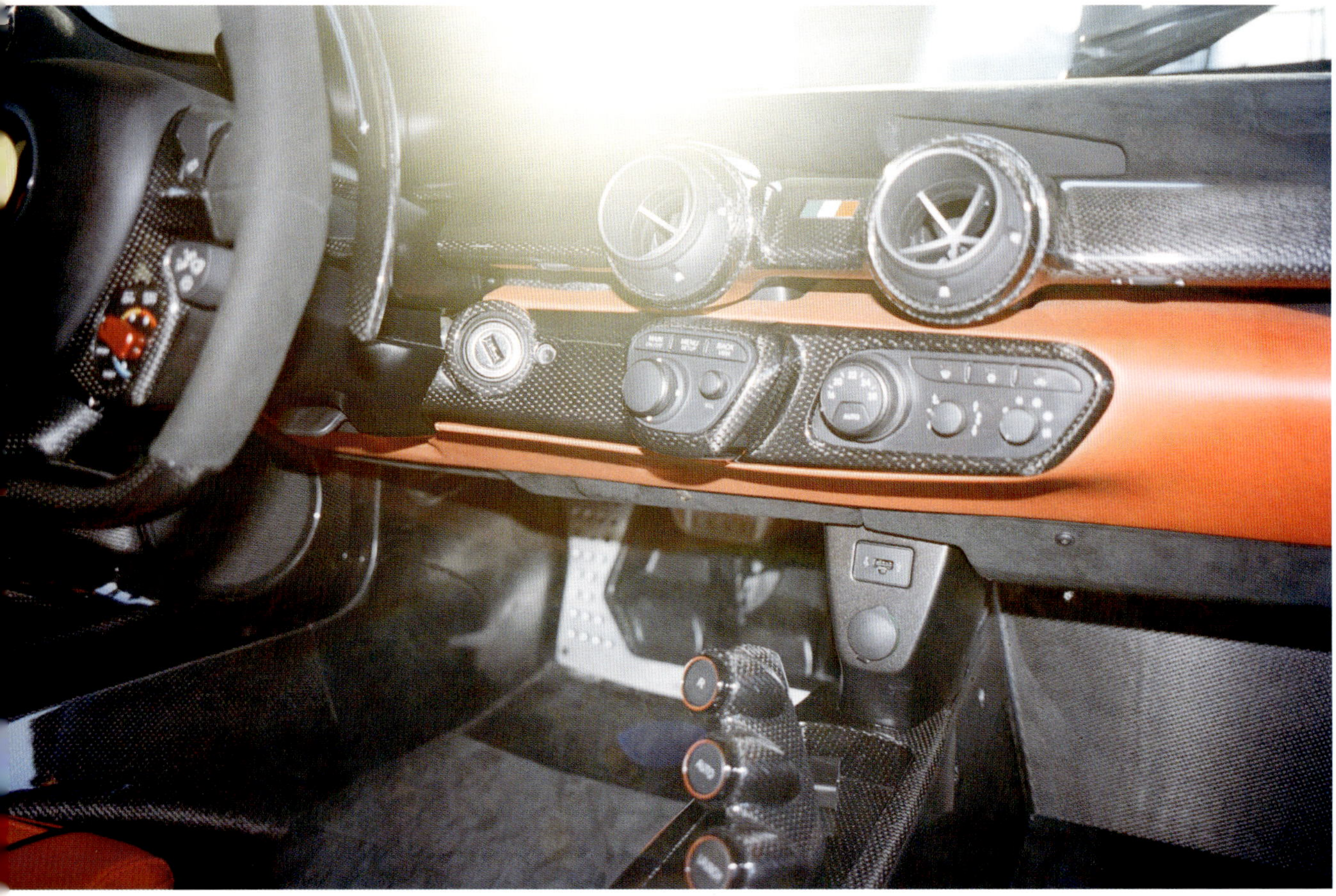

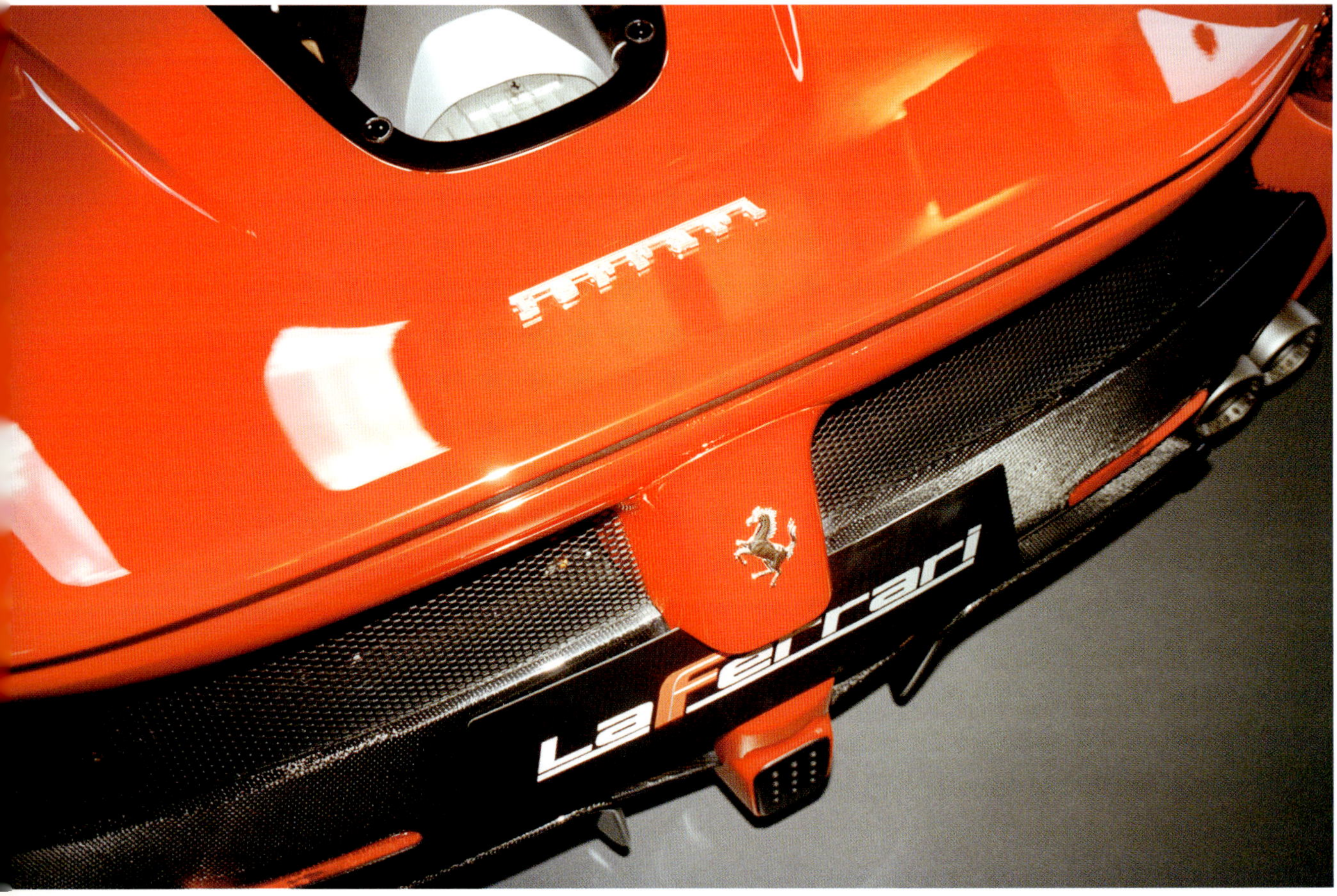

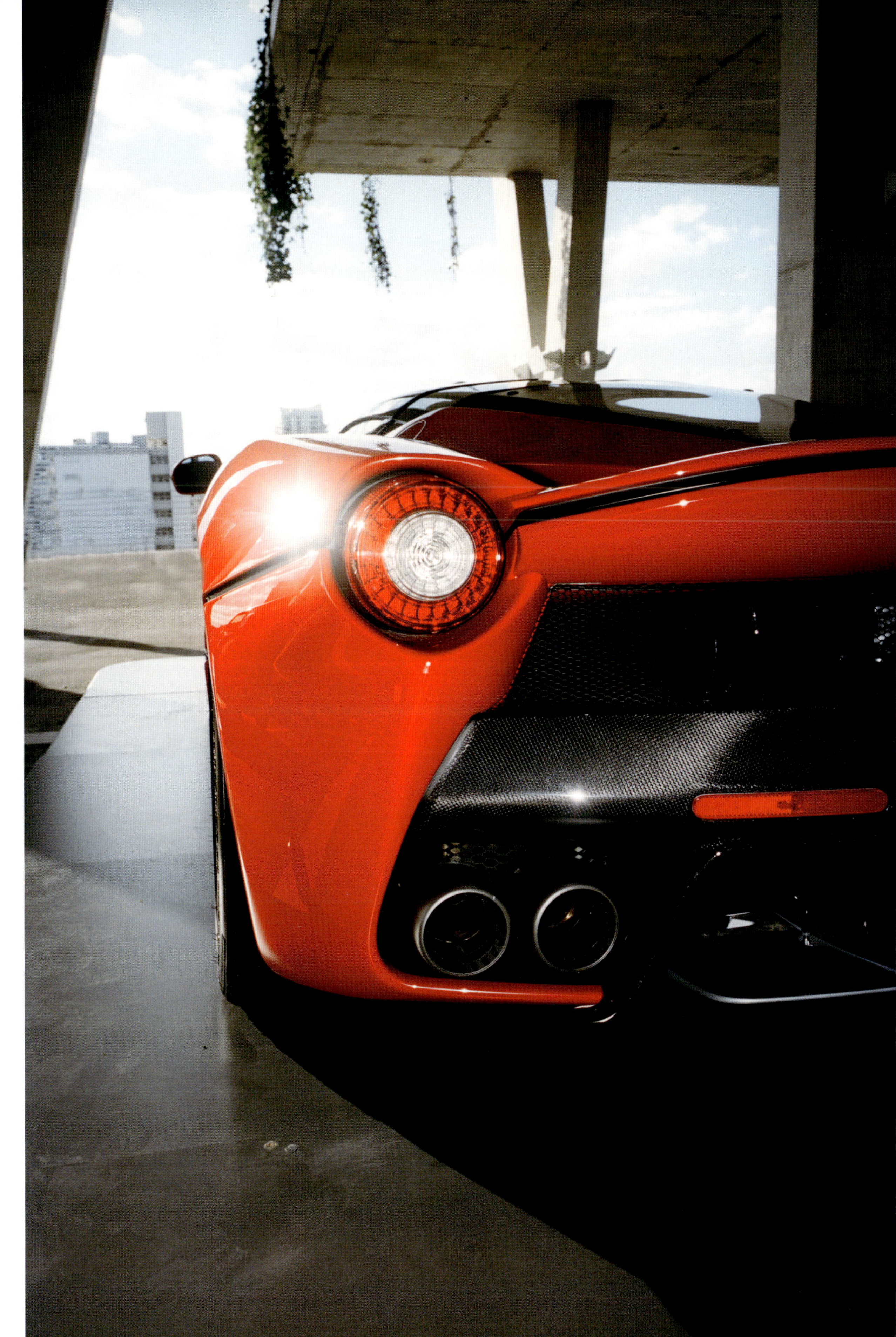

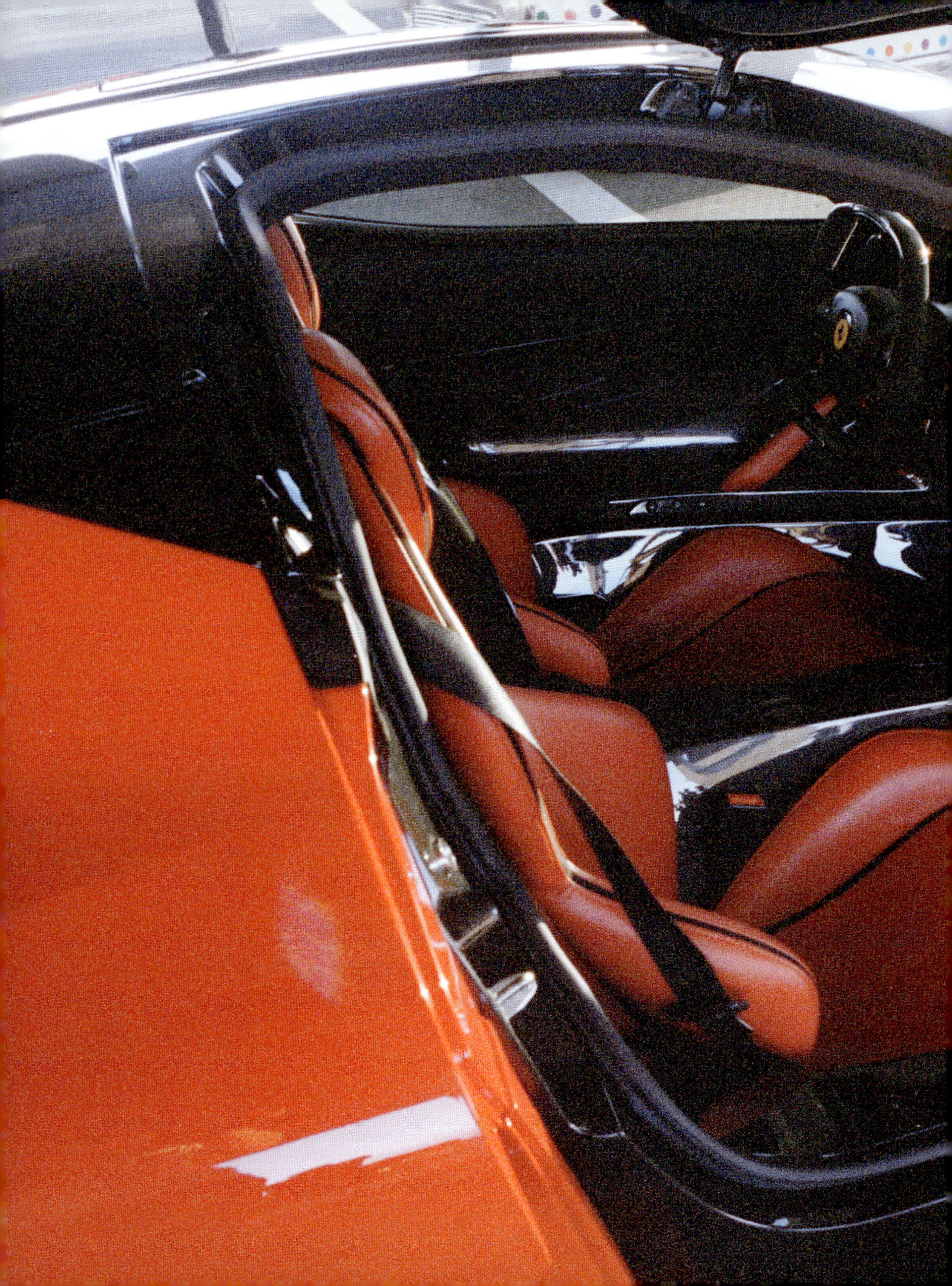

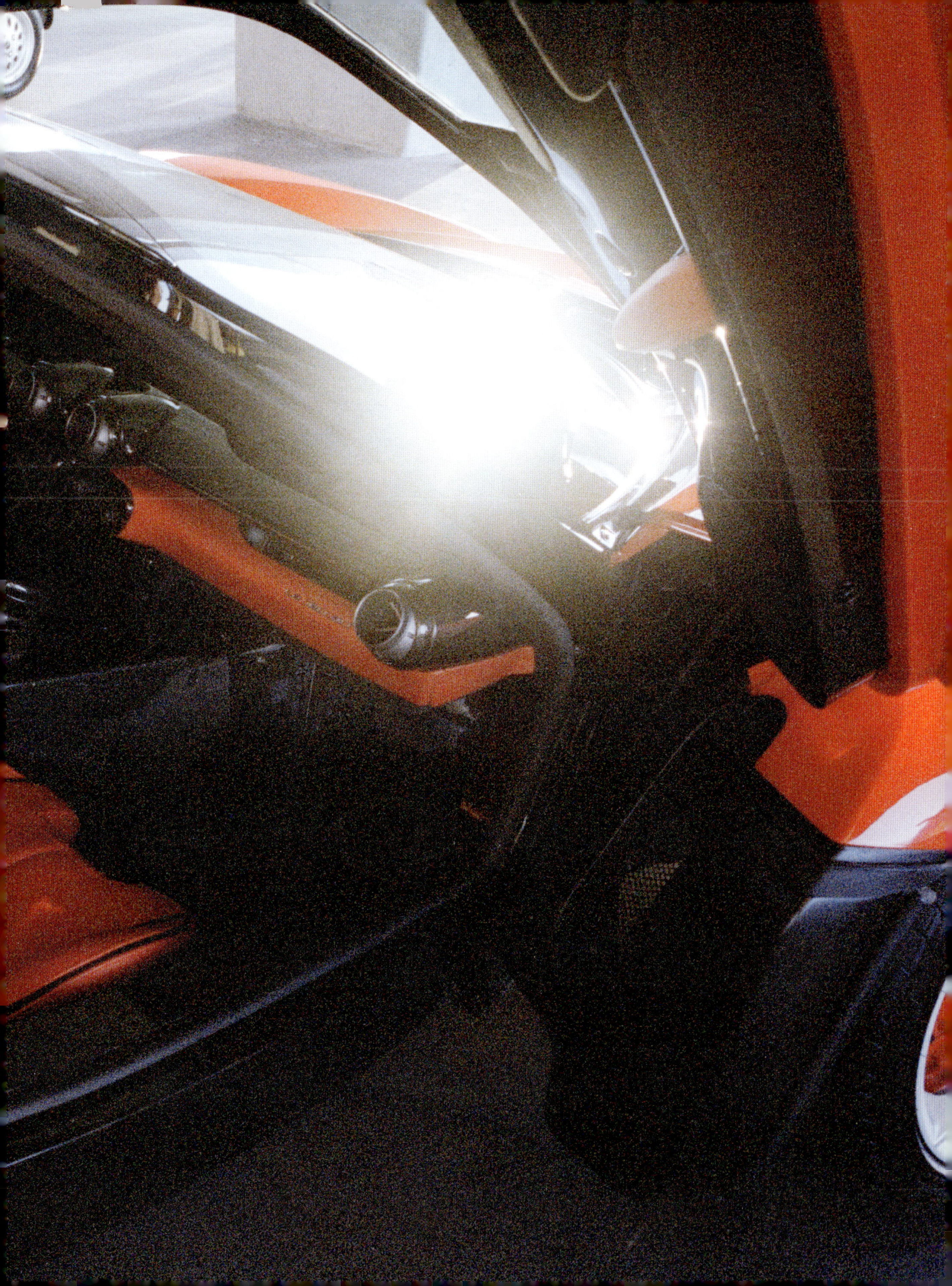

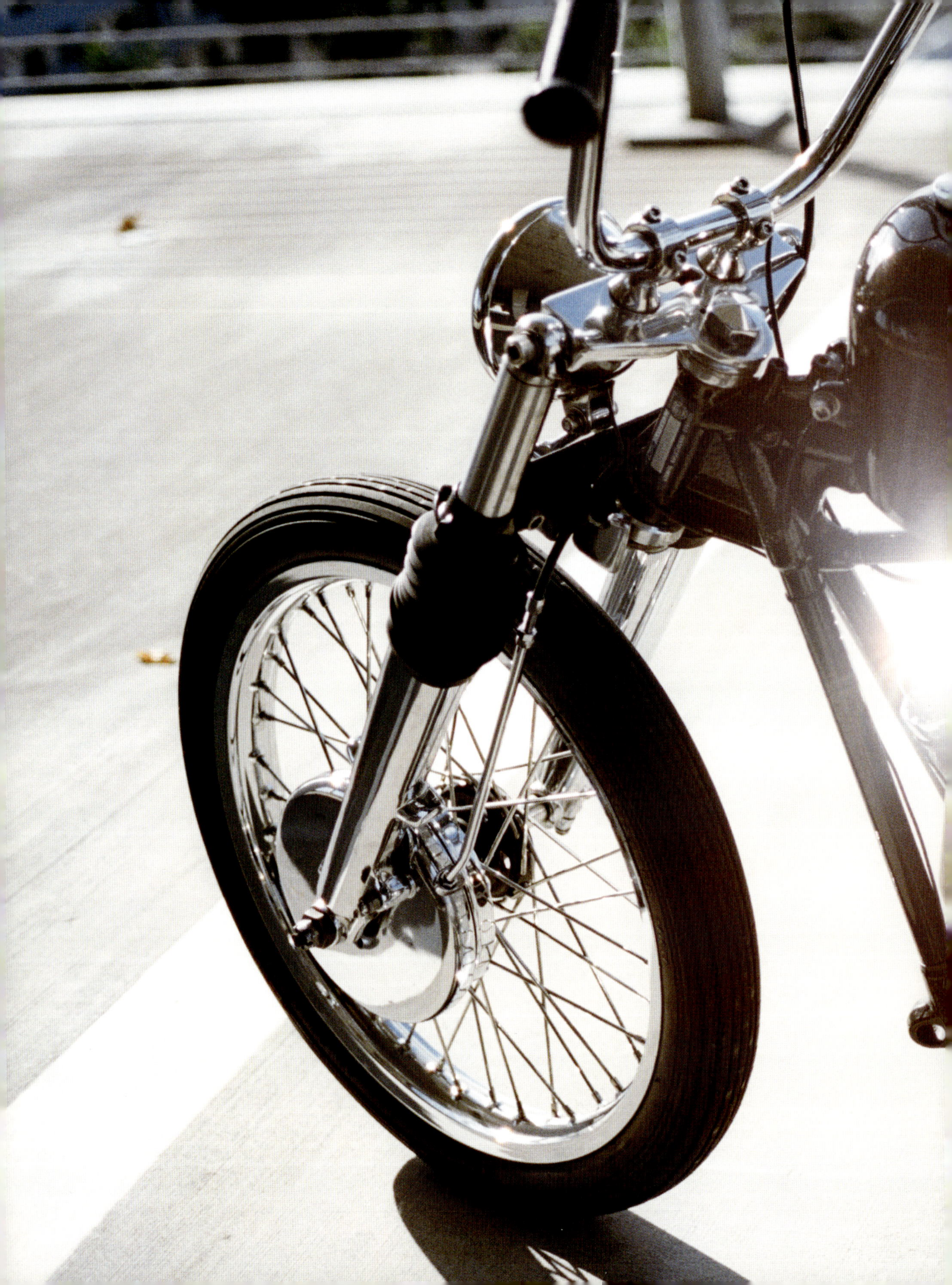

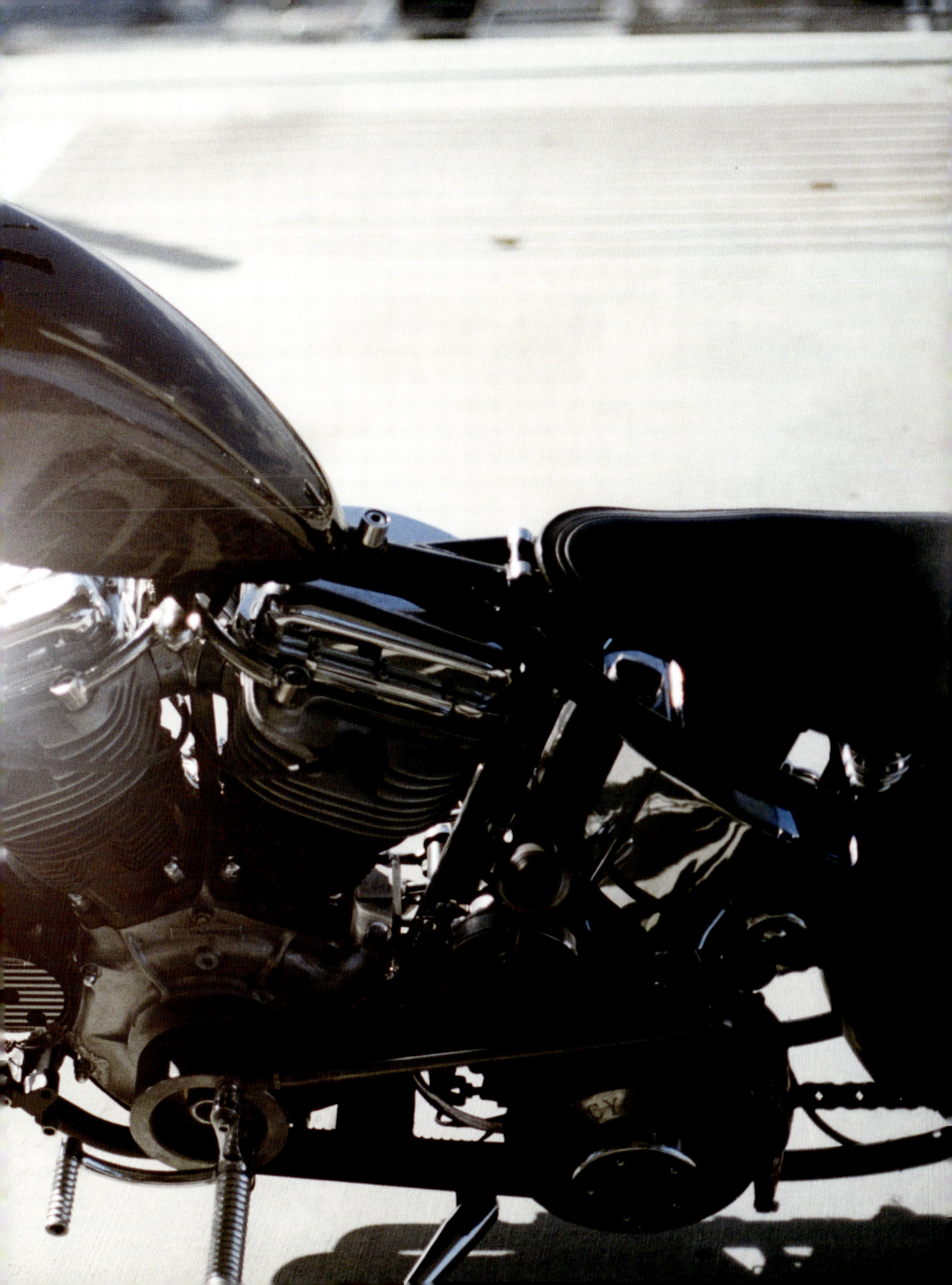

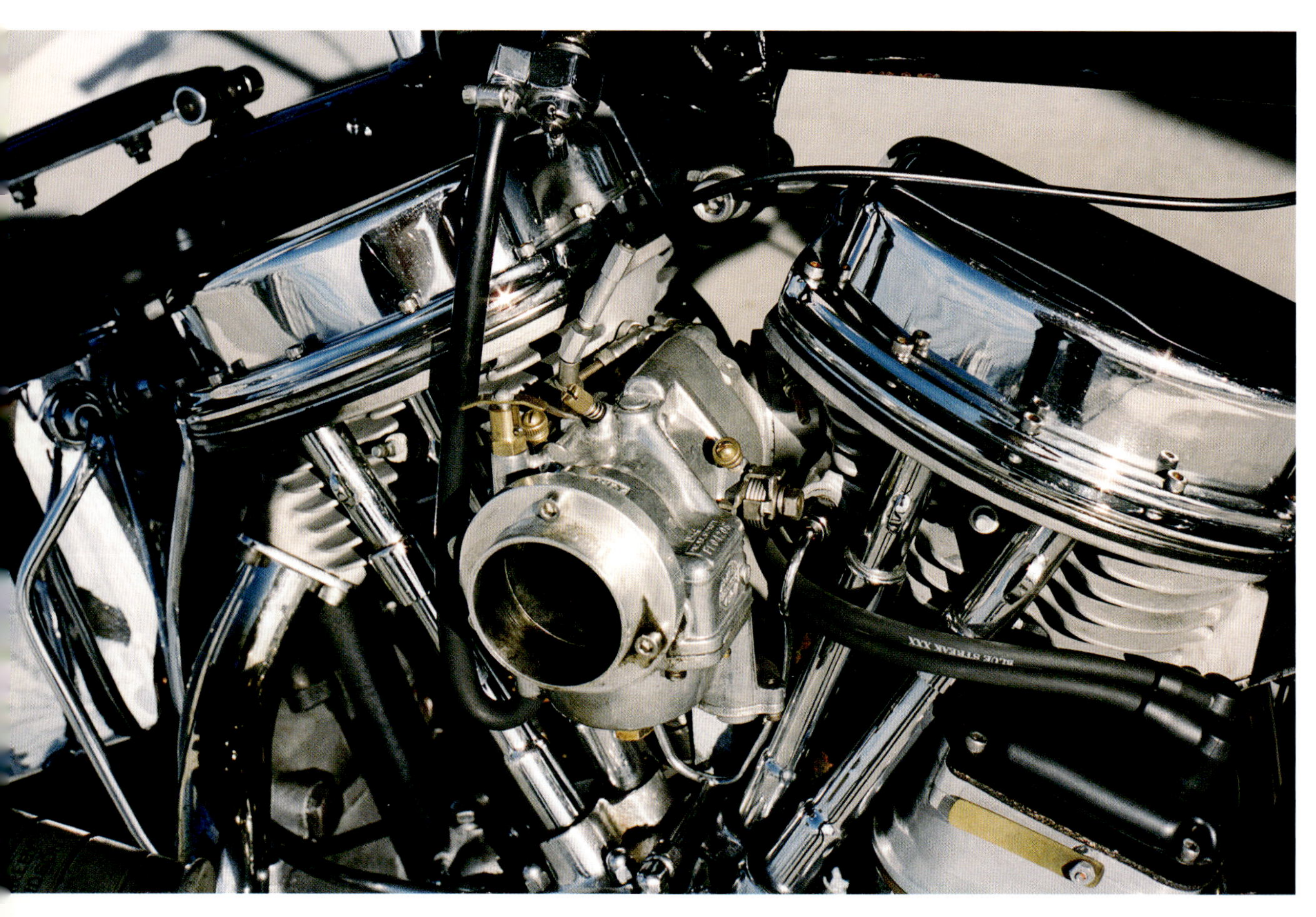
BLUE STREAK XXX

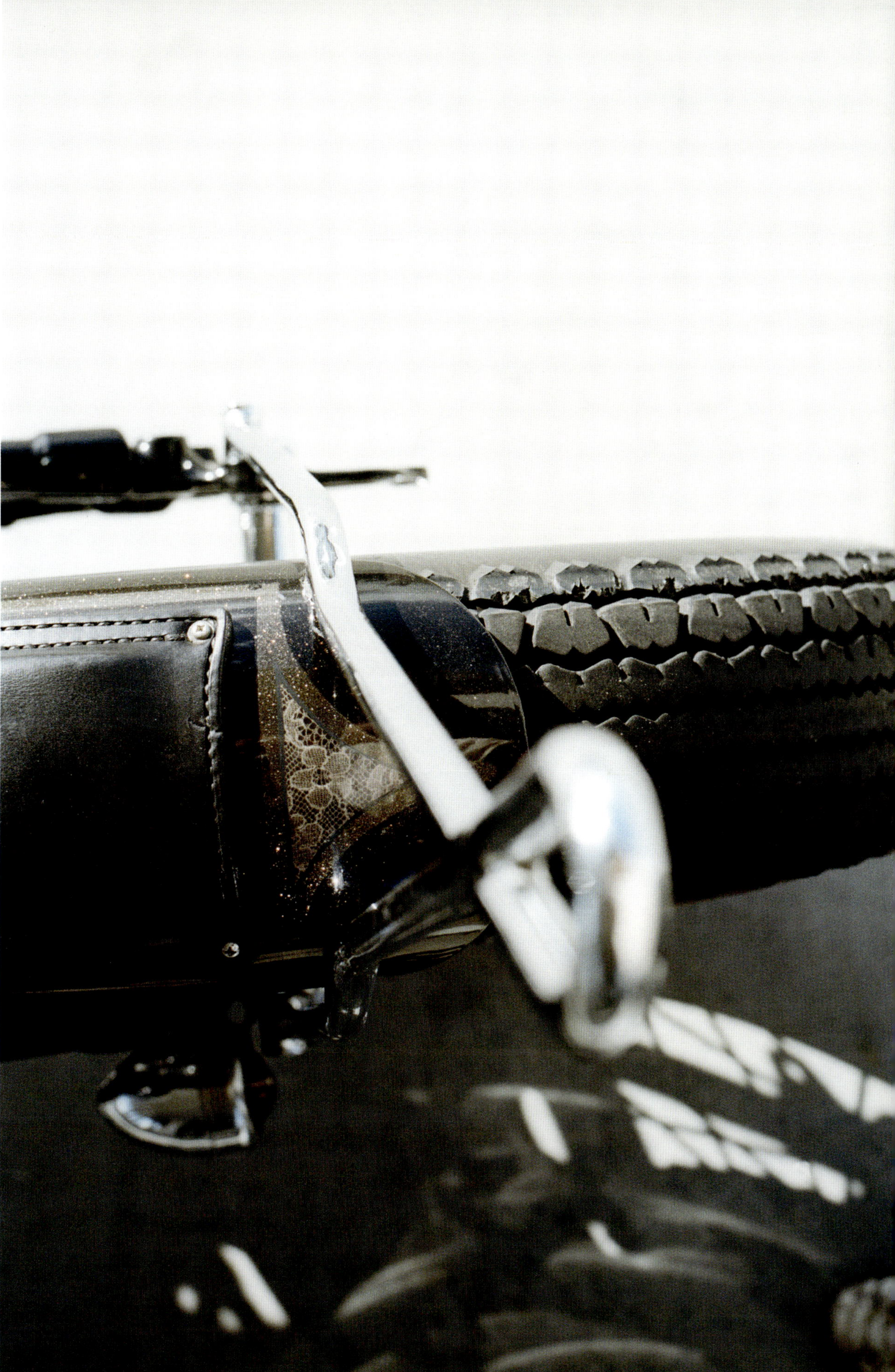

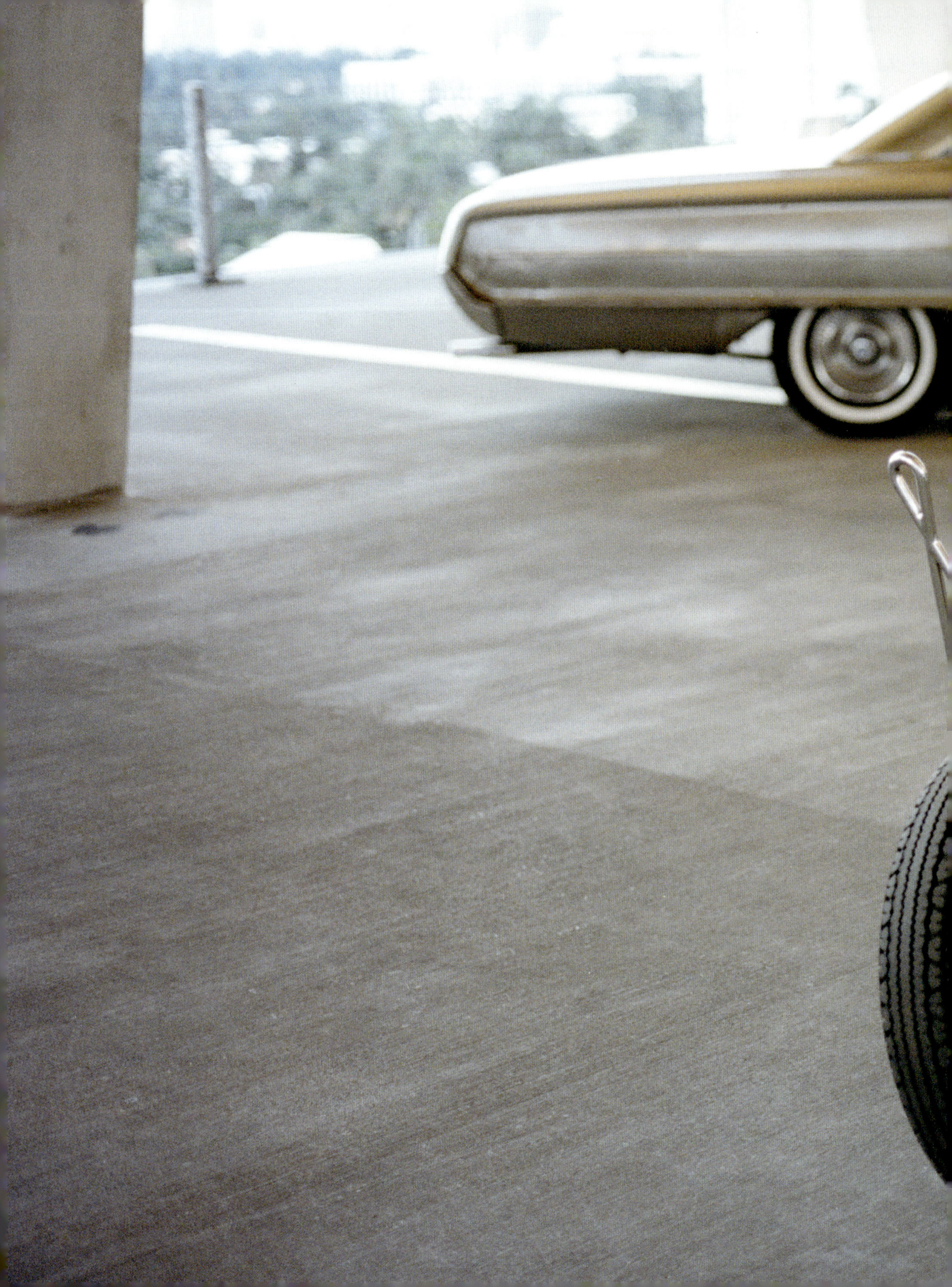

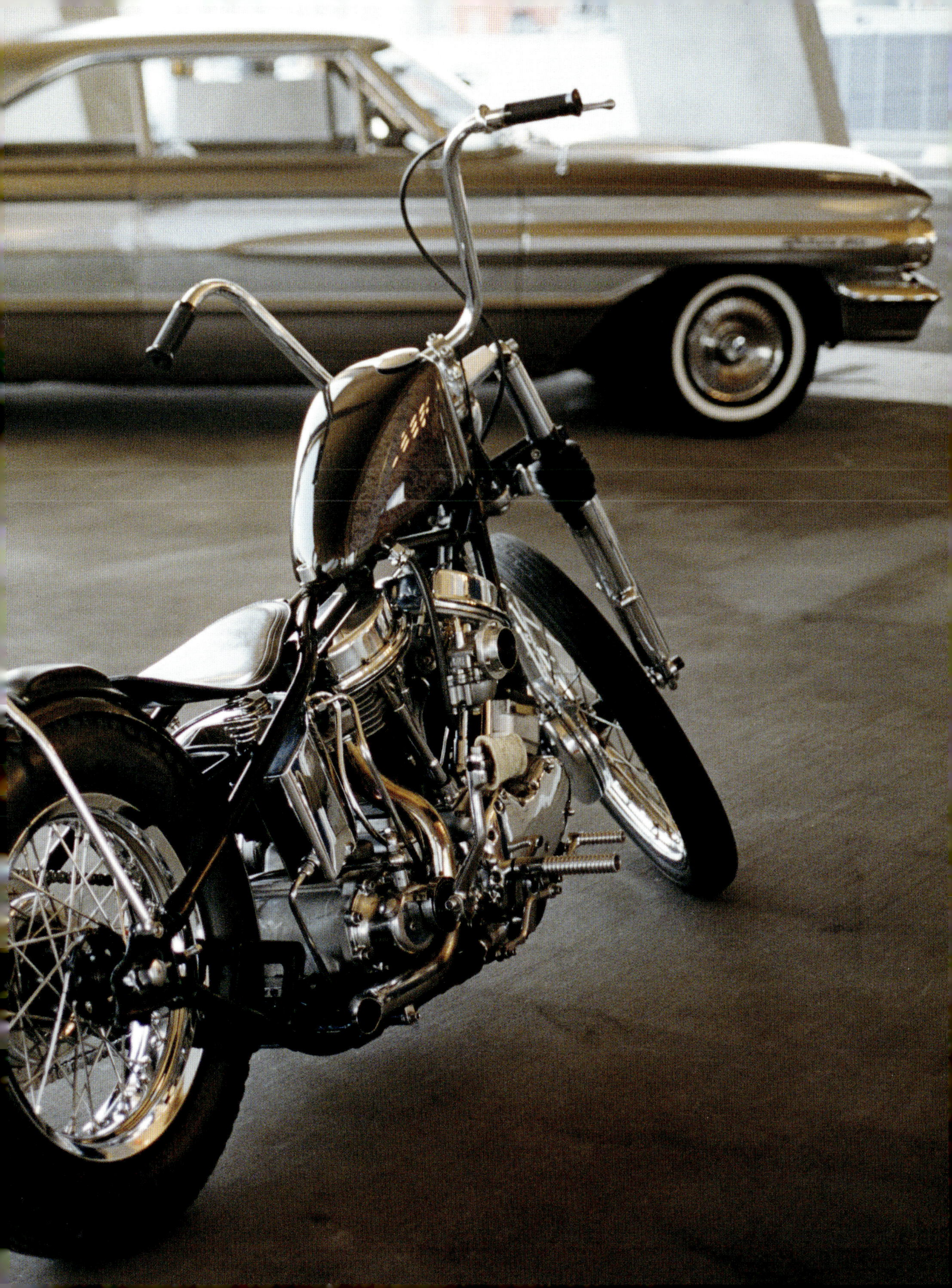

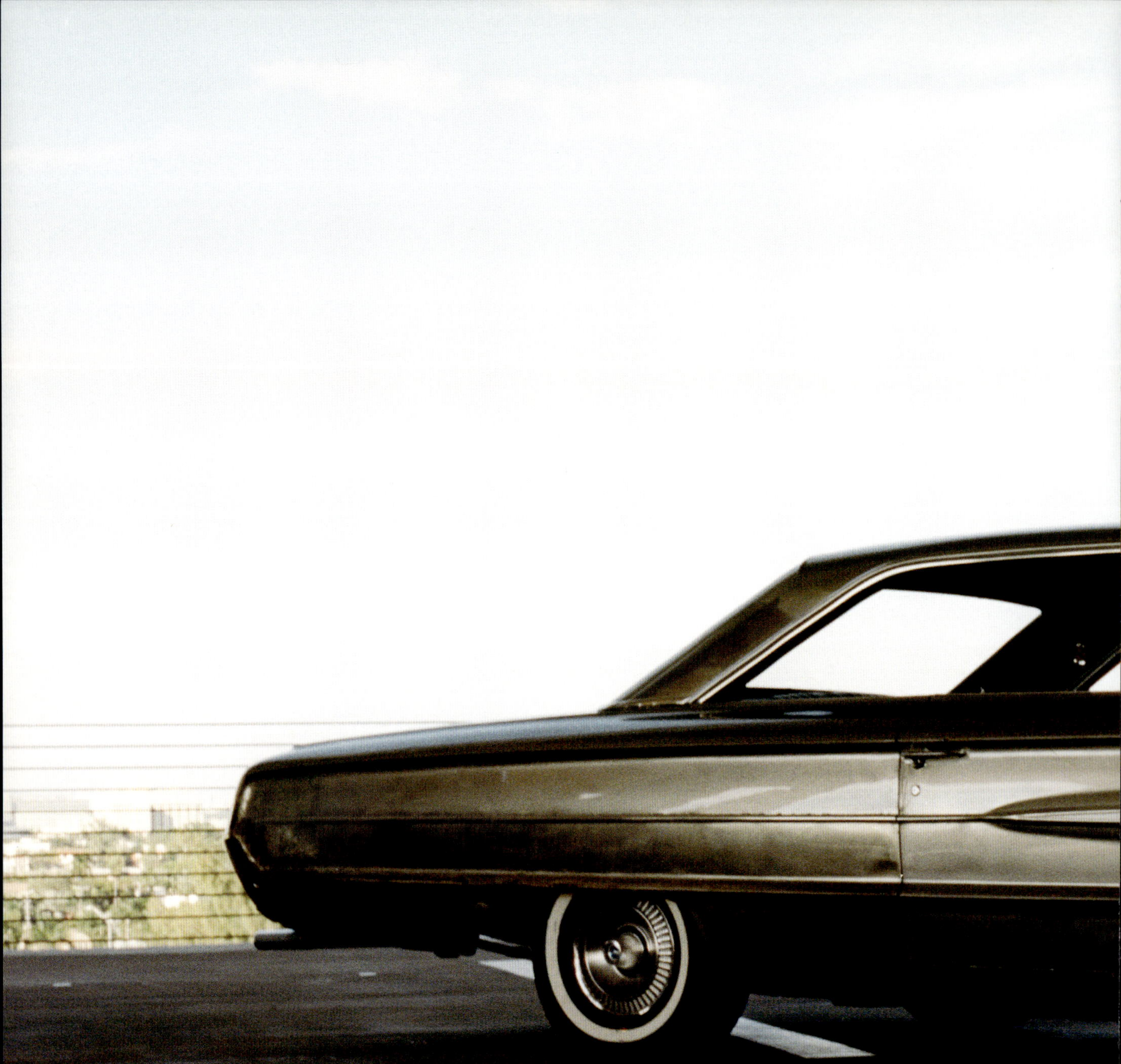

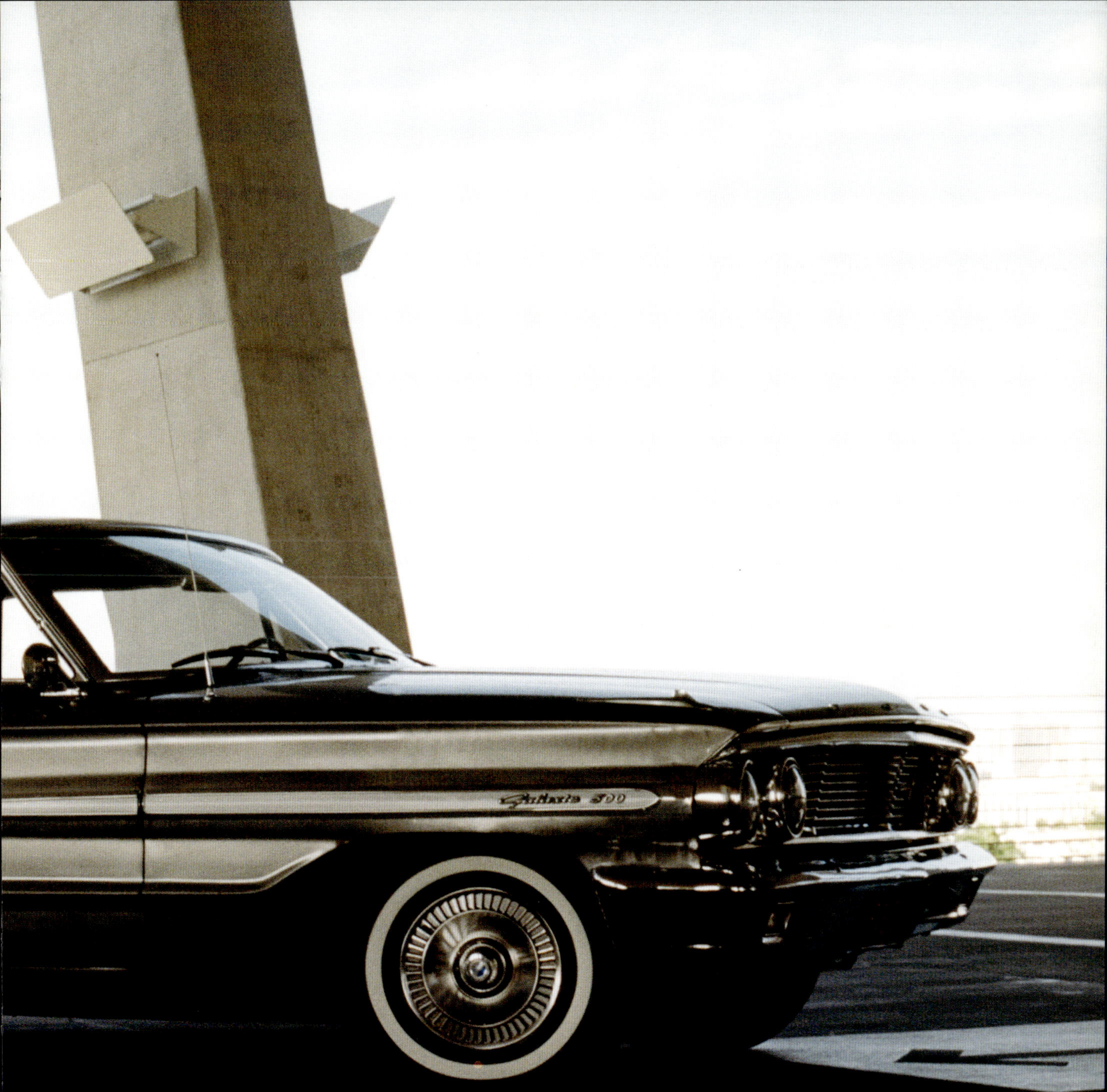
Galaxie 500

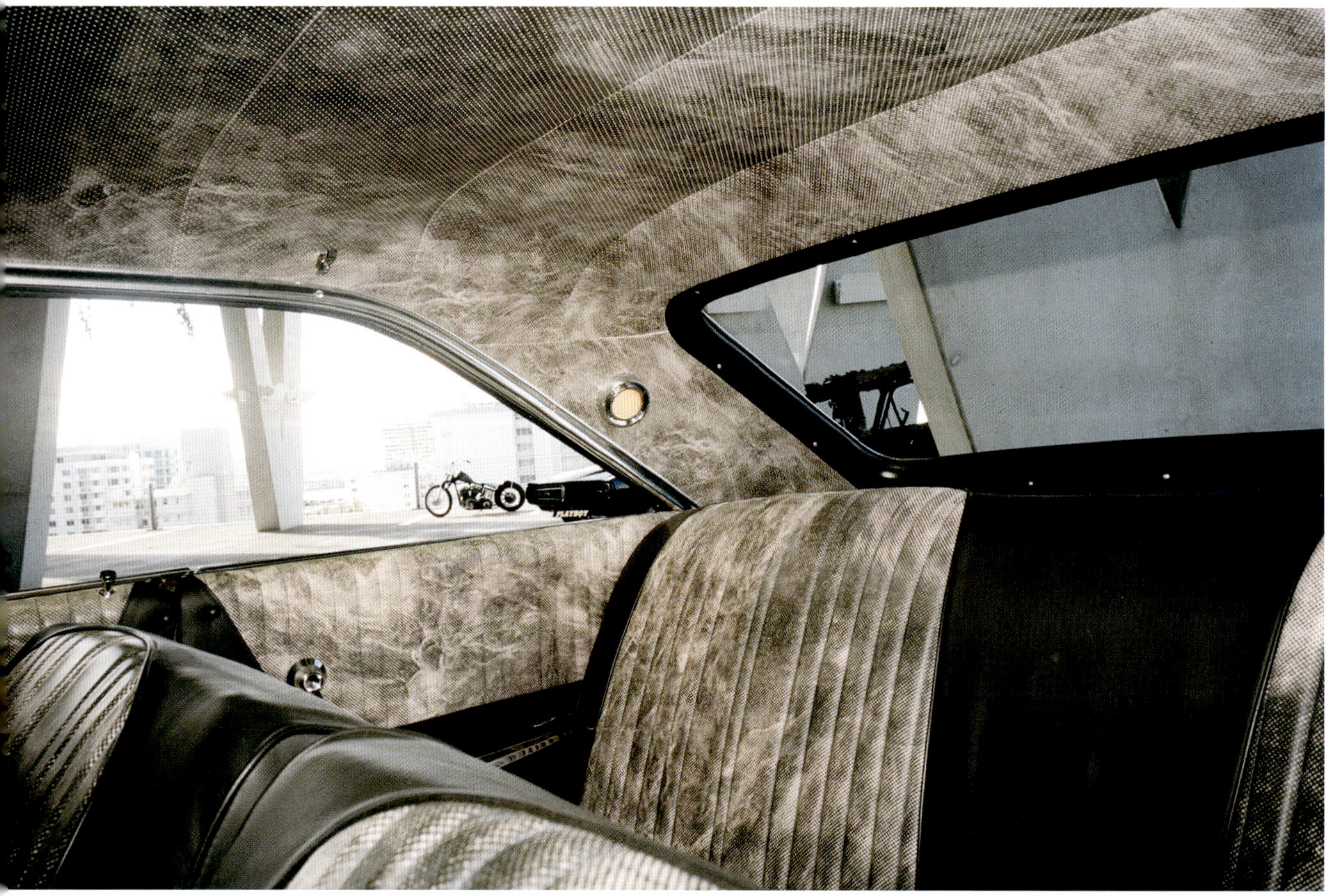

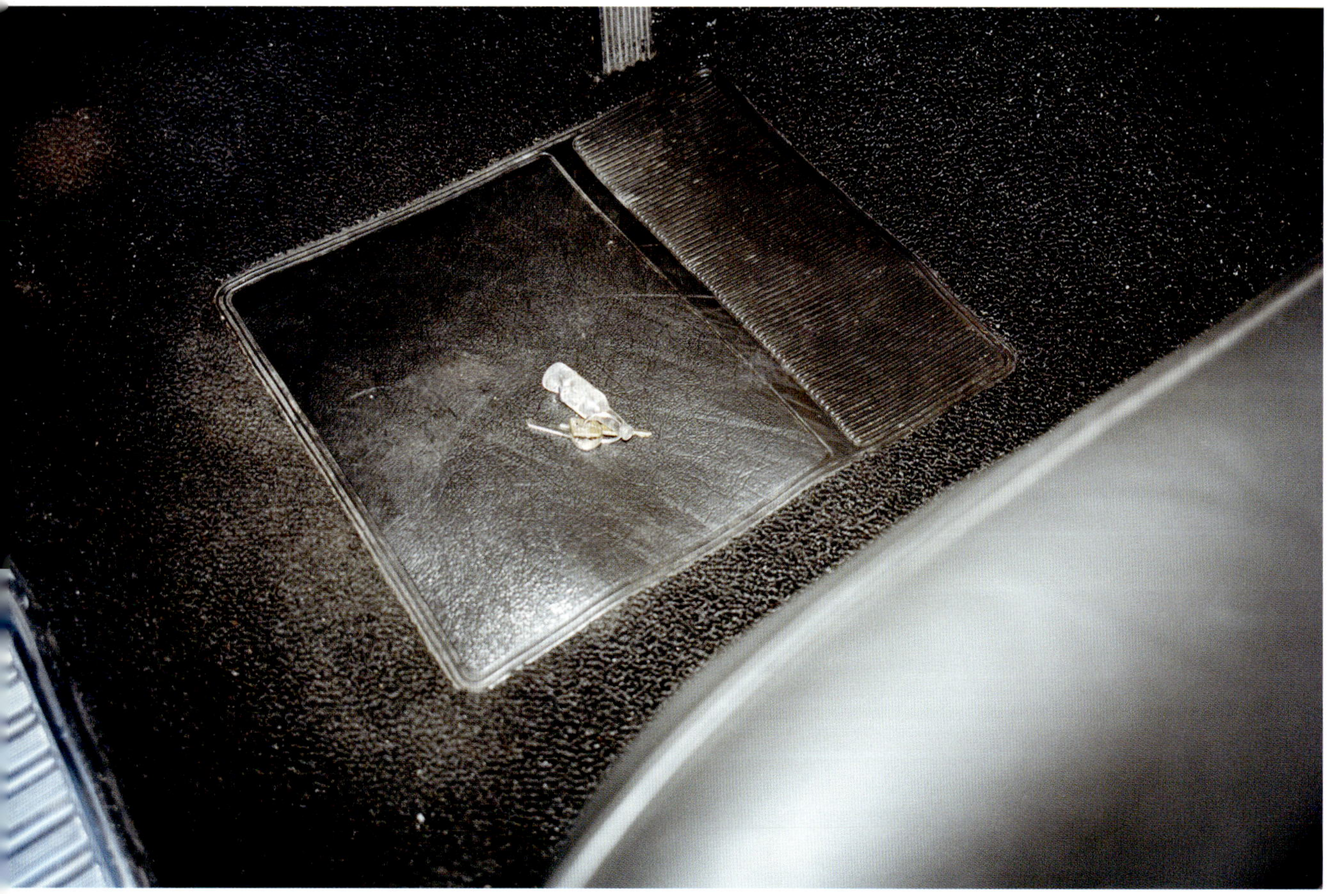

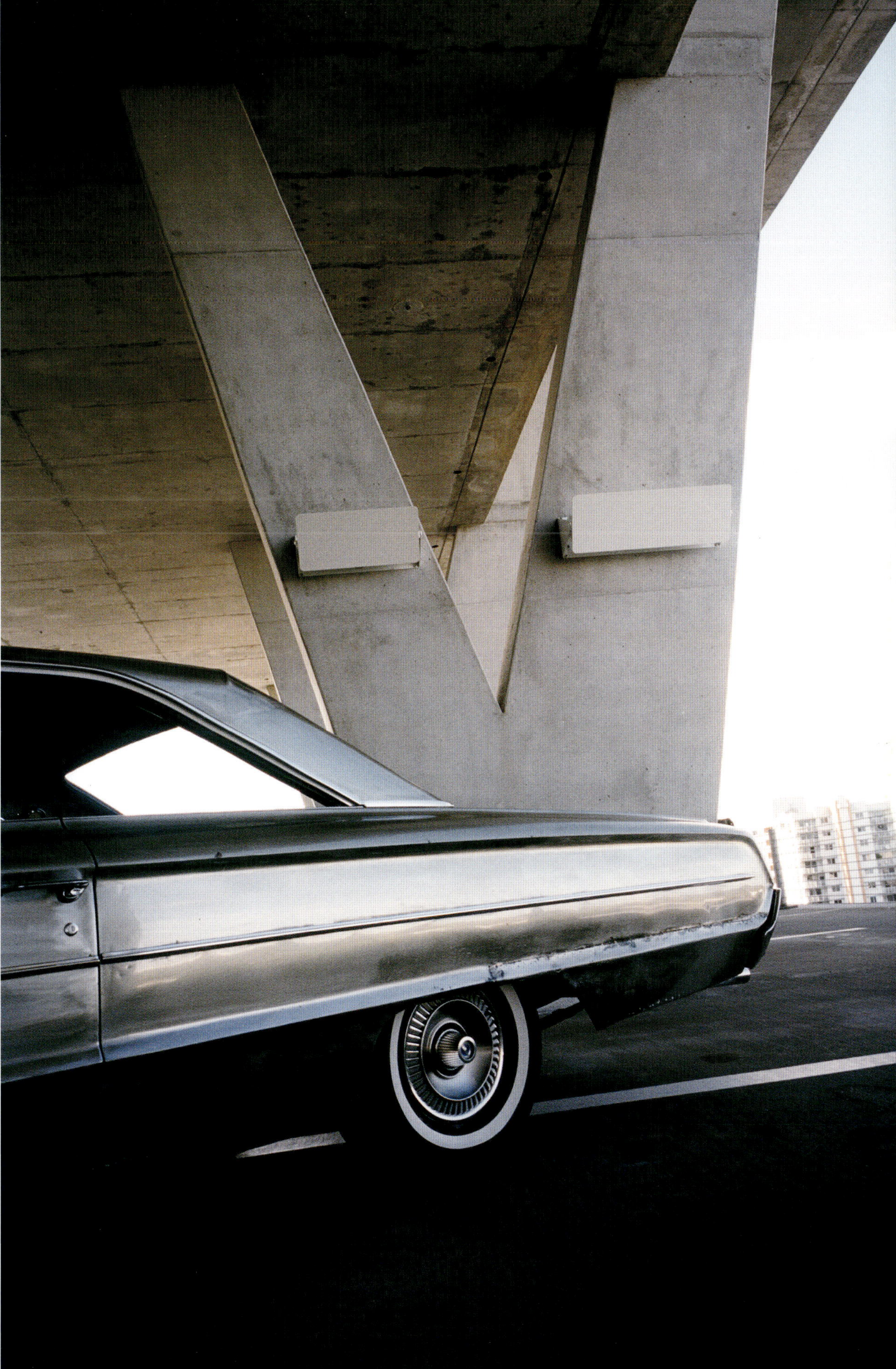

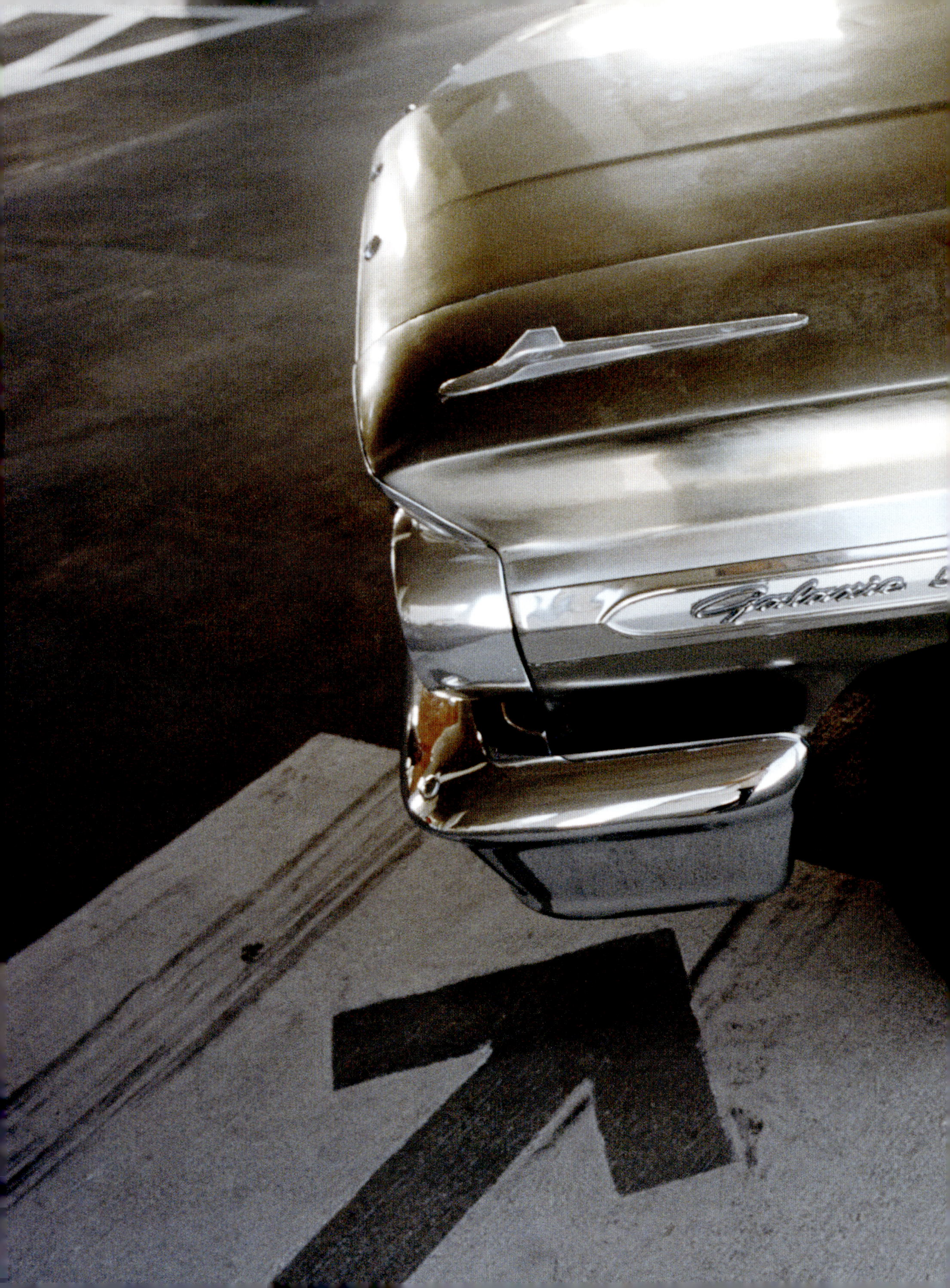
Galaxie

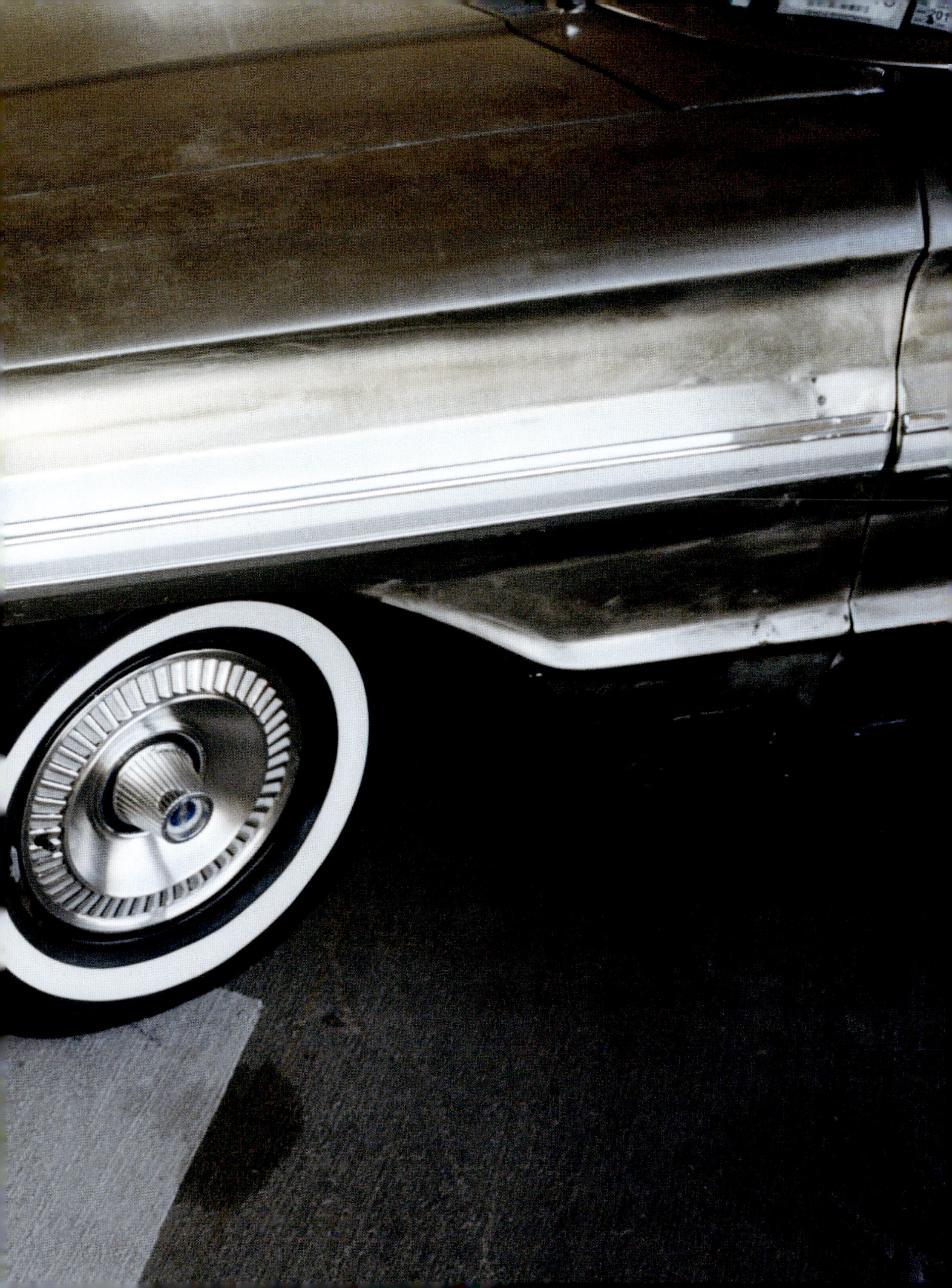

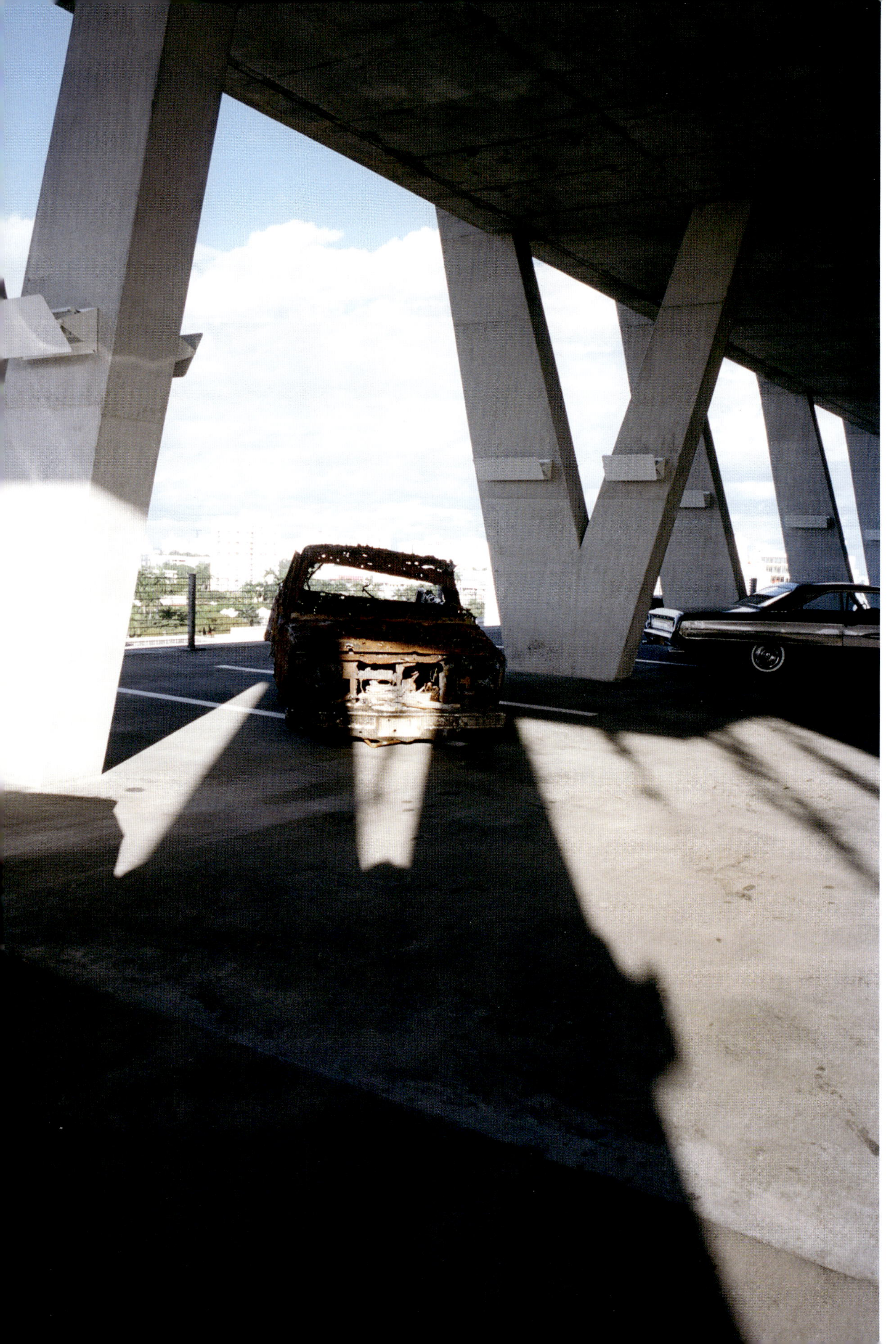

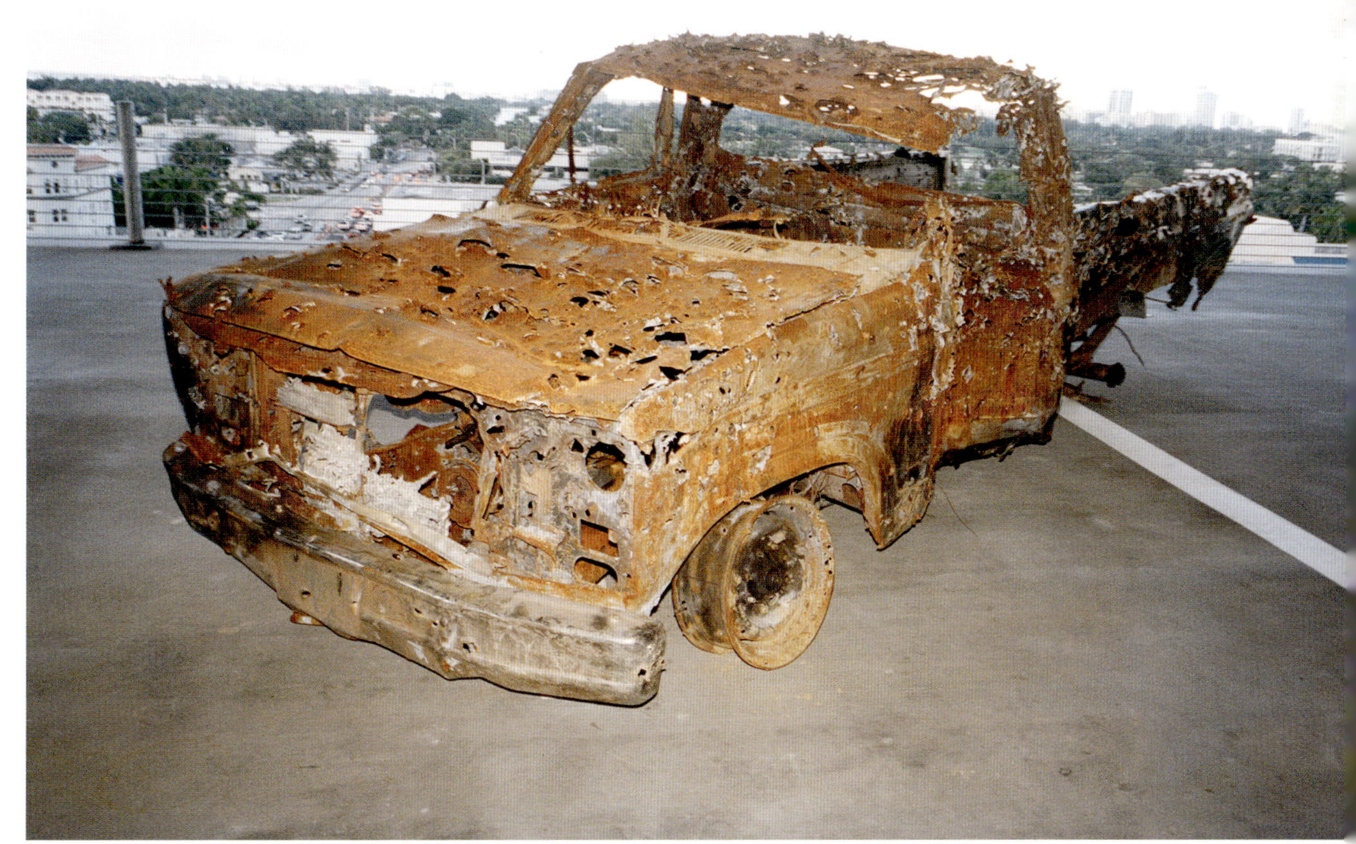

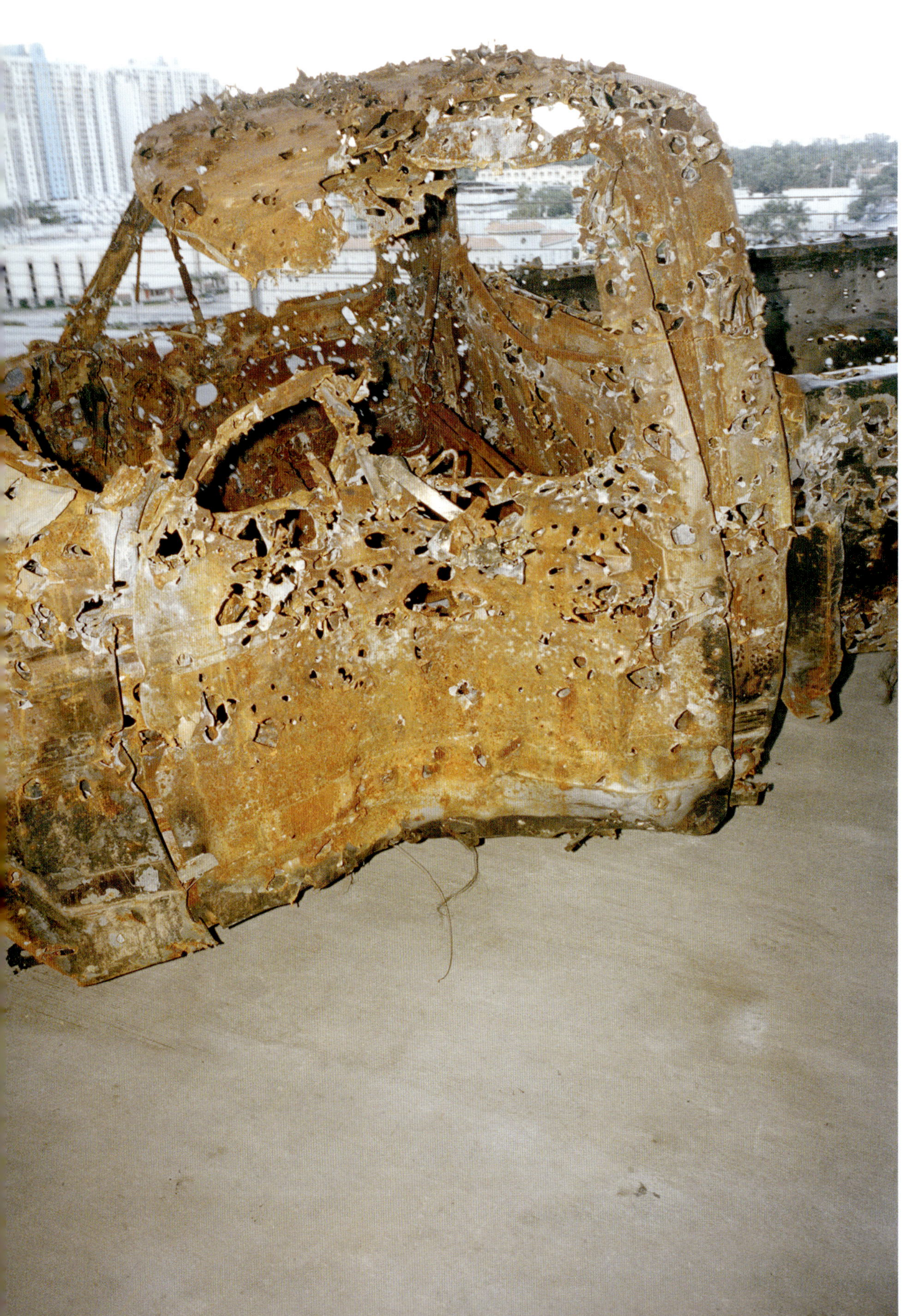

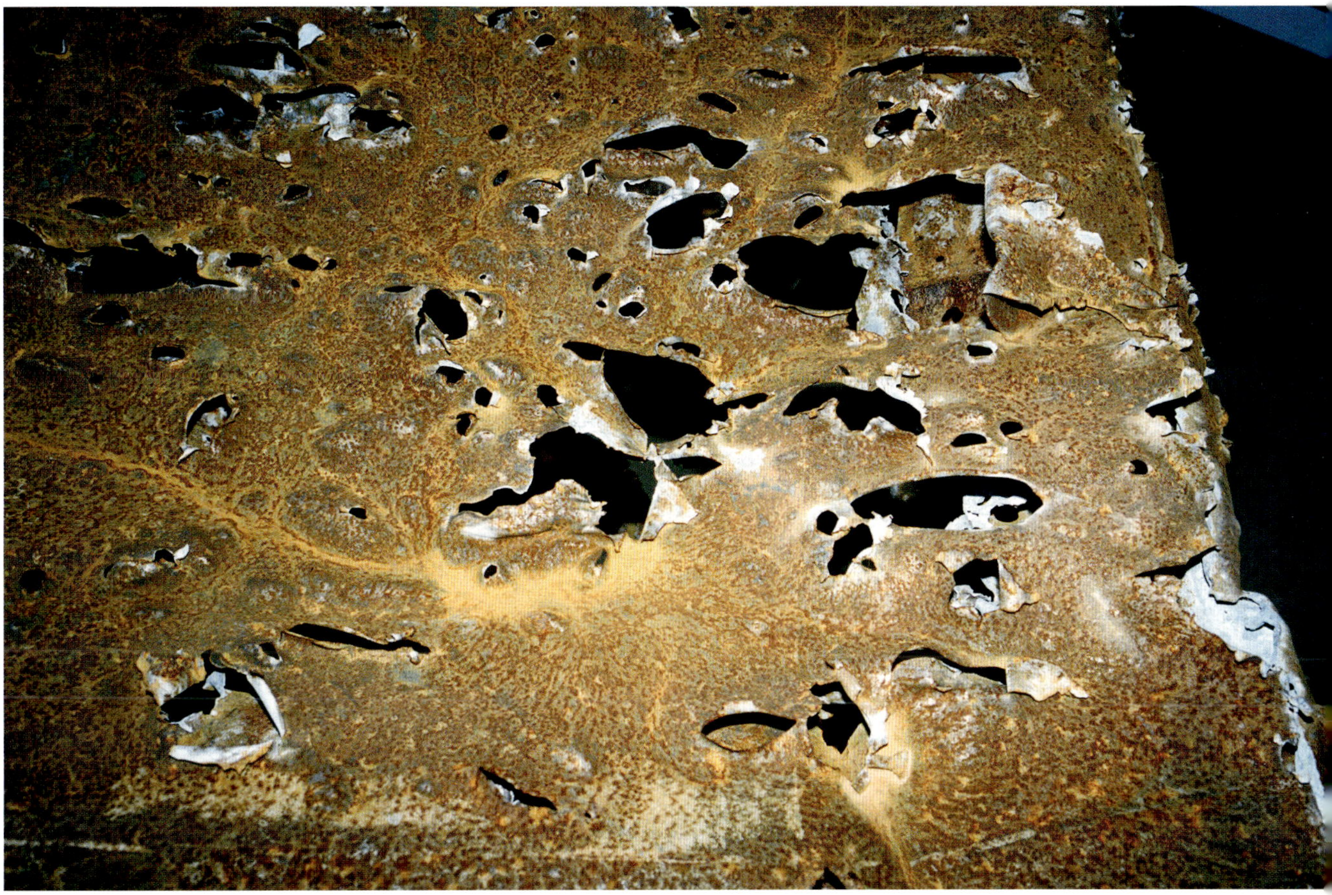

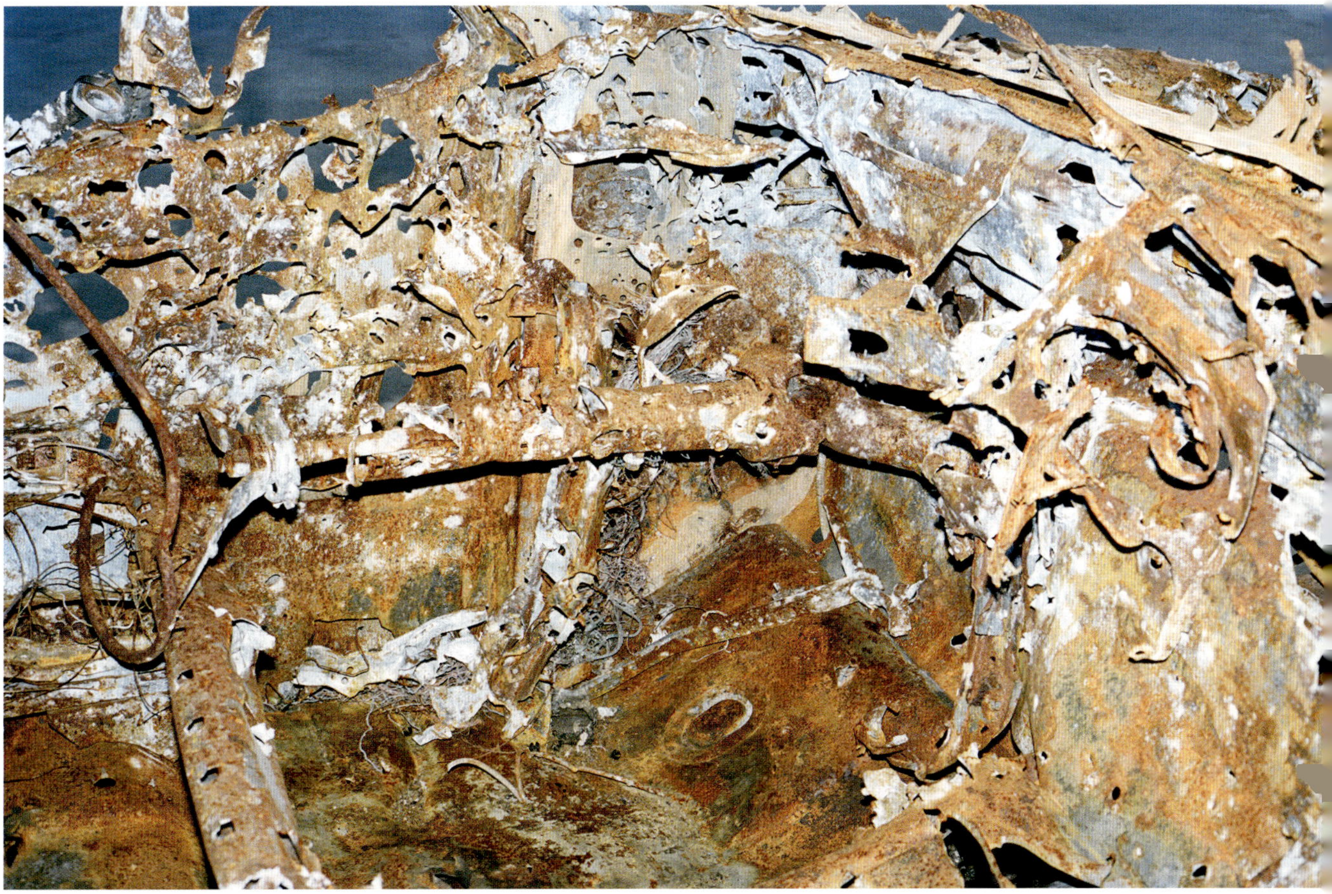

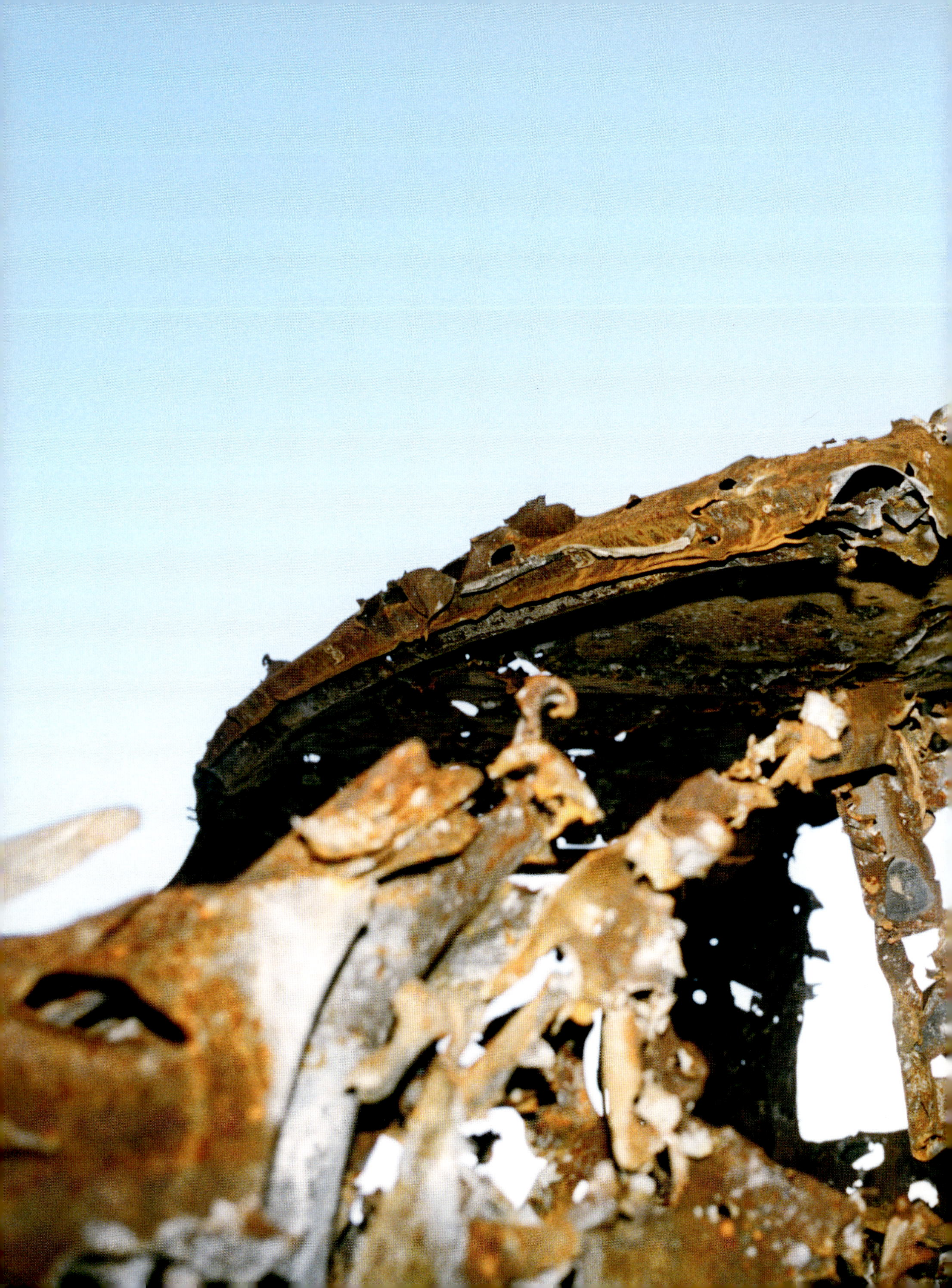

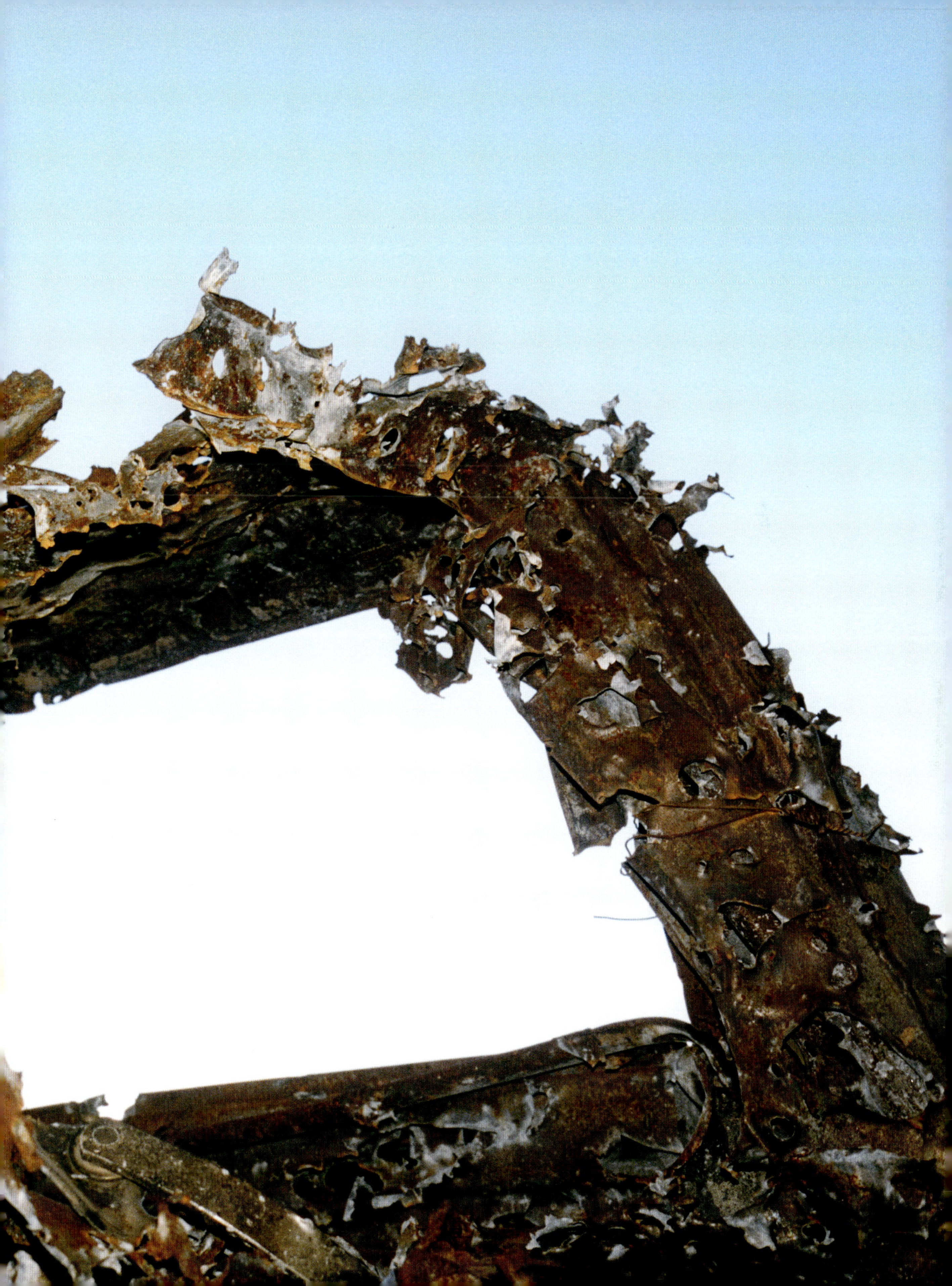

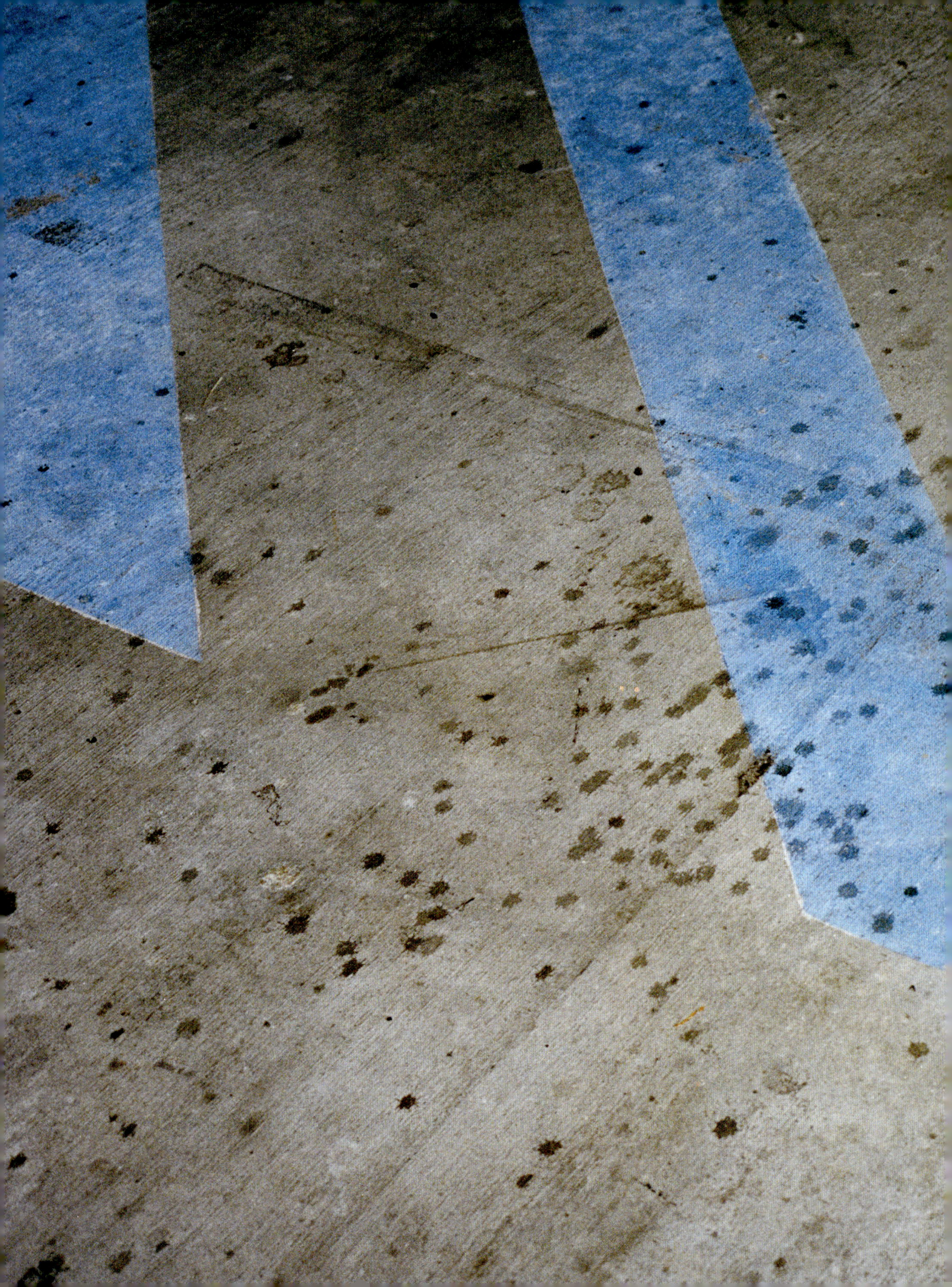

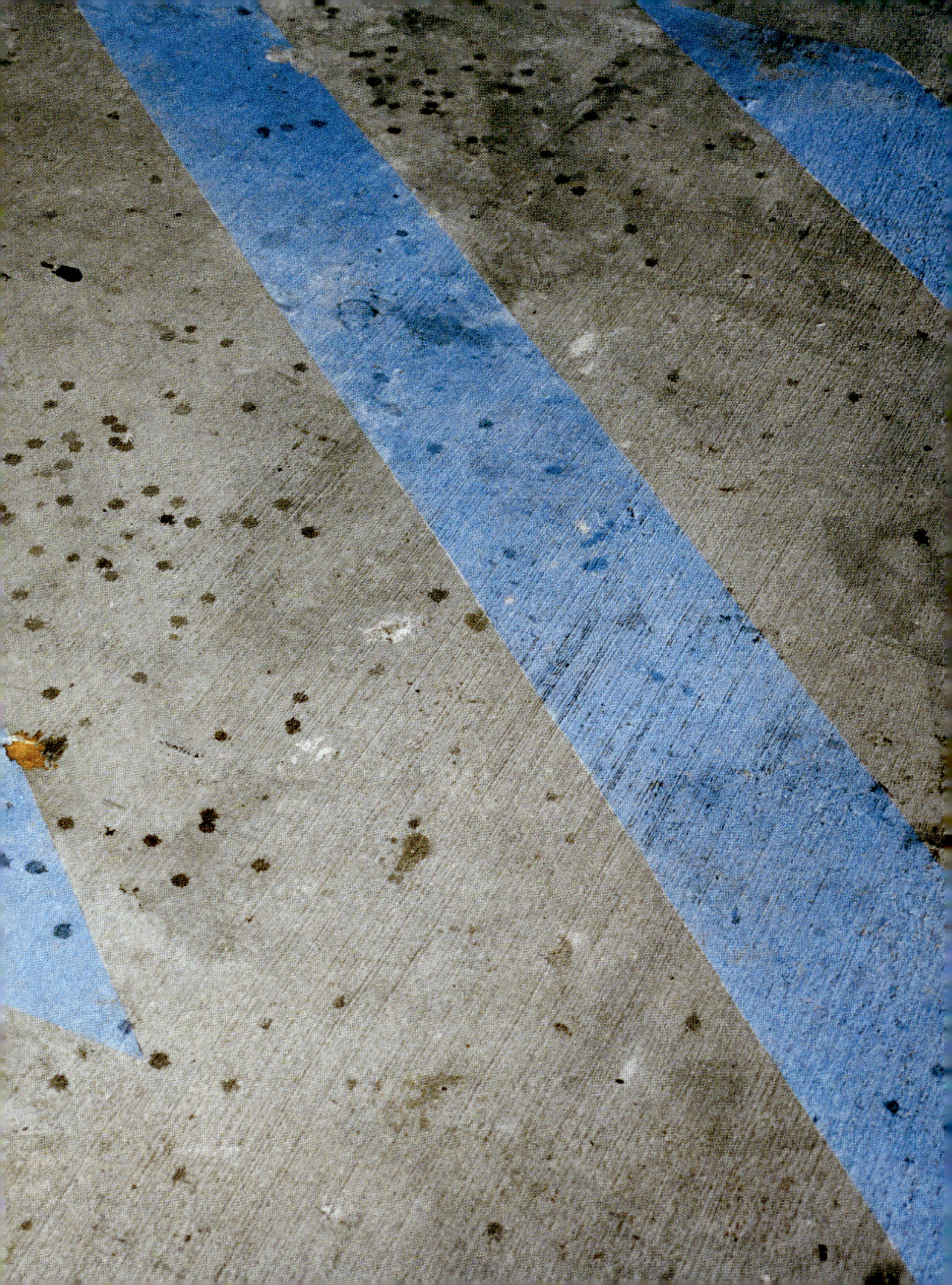

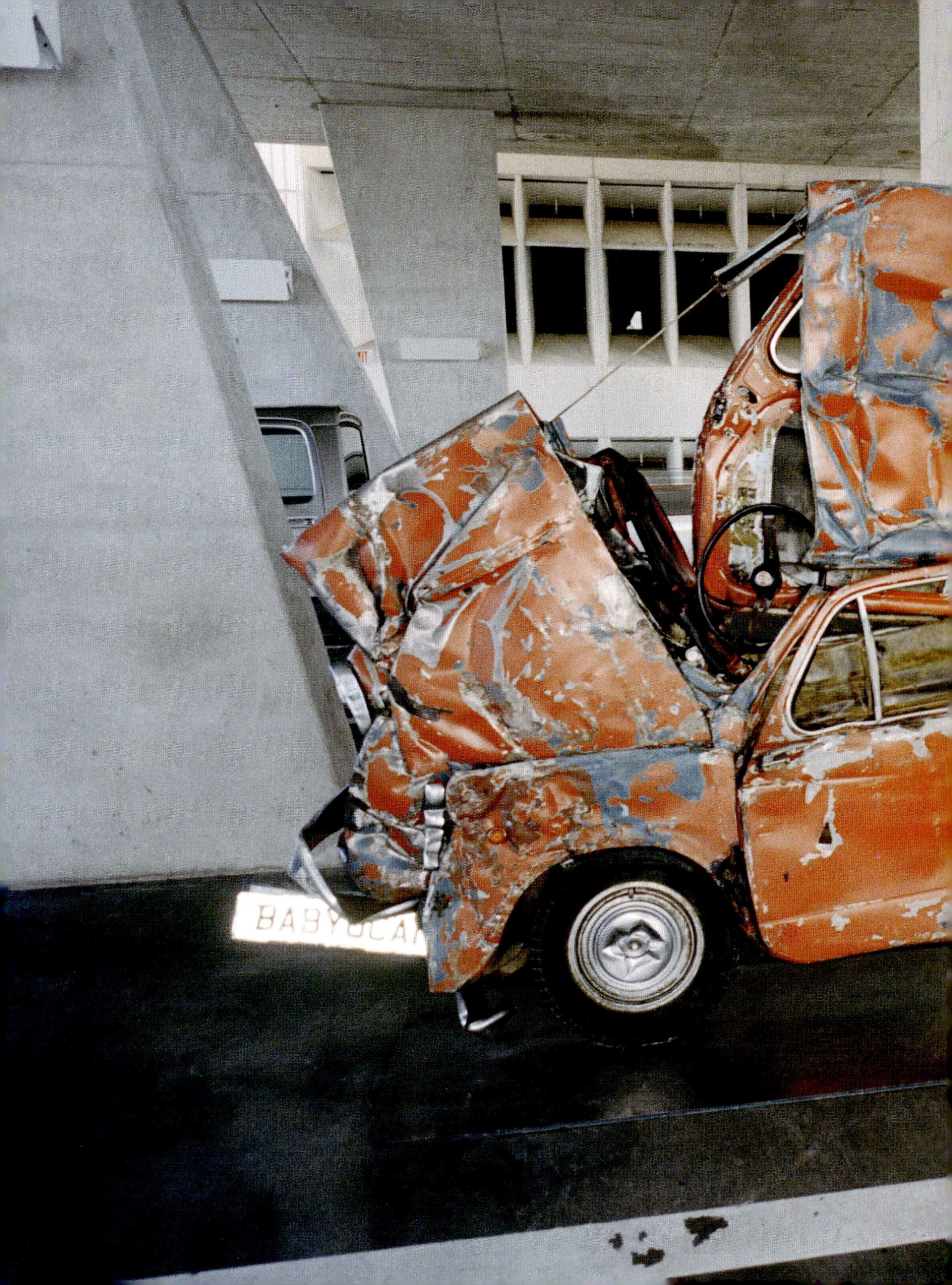

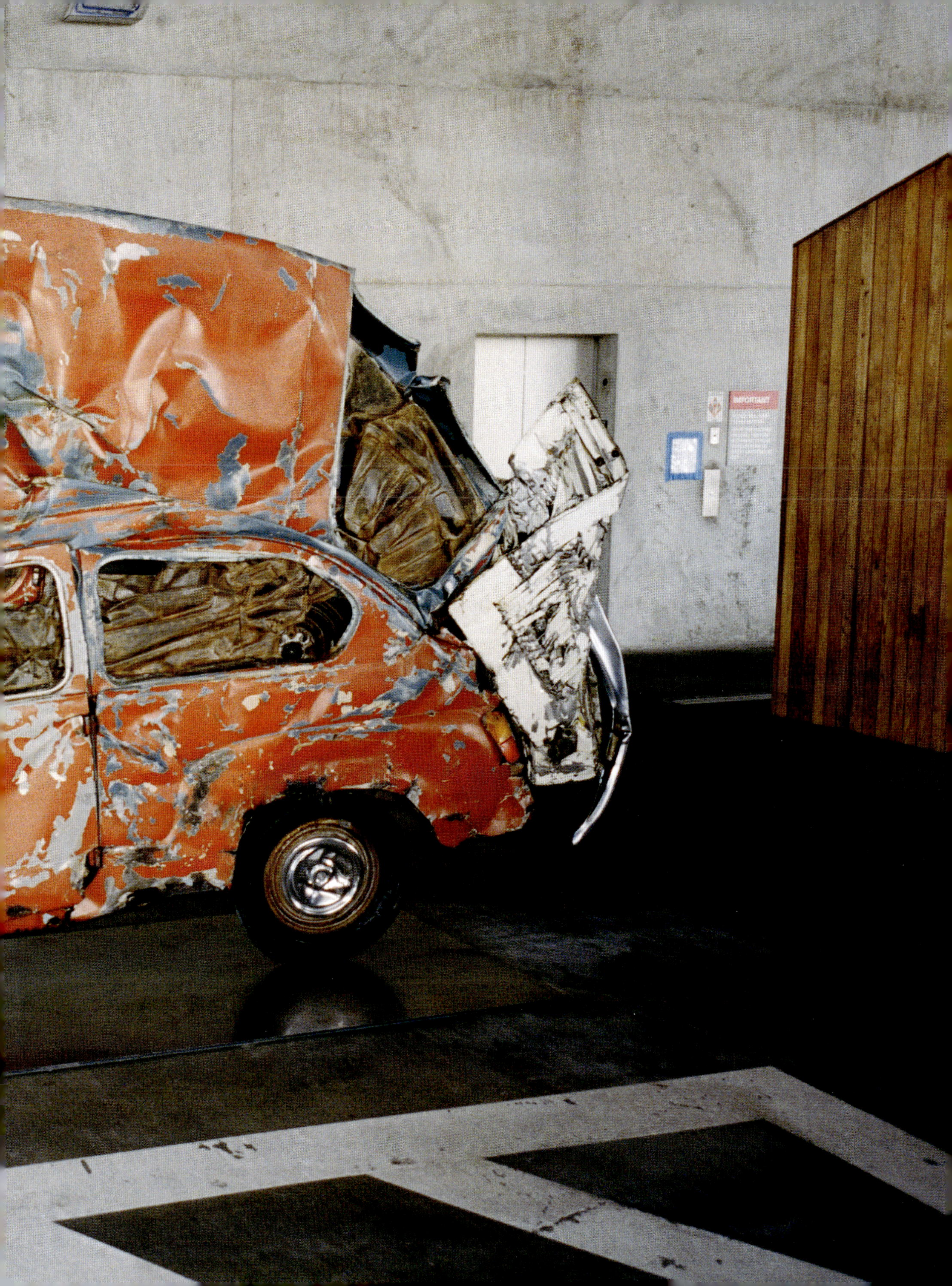
IMPORTANT

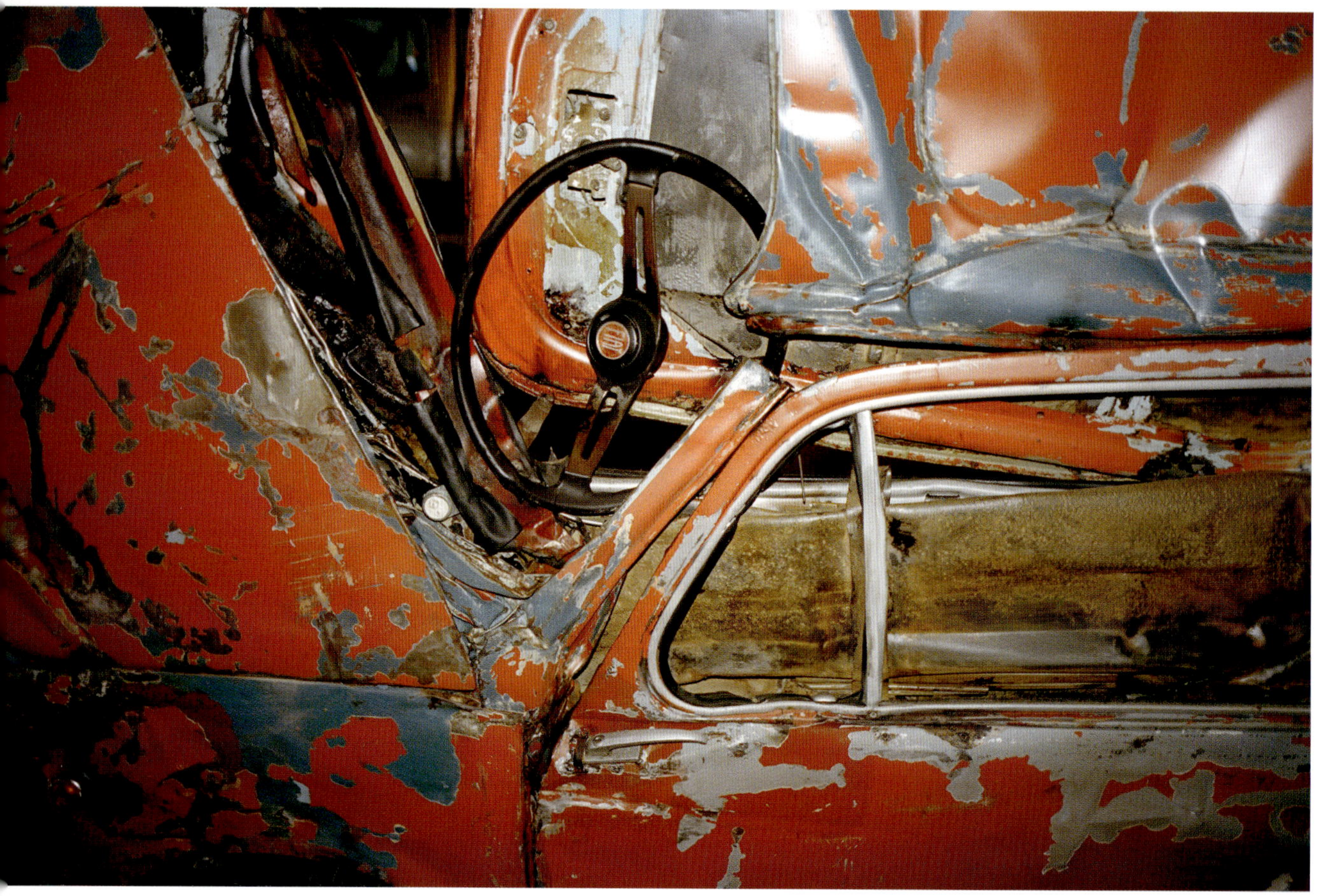

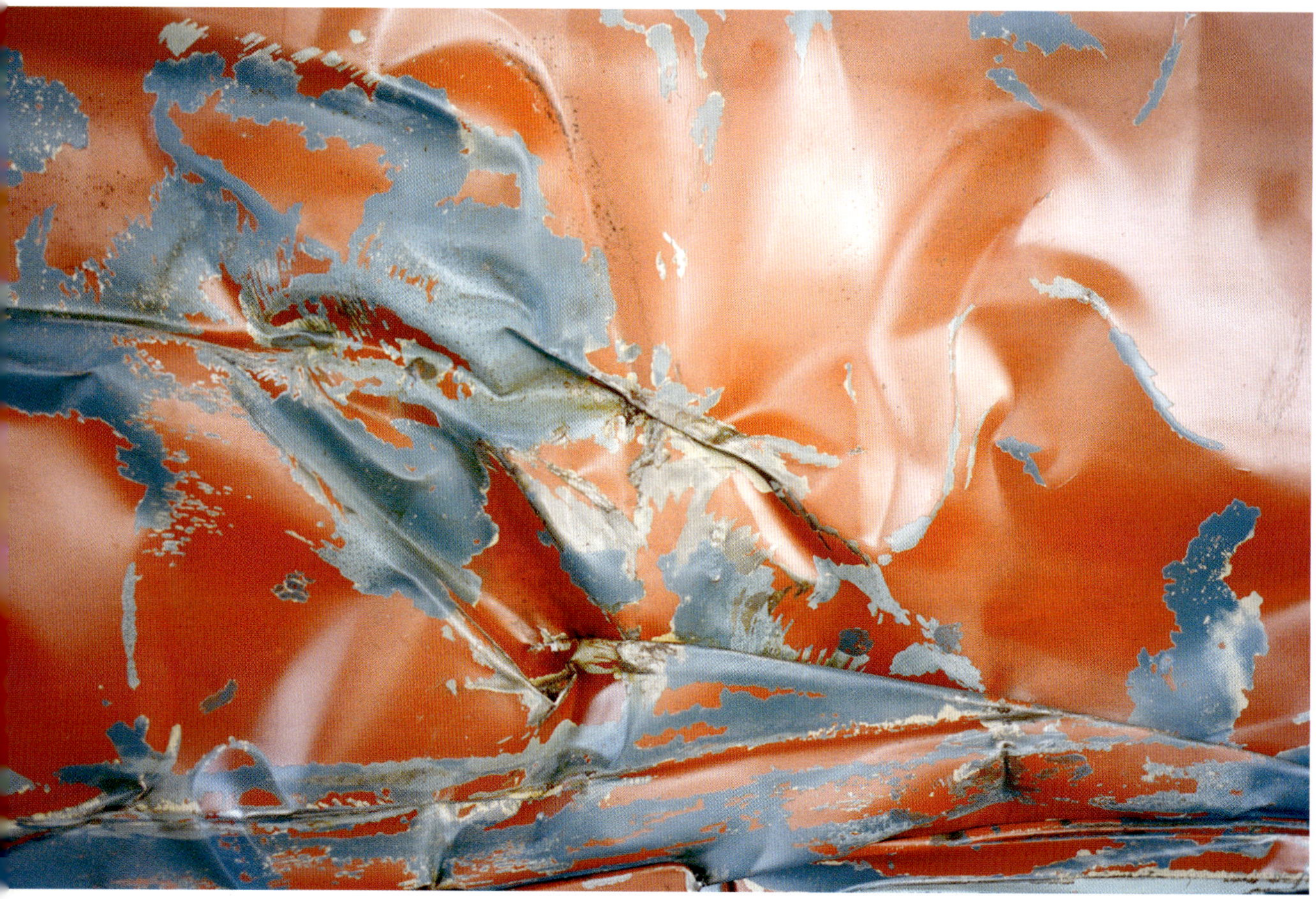

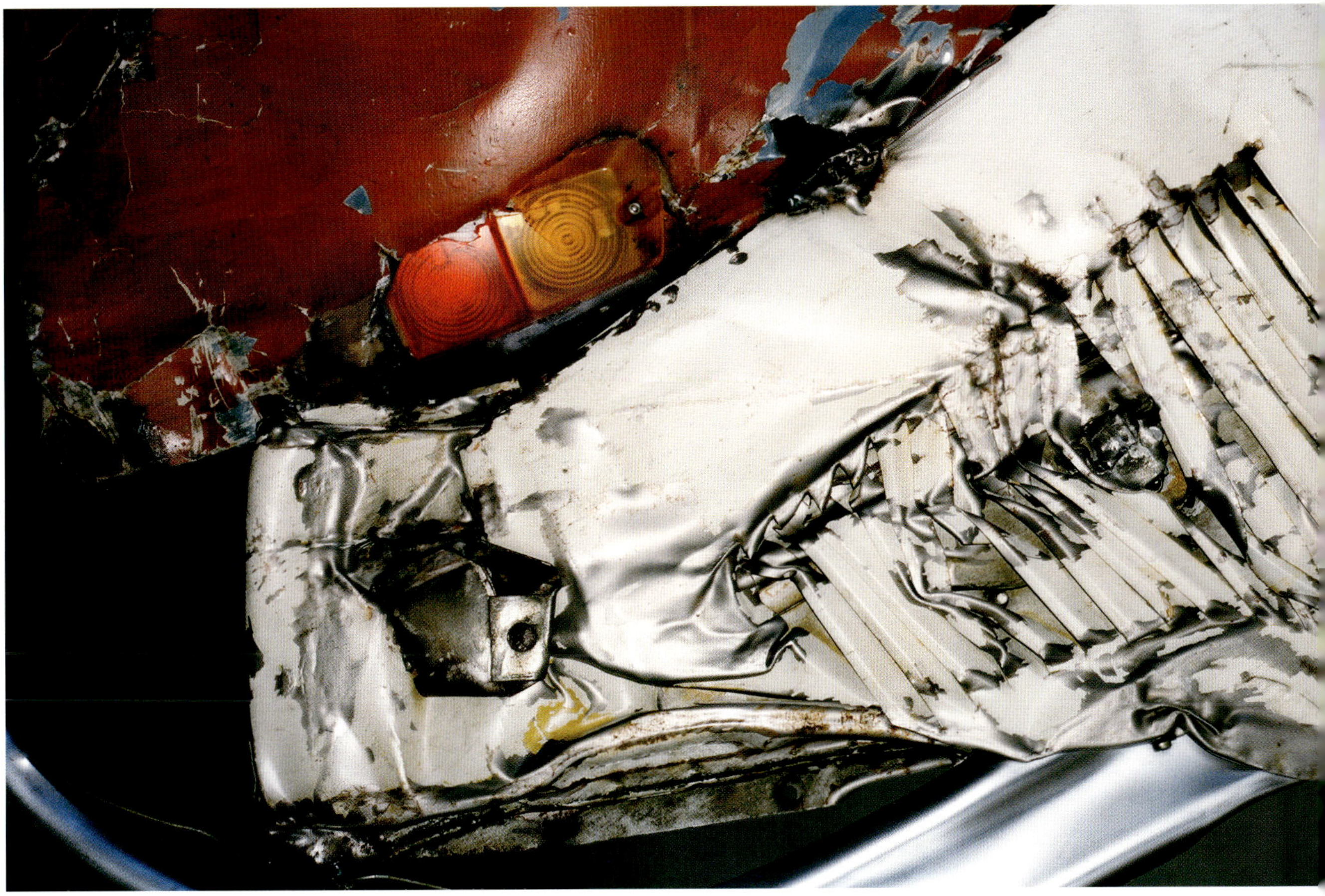

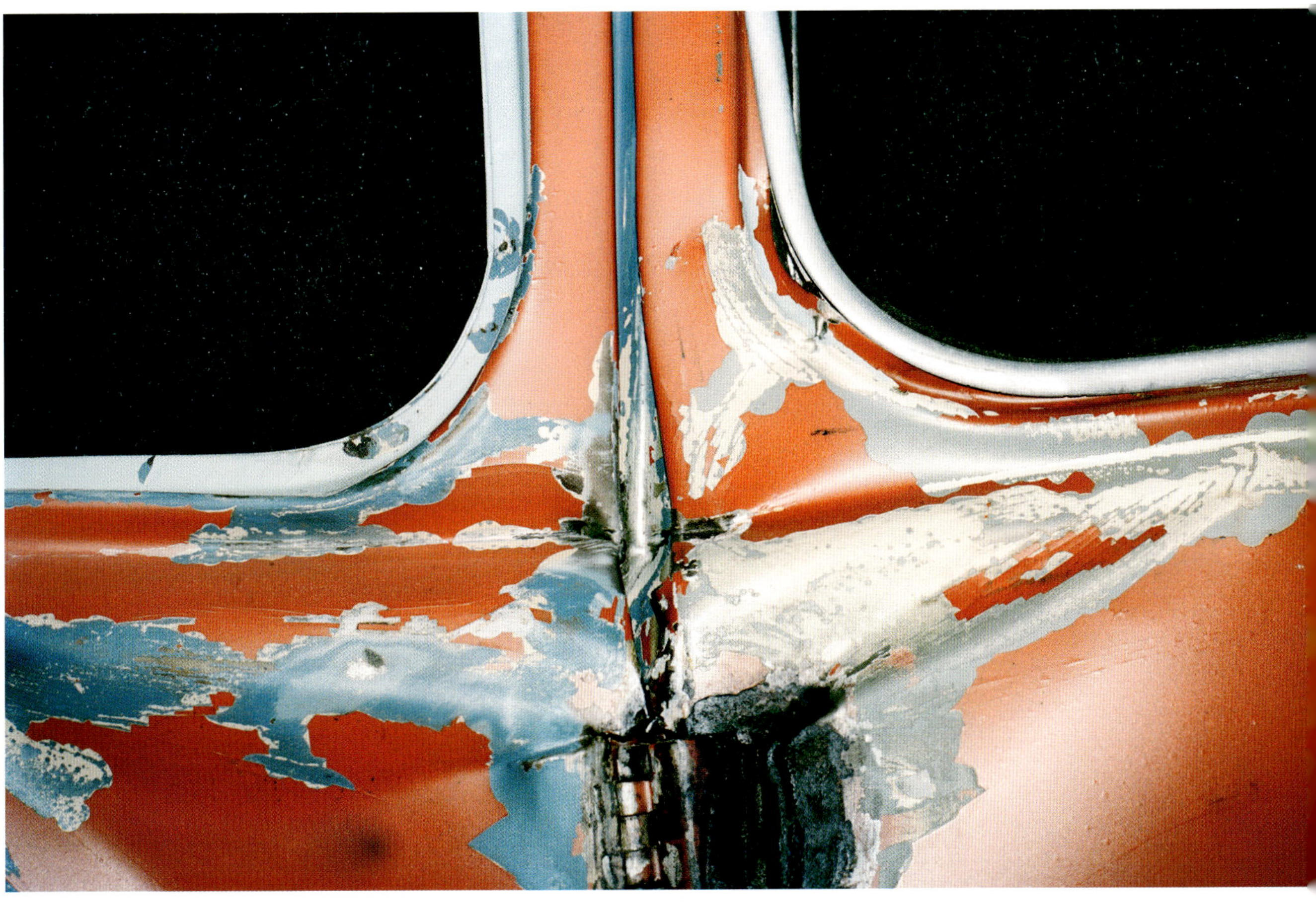

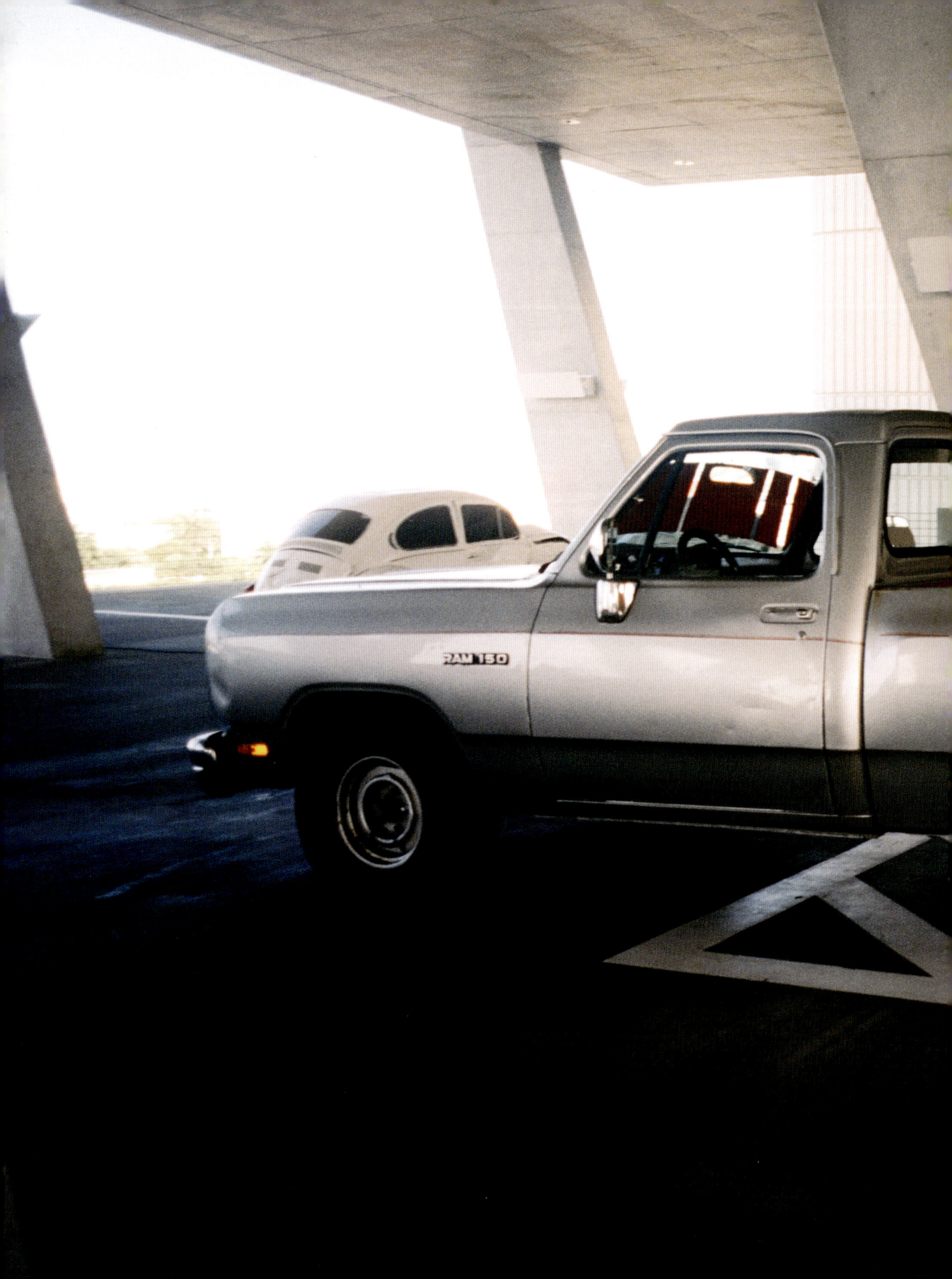
RAM 150

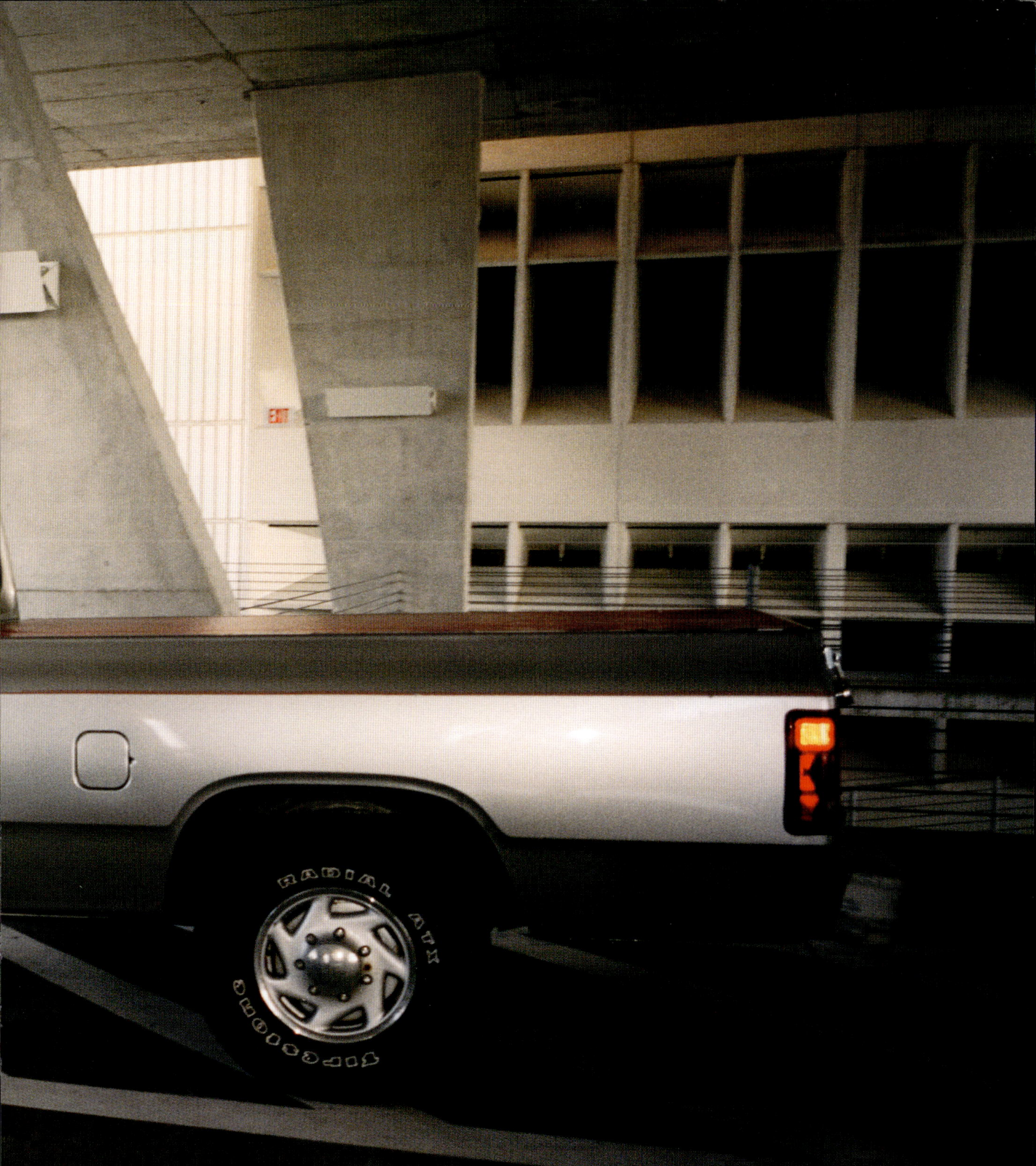
EXIT
RADIAL ATX

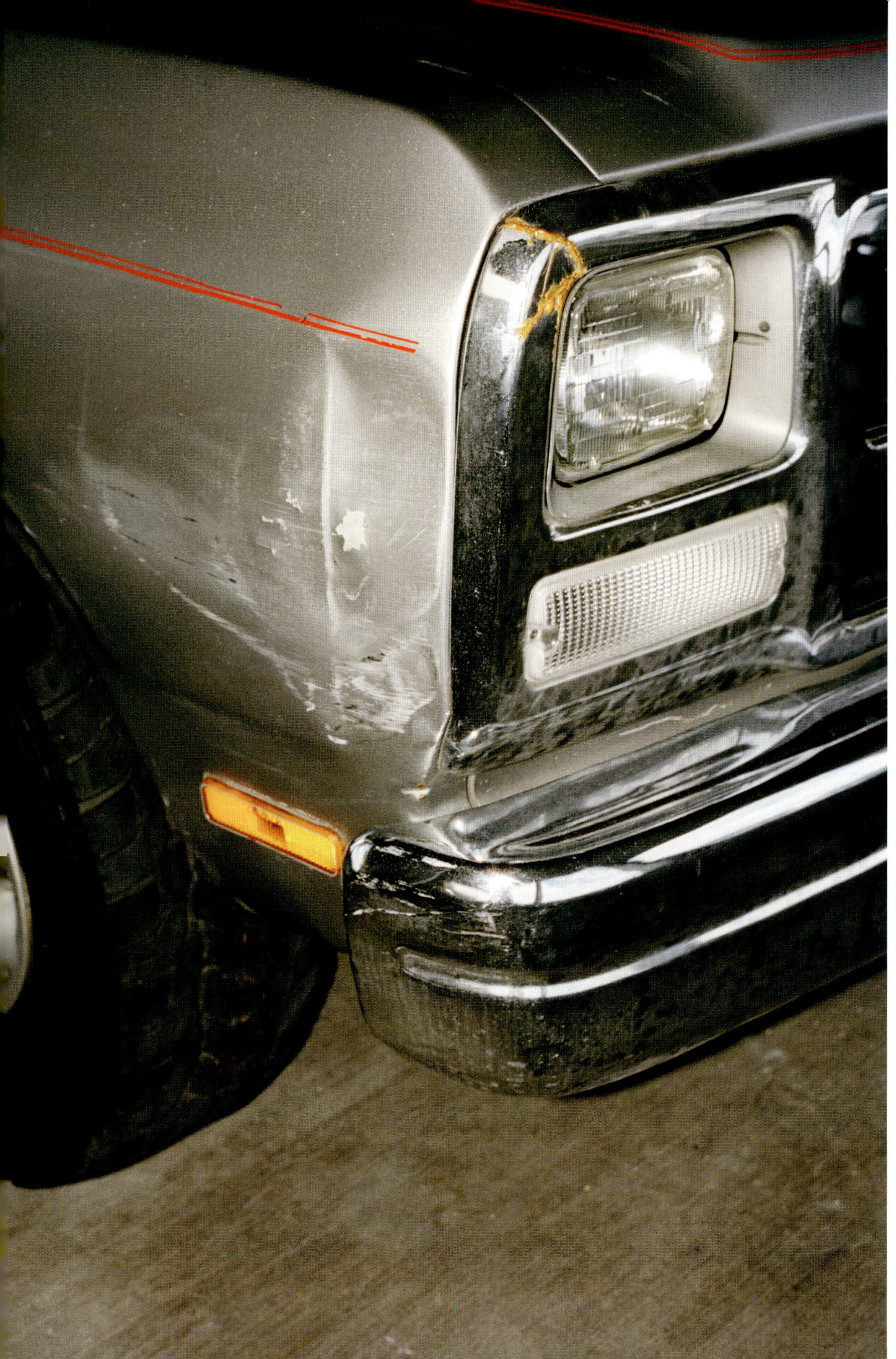

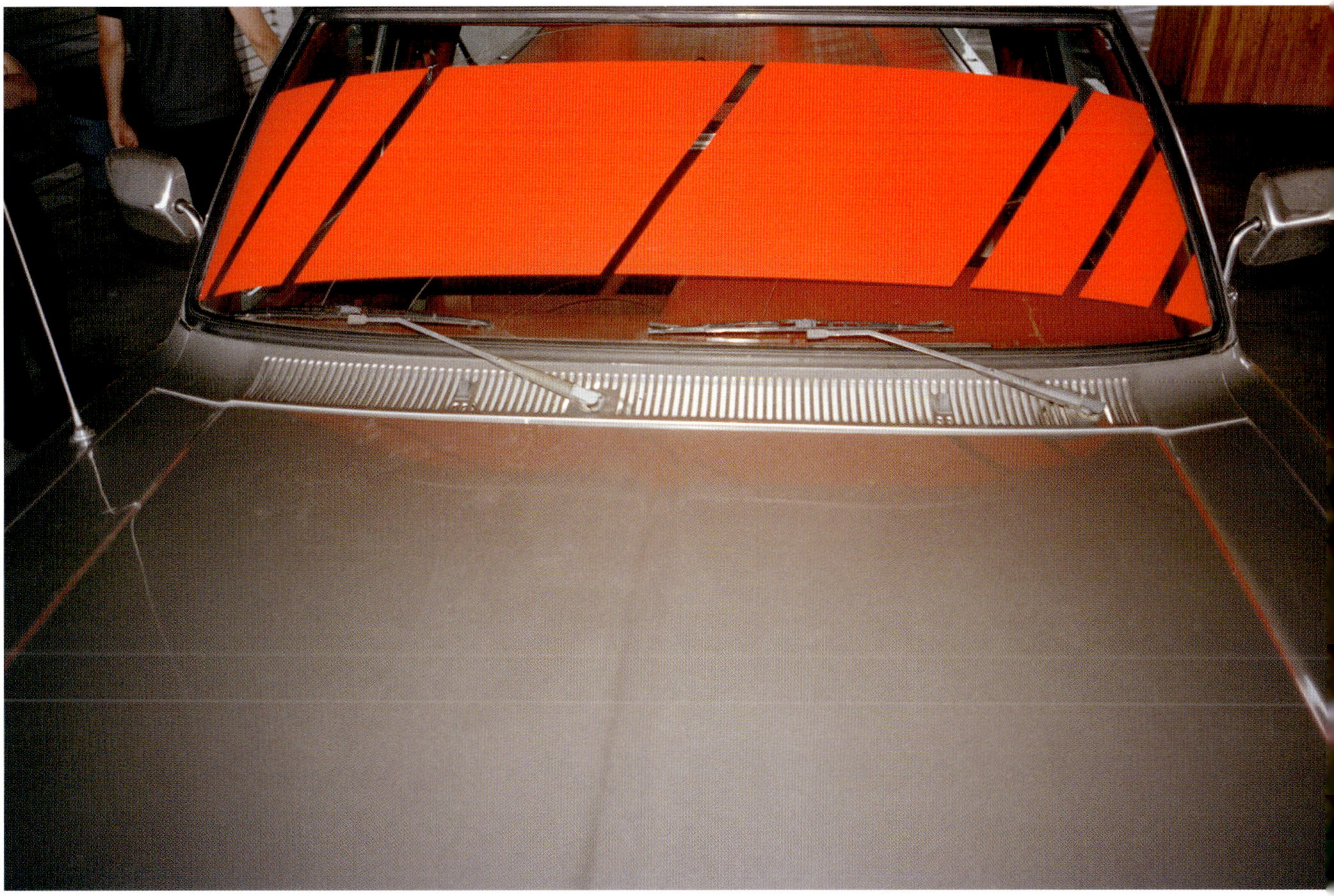

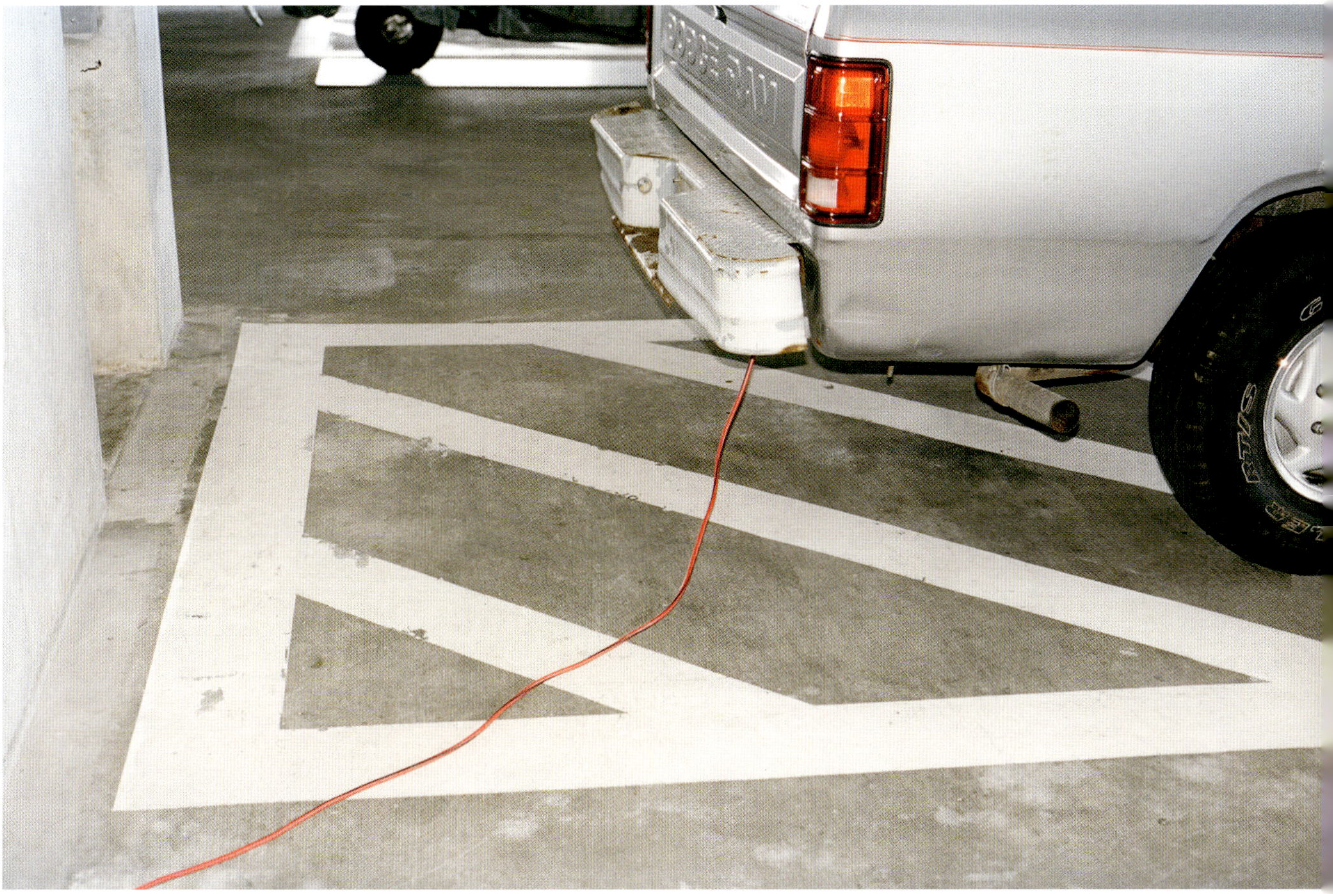

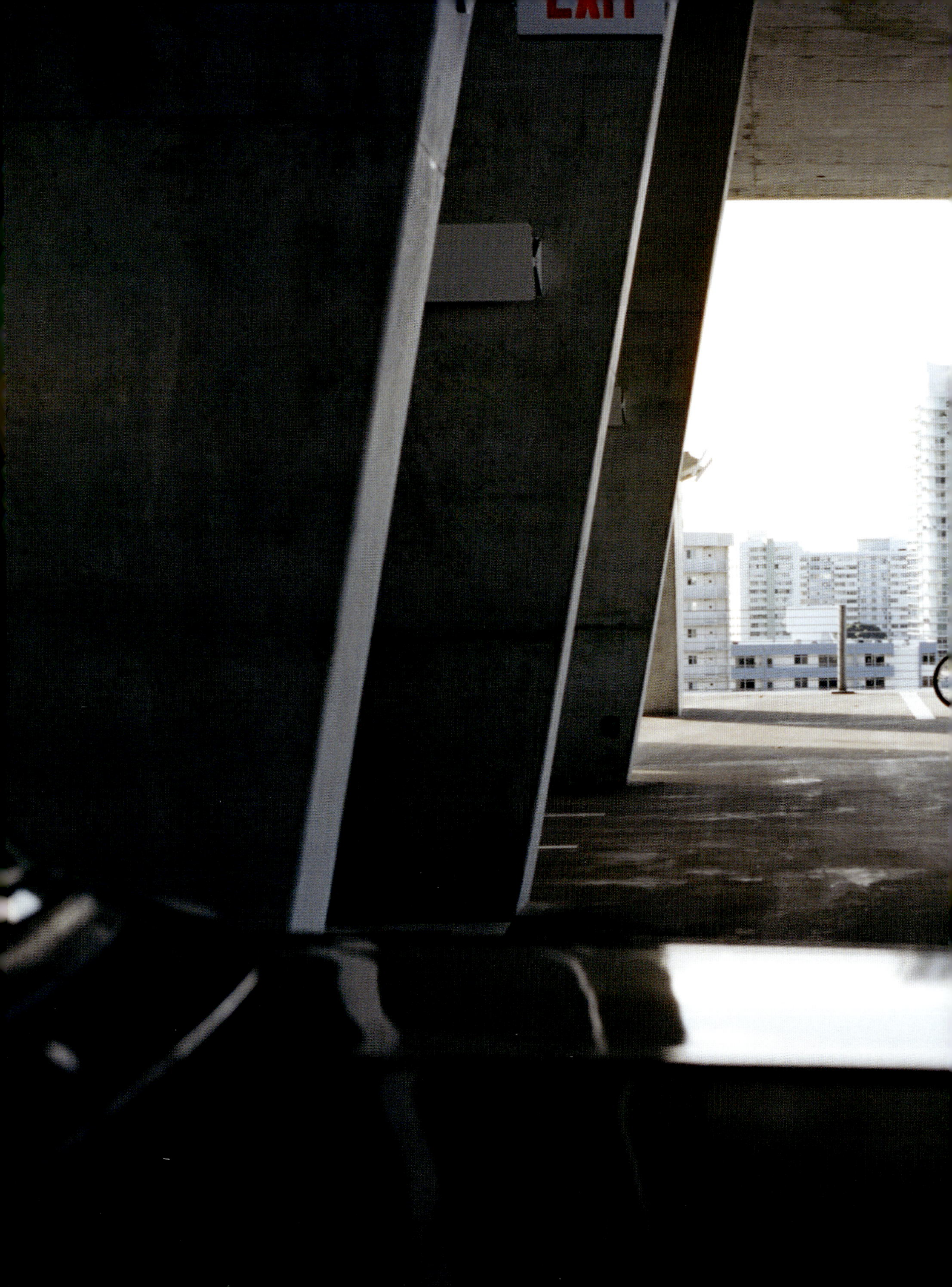

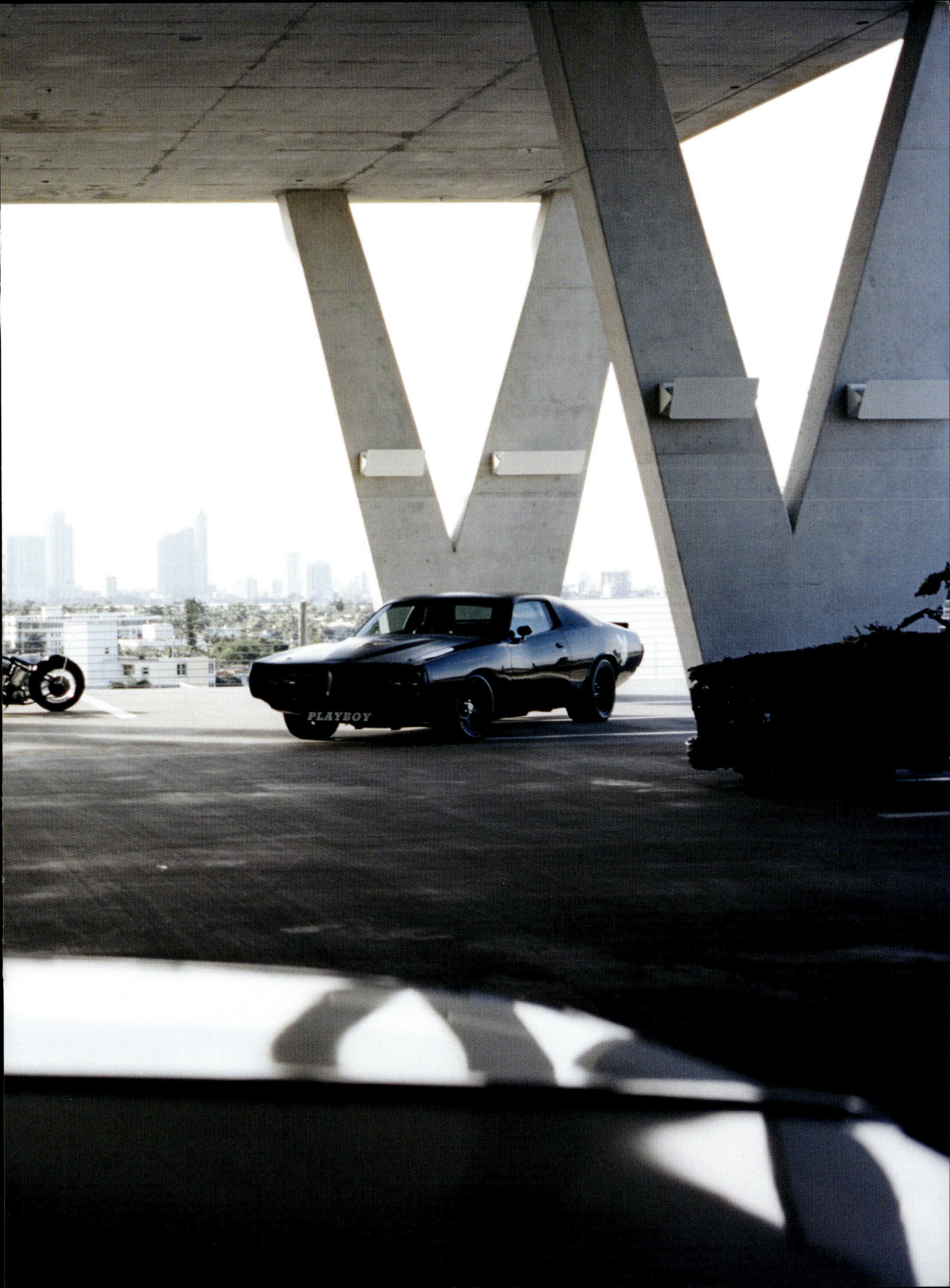
PLAYBOY

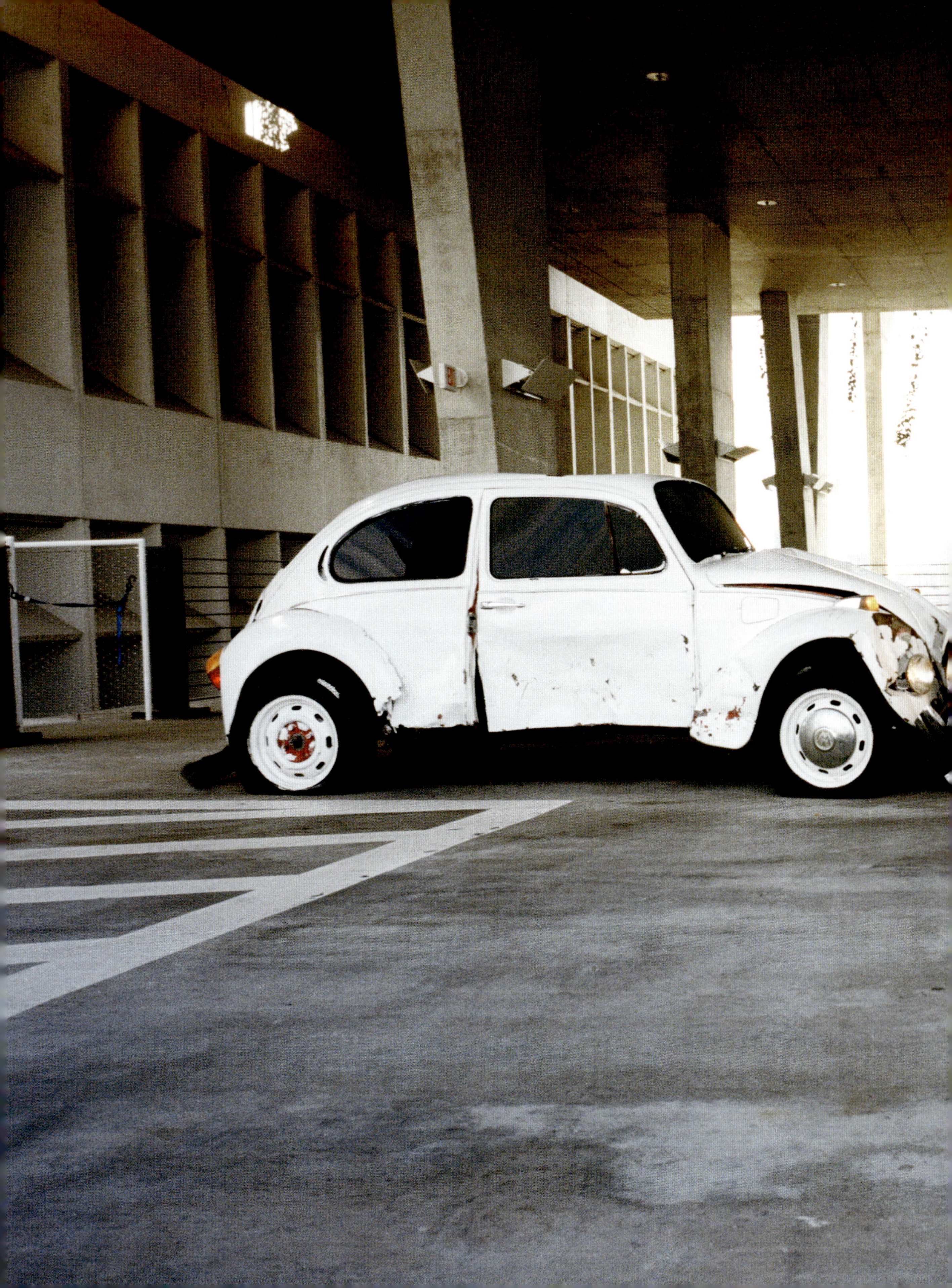

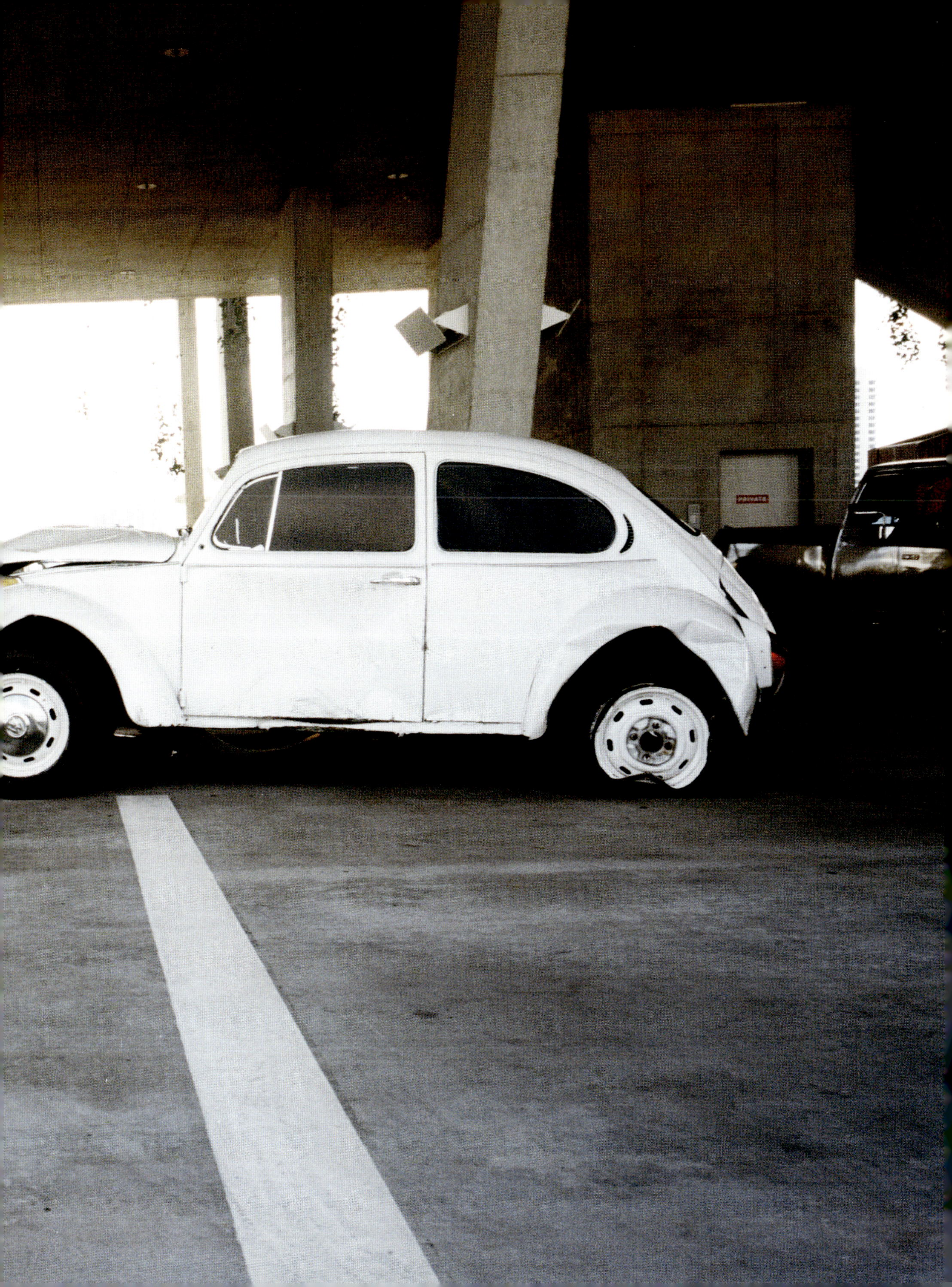

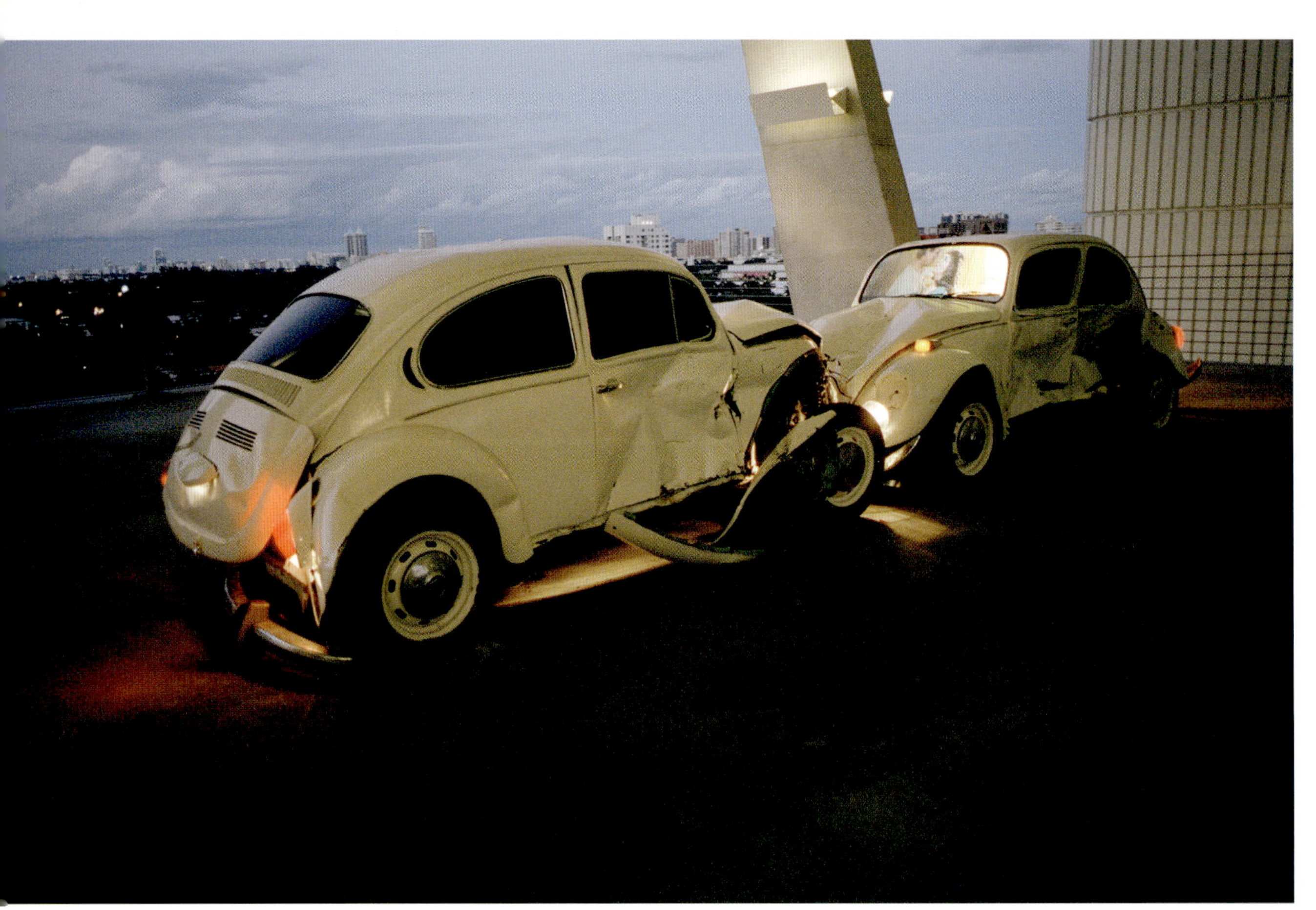

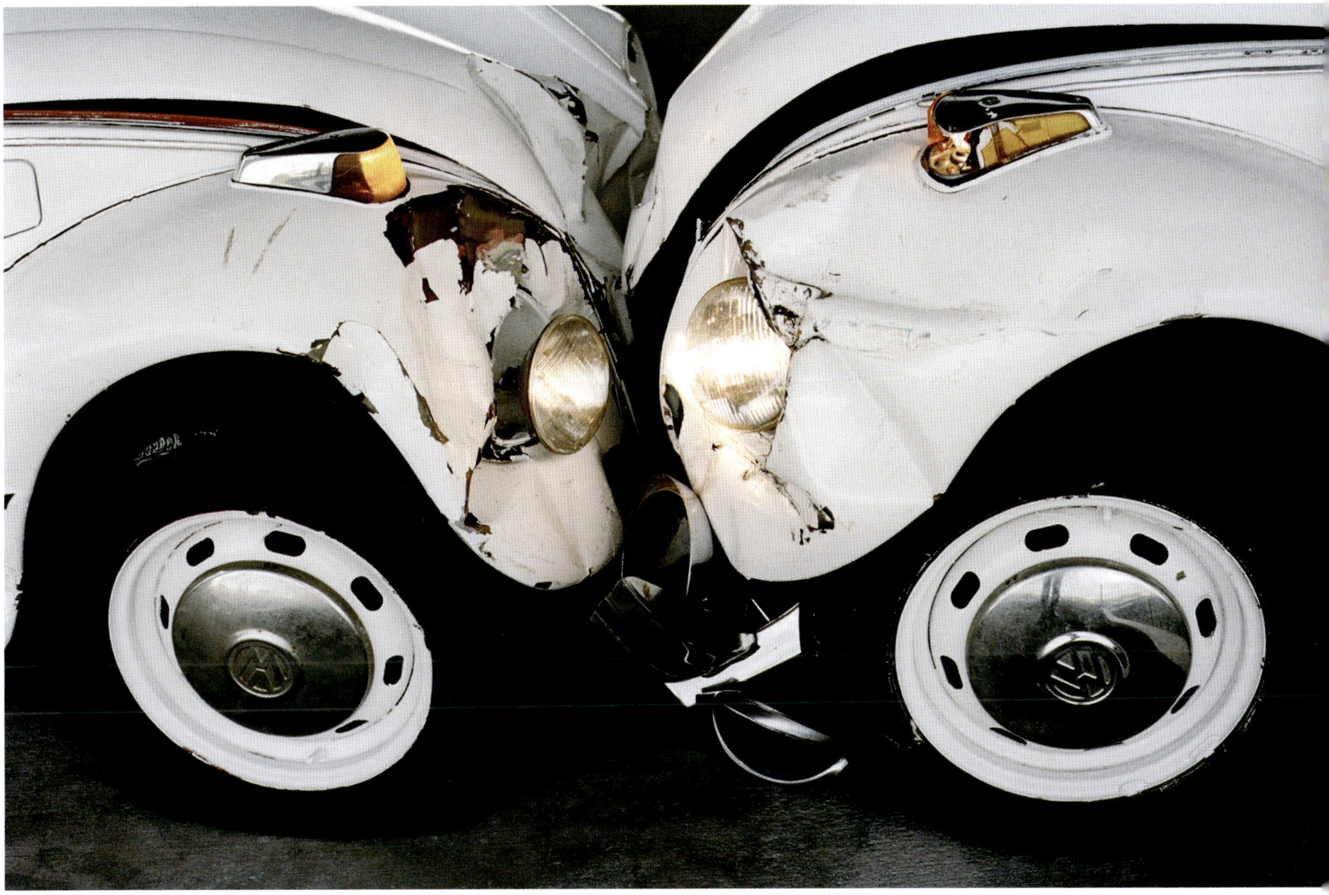

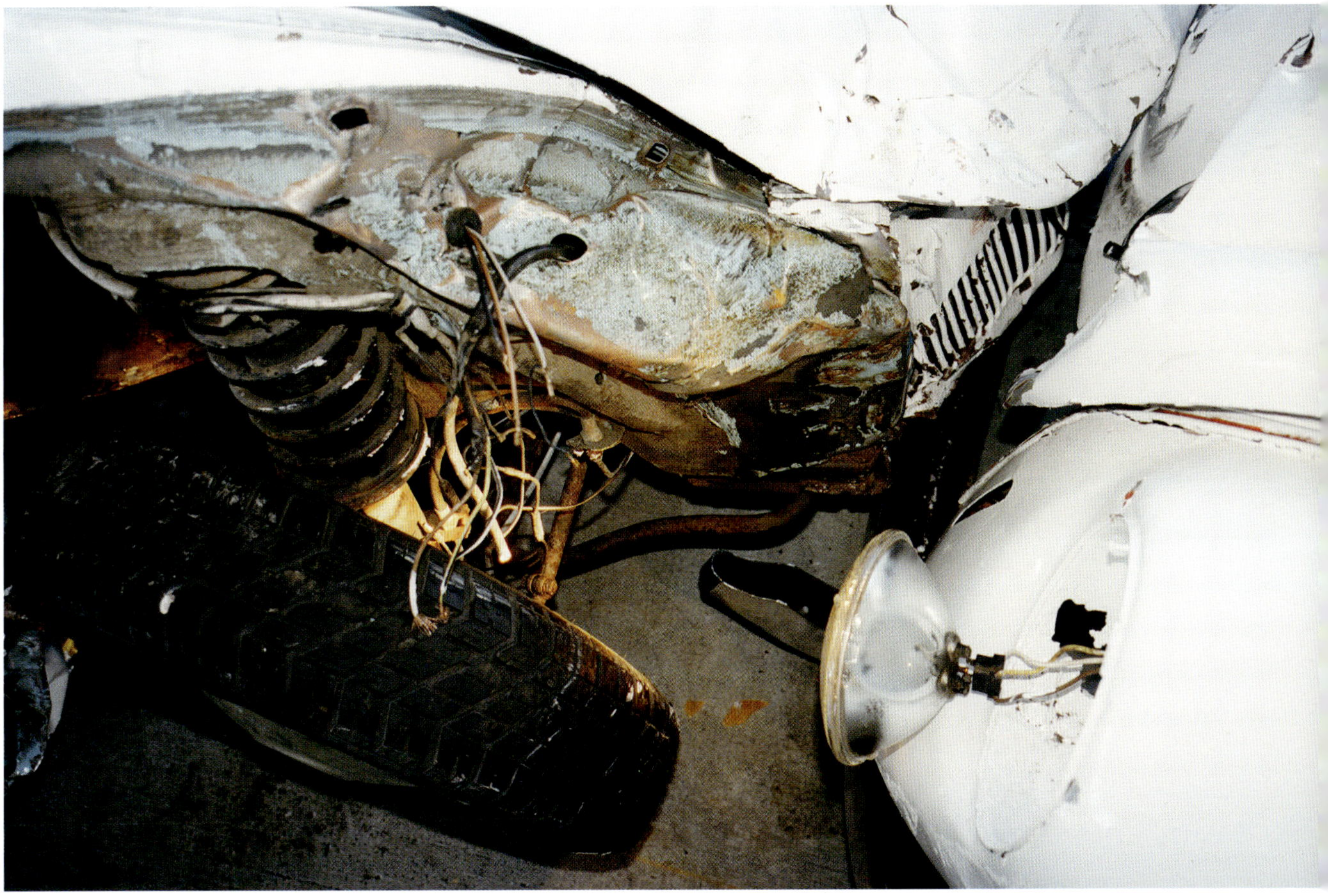

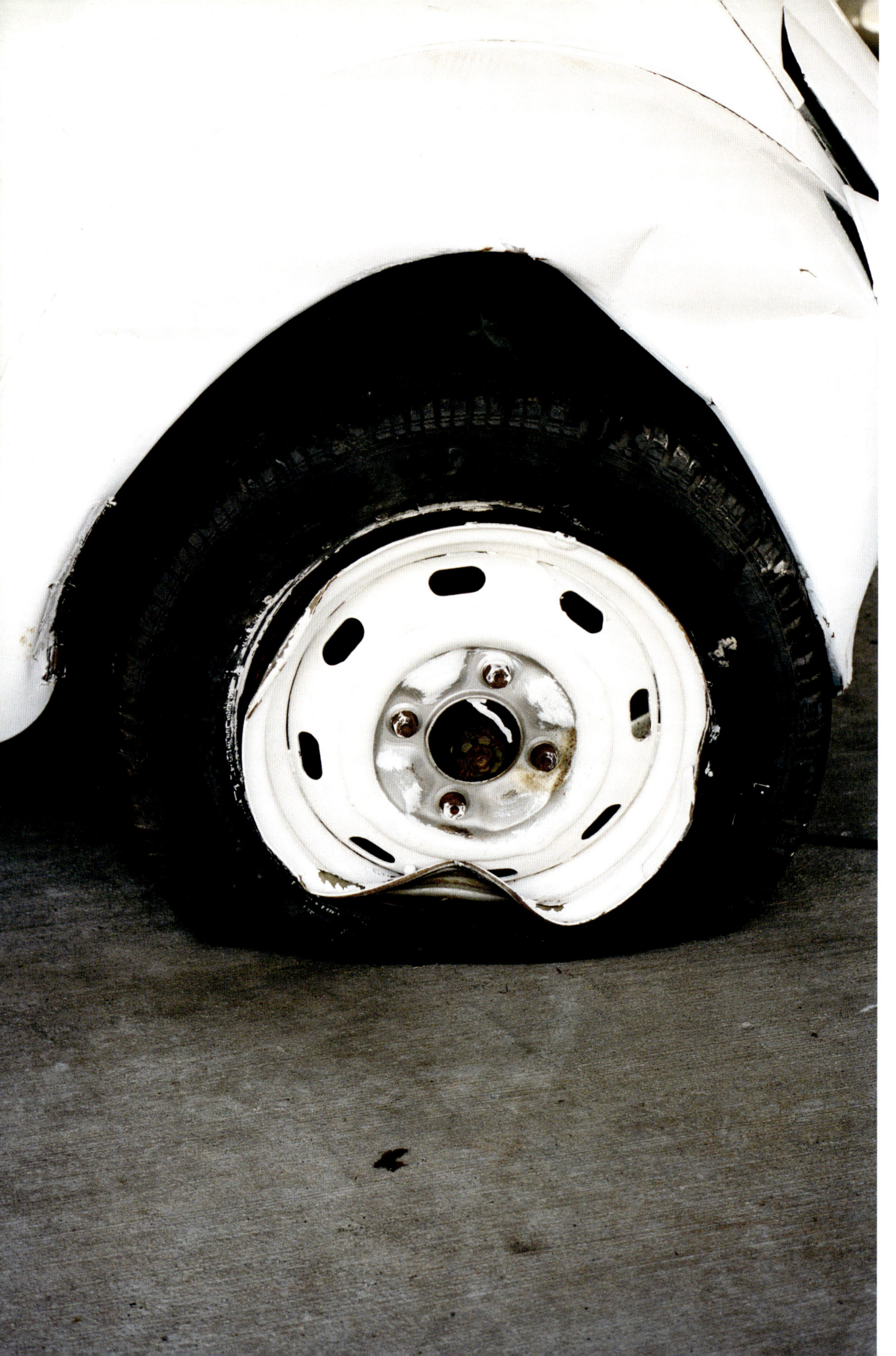

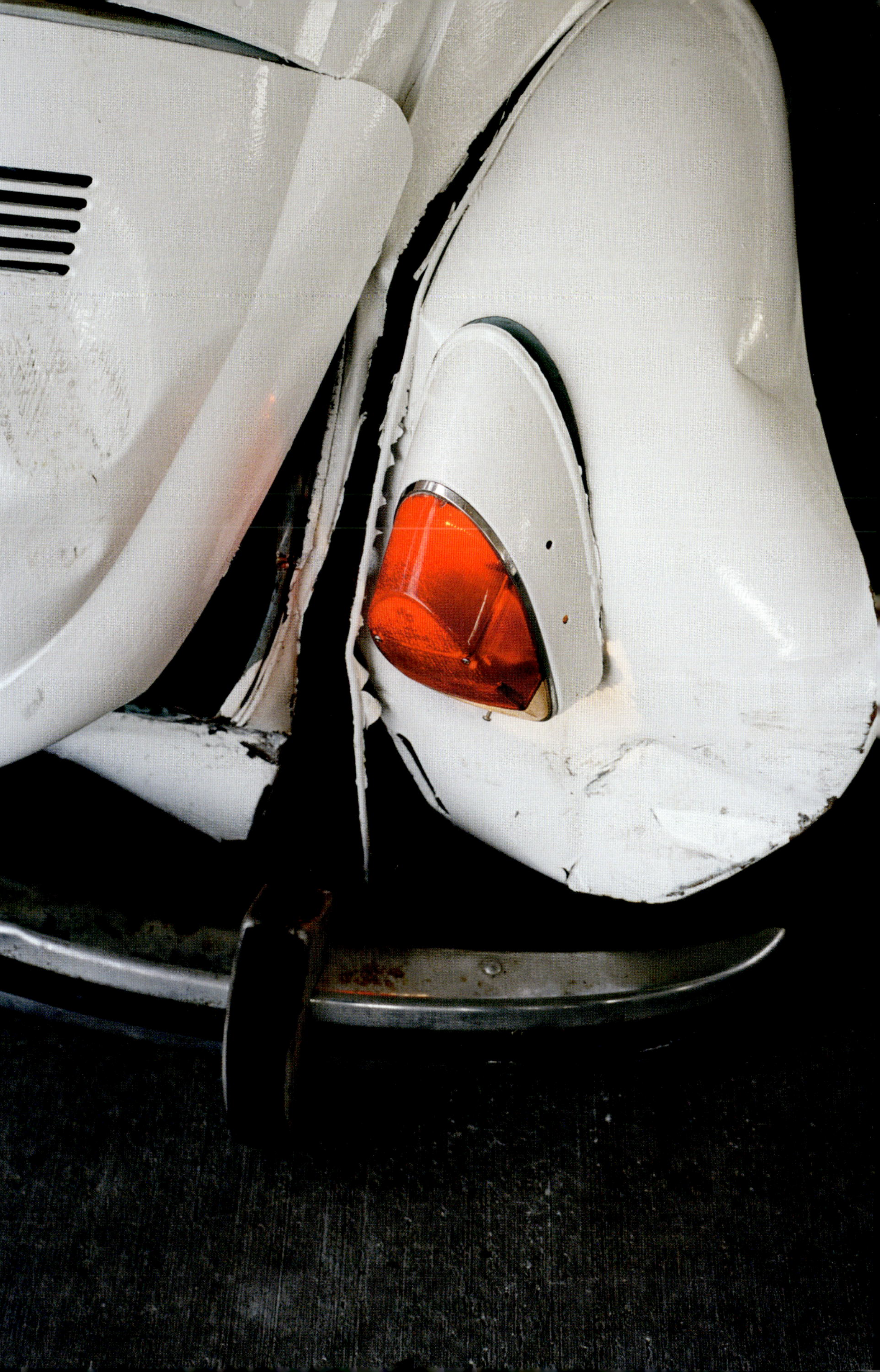

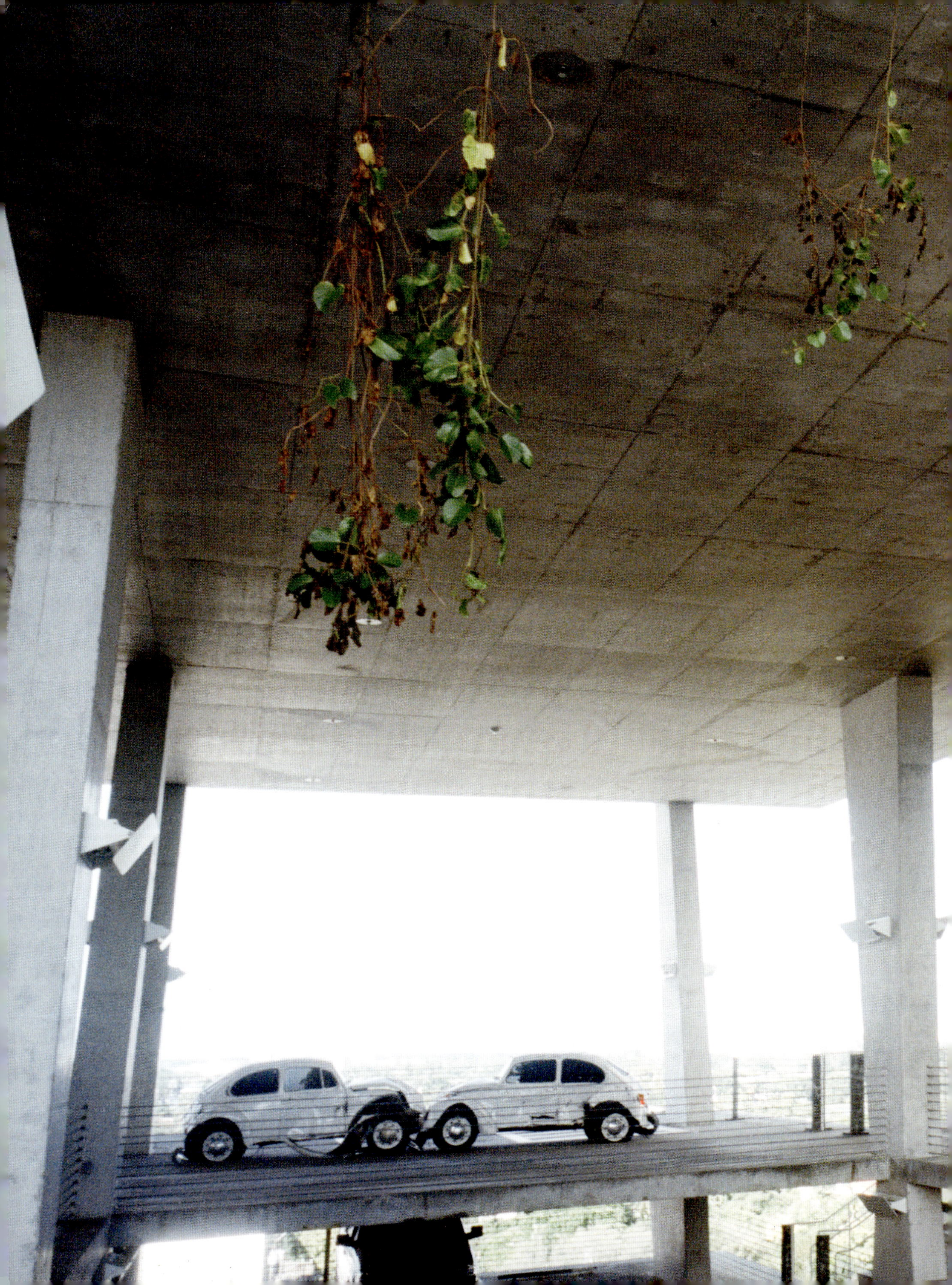

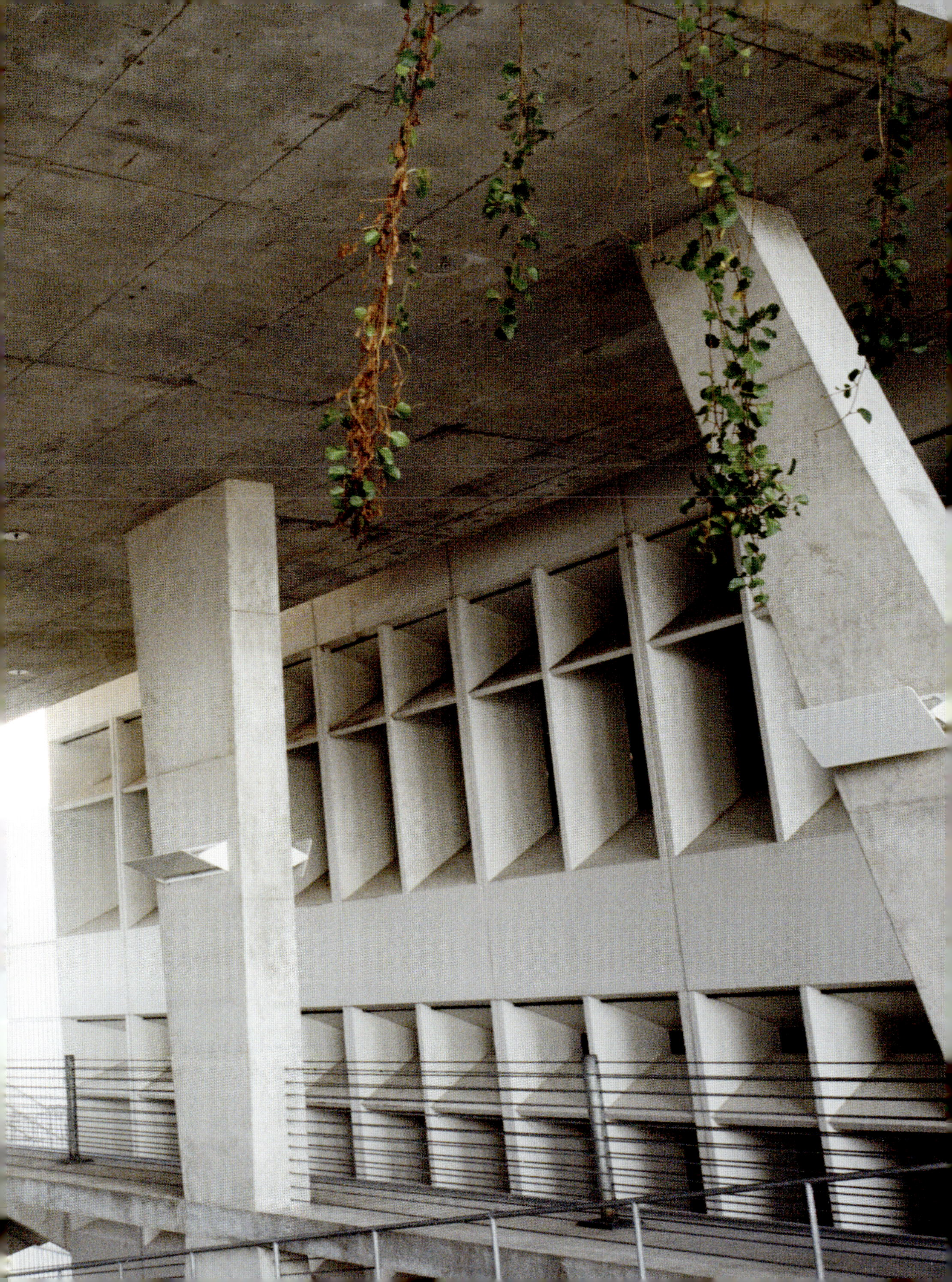

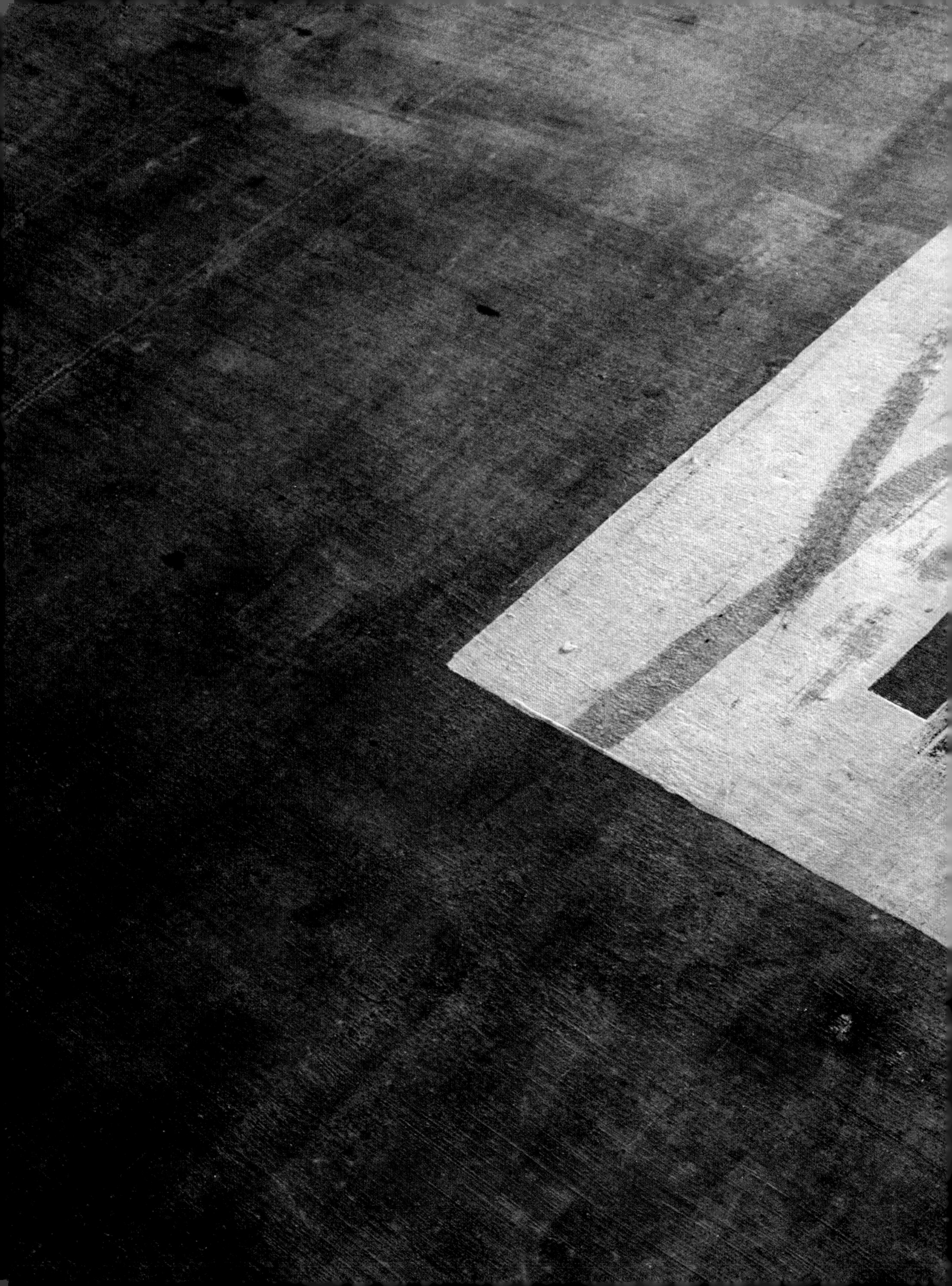

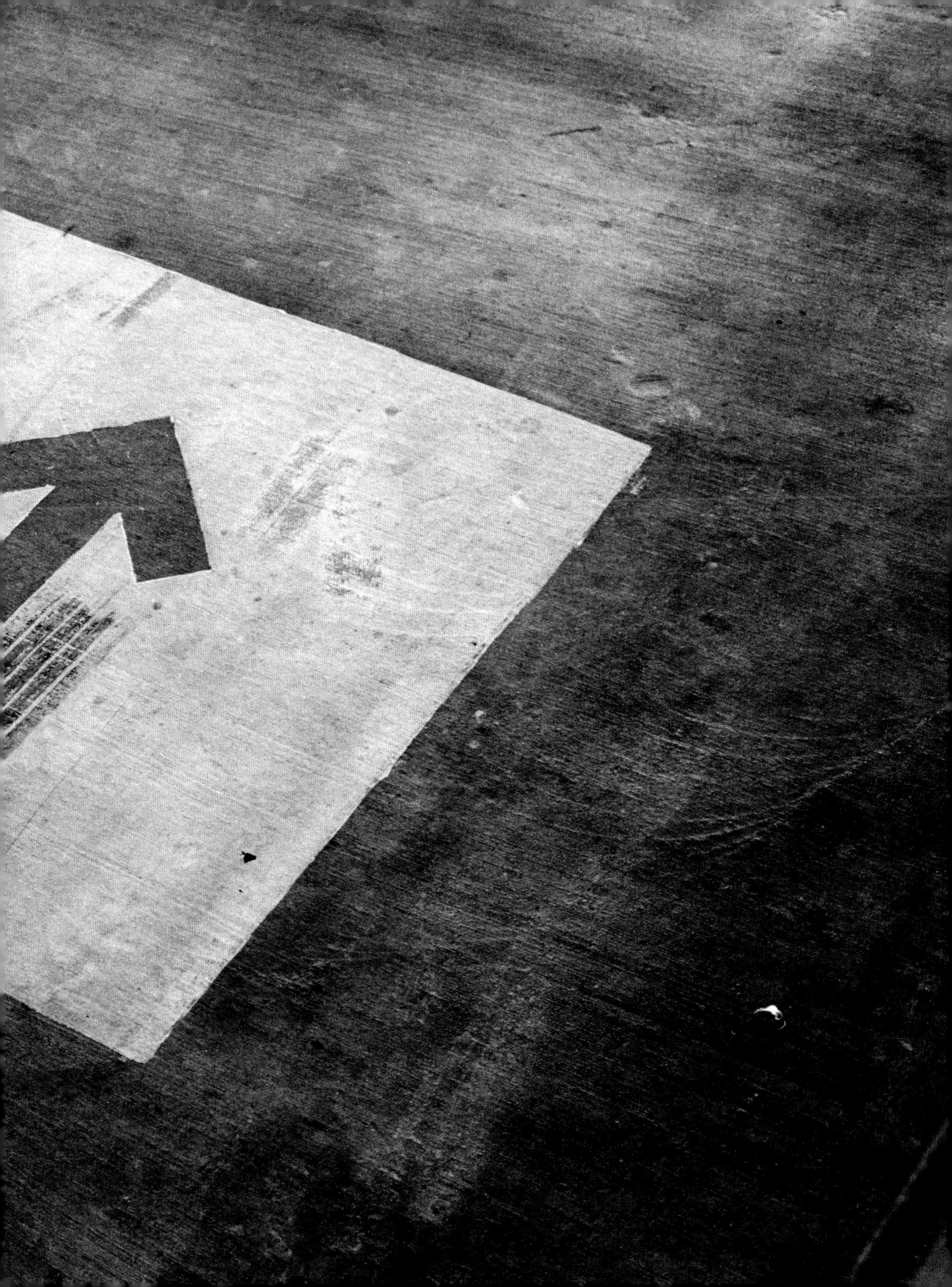

WORKS IN THE EXHIBITION

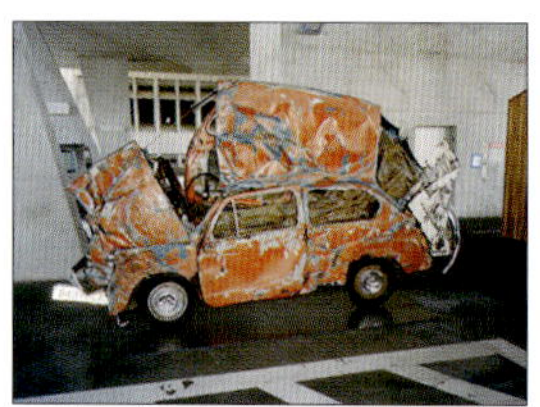

Ron Arad
Pressed Flower (Baby You Can)
2013
Fiat 600, steel
83 x 150 x 40 inches

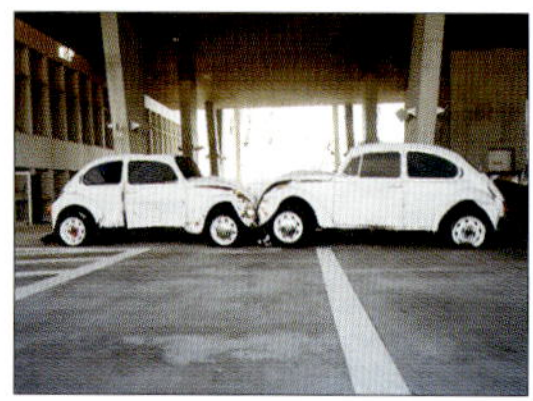

The Bruce High Quality Foundation
Art History with Passion
2013
Two Volkswagen Beetles
video components
326 x 62 x 64 inches

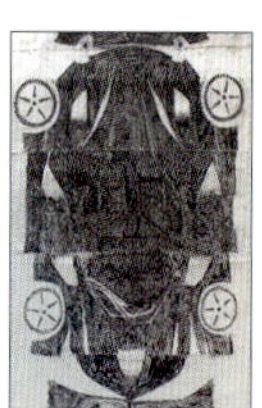

Joshua Callaghan
F150 2D
2013
Charcoal rubbing on unstretched canvas
300 x 168 inches
Edition of 2

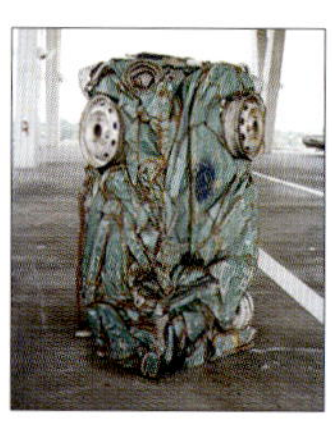

César
Compression Voiture Venise
1995
Compressed car
59 x 23 ½ x 23 ½ inches

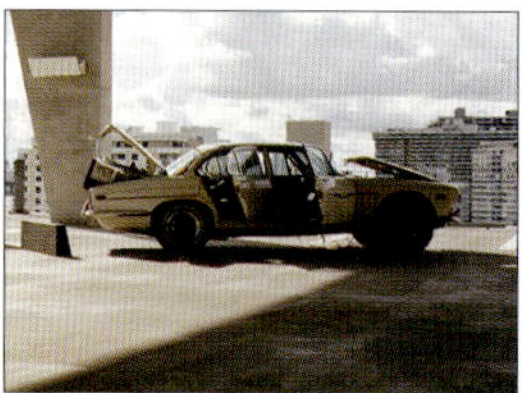

Dan Colen and Nate Lowman
Welfare Mothers Make Better Lovers
2008
White 1973 Jaguar, speakers, speaker wire, DVD players, amps, stereos, Christmas tree
Dimensions variable

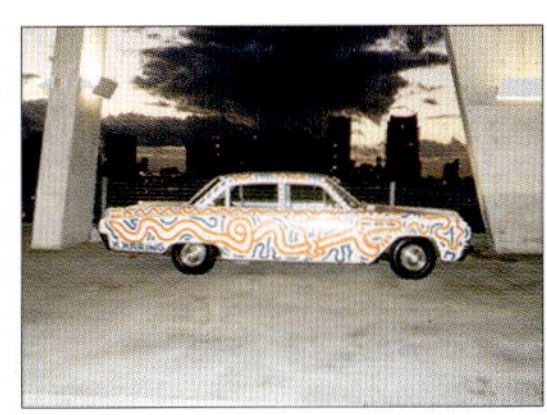

Keith Haring
Untitled (Car)
1986
Enamel on 1963 Buick Special
189 x 71 x 54 inches

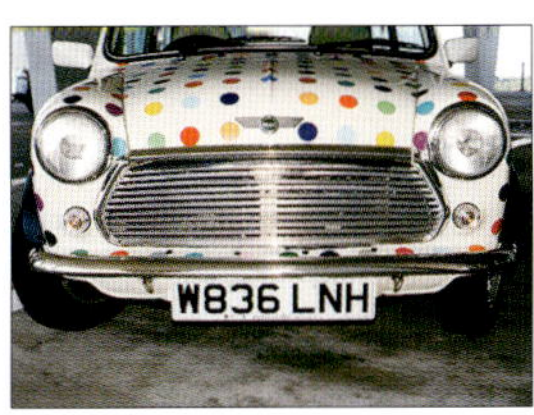

Damien Hirst
Untitled (Spot Mini)
2000
Automotive paint on Mini Cooper
52 ¾ x 70 x 120 inches

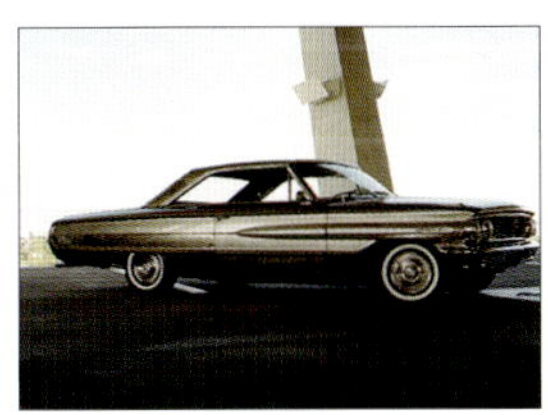

Jacob Kassay, Olivier Mosset, and Servane Mary
Ford Galaxie
2013
1964 Ford Galaxie 500
210 x 81 ½ inches

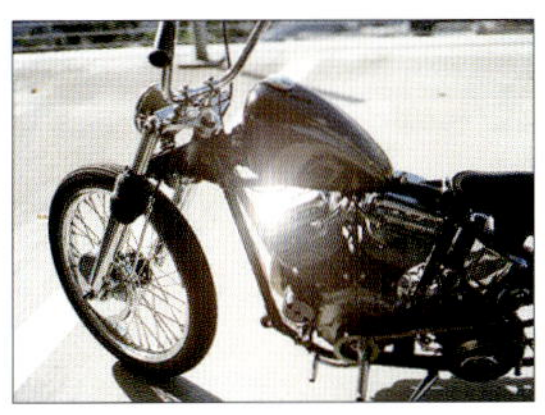

Olivier Mosset
Panhead
2007
1965 Harley Davidson FLH

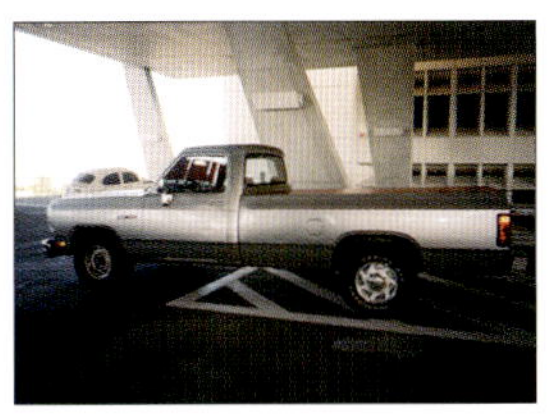

Virginia Overton
Truck
2013
1993 Dodge Ram 150, plastic tarp, vinyl decals, LED lights
Installation, dimensions variable

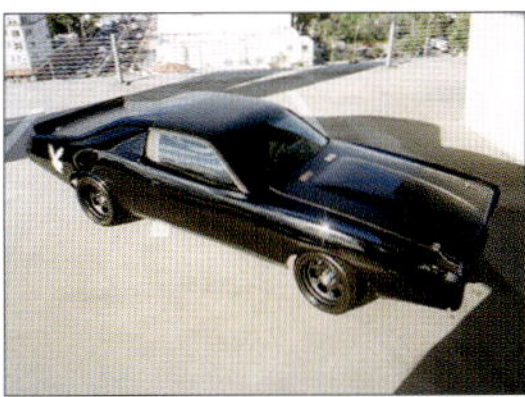

Richard Phillips
Playboy Charger
2013
1972 Dodge Charger
206 ½ x 80 x 53 inches

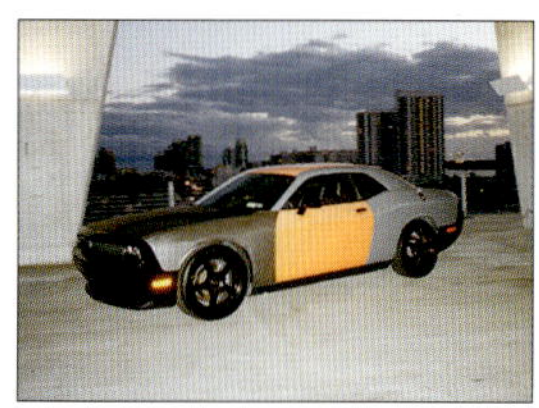

Richard Prince
Vanishing Point (The Artist Cut)
2012-13
2012 Dodge Challenger R/T
197 3/4 x 75 ¾ x 57 inches

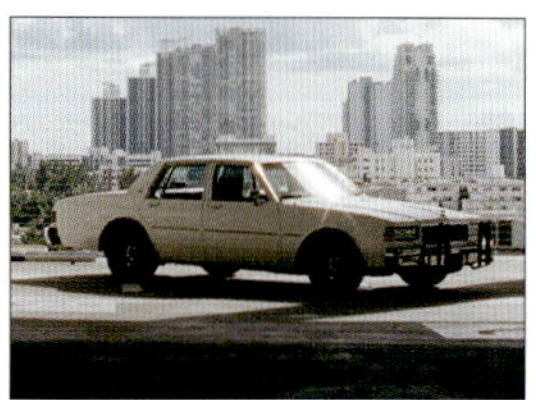

Tom Sachs
Untitled (1989 Chevy Caprice)
2007
1989 Chevrolet Caprice, mixed media
56 x 212 x 79 inches

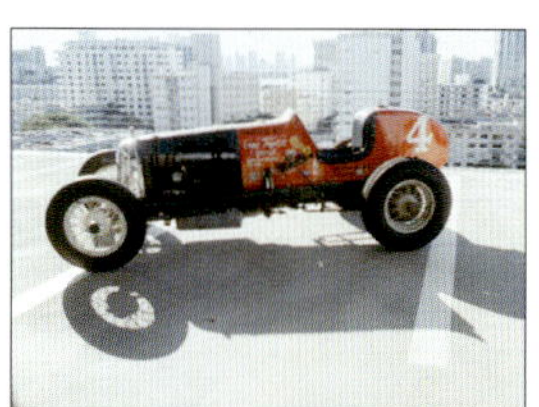

Salvatore Scarpitta
Ernie Triplett Special (S.A.L. Ernie Triplett Spl)
1968-1969
48 x 139 x 67 inches

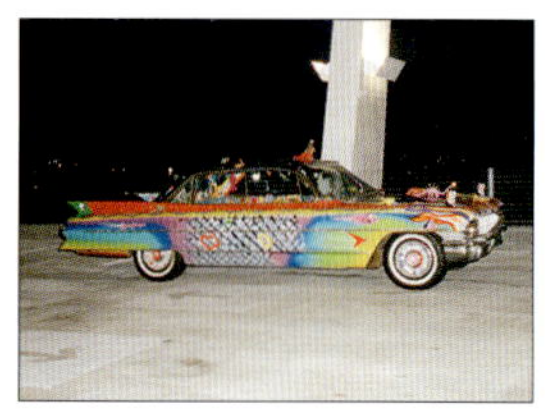

Kenny Scharf
Ultima Suprema Deluxa
1984
1961 Cadillac, mixed media, acrylic, spray-paint, found objects
68 x 78 x 22 inches

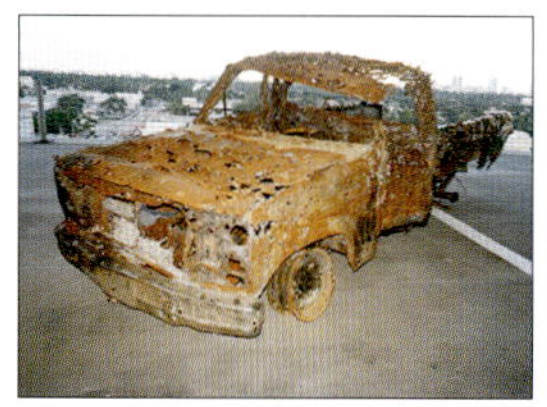

Lucien Smith
The sound of the engine still running and for the last time they locked eyes, together again in the end
2013
68 x 208 x 78 inches

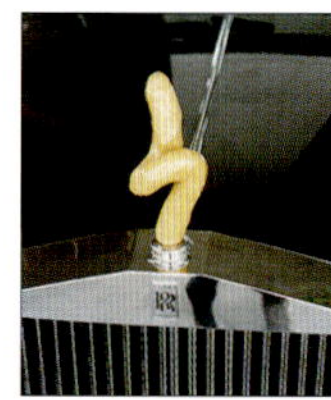

Franz West
Untitled
2007
Passstücke hood ornament, Rolls Royce

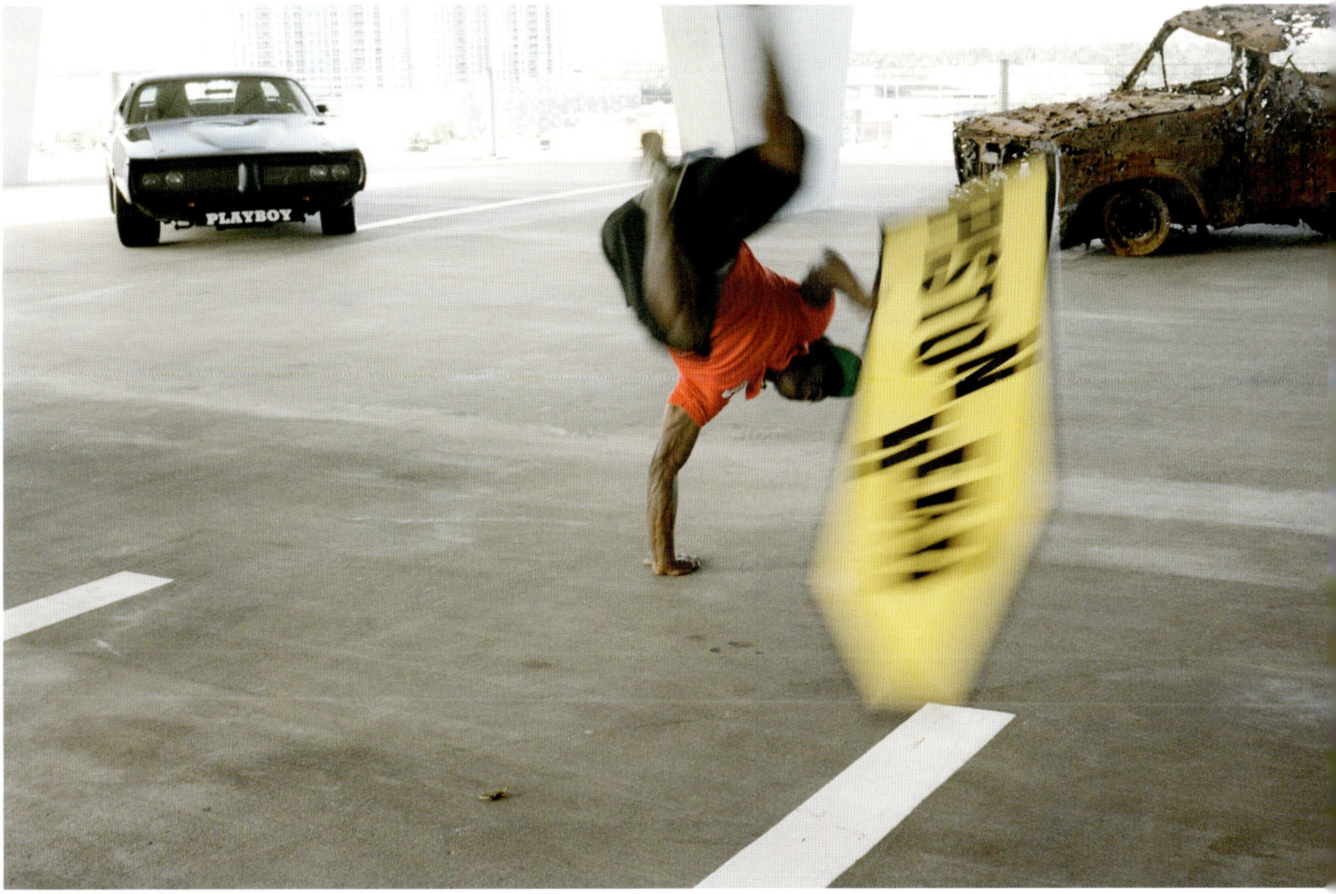

PLAYBOY

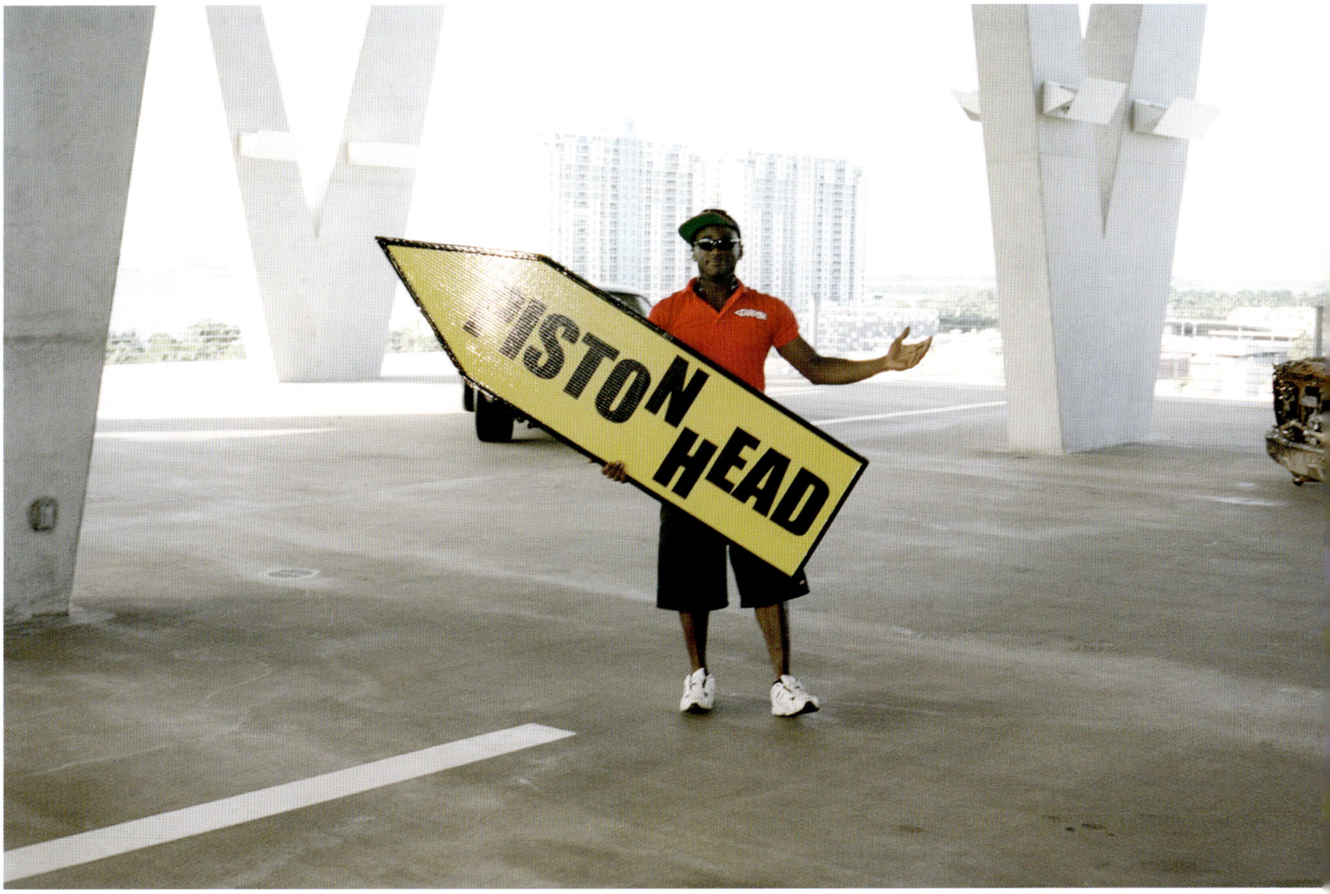

PISTON
HEAD

Published on the occasion of the exhibition
Piston Head: Artists Engage the Automobile
presented by Venus Over Manhattan
at 1111 Lincoln Road, Miami Beach, FL
December 3 - 8, 2013

Designed and edited by Josh Shaddock

Printed in the United States by The Avery Group at Shapco Printing, Inc., Minneapolis

Venus Over Manhattan
980 Madison Avenue, Third Floor, New York NY 10075
Tel: 212.980.0700 Fax: 212.980.5144
www.venusovermanhattan.com